THE GRAY LOBBY

THE GRAY LOBBY

Henry J. Pratt

The University of Chicago Press
Chicago and London

The University of Chicago Press, Chicago 60637
The University of Chicago Press, Ltd., London

© 1976 by The University of Chicago
All rights reserved. Published 1976
Printed in the United States of America

81 80 79 78 77 76 987654321

Photo credits: p. ii—Henriette Castex Epstein
(courtesy *Albany Times-Union*); pp. 8, 36,
104, 186—Nate Fine Photo

HENRY J. PRATT is associate professor of
political science at Wayne State University. He
is the author of *The Liberalization of American
Protestantism* and the editor of *Ethno-Religious
Politics.*

Library of Congress Cataloging in Publication Data

Pratt, Henry J   1934–
    The gray lobby.

    Bibliography: p.
    Includes index.
    1. Aged—United States—Political activity.
2. Aged—Legal status, laws, etc.—United States.
I. Title.
HQ1064.U5P68   301.43'5'0973   75-43232
ISBN 0-226-67917-9

for Myron Horowitz,
who taught me the importance
of asking the right questions

Contents

Acknowledgments

Writing a book can be a lonely venture. But in this case the undertaking has been greatly lightened—and at times even made a decided pleasure—through help and support from several persons. A colleague and friend, Dale Vinyard, was both instrumental in stimulating my initial interest in aging and in keeping up my spirits along the way. Equally supportive has been another Wayne State University colleague, Charles J. Parrish, who was involved in arranging a leave of absence for me to write and do research and who was instrumental, along with Wayne State University vice president Ronald Haughton, in my obtaining financial assistance from the University of Michigan-Wayne State Institute of Gerontology. Still another colleague, Clifford Kaufman, was especially helpful as I struggled to work out some conceptual problems.

Byron Gold, currently a faculty member in the School of Social Service Administration at the University of Chicago and formerly deputy to the chairman of the 1971 White House Conference on Aging, graciously gave me the benefit of his thinking at an early stage and continued to manifest interest in the successful completion of this work. Another Chicago faculty member, Theodore Marmor of the Department of Political Science, brought to bear his impressive social policy expertise in evaluating an initial draft of the manuscript. No one has been more uplifting and constructively critical than Robert Binstock of Brandeis, himself a student of aging politics with few peers in the profession. Frederick Eisele of Pennsylvania State University, in several long-distance phone conversations, helped keep alive my enthusiasm and direct my attention along fruitful paths.

My considerable gratitude goes to Peter A. Corning of Stanford University and Nancy Gina Bermeo, a Ph.D. candidate at Yale, who endured with me the special rigors of joint authorship (Corning in Chapter 5, Bermeo in Chapters 6 and 11). It was mostly through forbearance and dedication on their part that we managed to come through it all still smiling. Thomas Buchberger, my research assistant during the crucial early weeks, also merits warm appreciation, particularly for his help in the preparation of Chapter 3.

This work would not have been possible without the willing cooperation of people in Washington who are involved professionally in the aging field. I am especially indebted to Bernard Nash and James Sullivan of the American Association of Retired Persons, William Hutton and Nelson Cruikshank of the National Council of Senior Citizens, Alfred Abrams of the National Council on the Aging, and Thomas G. Walters of the National Association of Retired Federal Employees—all of whom interrupted busy schedules for the purpose of interviews. I am no less grateful to the two past commissioners on aging, John Martin and William Bechill, and to an authority on aging matters on Capitol Hill, Congressman H. John Heinz III of Pennsylvania, all of whom were indispensable in providing factual information and helping to interpret events.

There is also a sense of indebtedness to the students in my graduate seminar on public policy and the aged at Wayne State University. In their reactions to an initial draft of this work they managed to be both gentle and yet unsparing in their criticism. Susan Lanser, Patricia Moll, and Chris Dobrovich, each of whom at one time or another helped type the manuscript, deserve my gratitude for their unflagging and cheerful efforts.

I have benefited from what all these people have offered; yet, needless to say, the final responsibility for any errors or omissions or faults in logic lies squarely on me, not on their kind shoulders.

THE GRAY LOBBY

1 Introduction

The federal government's response in the 1960s and '70s to the needs of the nation's elderly population has been, to say the least, remarkable. Whereas other disadvantaged groups have had a difficult time achieving even modest levels of public sympathy and support, retirees and other older Americans have come to enjoy high political visibility and equally high levels of official concern and action.

An important aspect of the change has been enactment of new legislation. Beginning with the passage in 1965 of Medicare (P.L. 89–97) and the Older Americans Act (P.L. 89–73), Congress enlarged and broadened the range of statutory old-age protections. The more recent actions have included a nutrition program to provide meals for the elderly, enacted in 1972 as an amendment to Title VII of the Older Americans Act, and the establishment of an income floor for older persons by replacing the long-standing Old Age Assistance Program (OAA) with the federally-financed Supplemental Security Income Program (P.L. 92–603). Additionally, Congress has recently made age discrimination in employment illegal (P.L. 90–202). The law applies to workers under sixty-five years old but is indicative of a concern for older persons generally. Congress has also amended the Housing Act by authorizing federal loans for old people's housing and has enacted legislation providing for federal standards for private pension plans (P.L. 93–106).

By no means least important among recent congressional actions have been the increased benefits under social security, including establishment of a cost-of-living escalator clause. To finance these expansions of benefits the lawmakers have voted to increase substantially the Social Security payroll tax. The increase enacted in 1972 was the biggest since the Korean War and, surprisingly, was passed, as a *New York Times* analyst remarked, ''at a time of the 'taxpayers' revolt' at the federal, state and local levels. It was at a time when George Wallace was appealing to a sense of frustration in the middle and lower-middle classes, telling them the tax system was unfair. It was an election year.''[1] Yet the act passed easily, and in 1974 Congress voted to boost benefits a further 11 percent.

The increase in Social Security benefits has been the primary factor in the substantial enlargement of federal age-related spending, which increased

from $25 billion in fiscal year 1967 (15.8 percent of federal expenditures) to
$229 billion in fiscal 1972 (20.2 percent of the federal total). Moreover, as a
recent Health, Education, and Welfare Department study makes clear,
federal old-age spending increased by an even greater percentage in those
"discretionary" programs like housing, food distribution and food stamps,
research and development, and veterans' programs, where no separate trust
fund is involved from which retired persons draw benefits as a matter of legal
right. The total of all "discretionary" spending increased 2.6 times between
1967 and 1972, from $457 million to $1.2 billion. One part of this increase,
namely, appropriations under the Older Americans Act, has been especially
noteworthy; here spending levels have soared from $7.5 million in fiscal
1966 to a presidential request for fiscal 1975 of $202.6 million.[2]

Not all of the important changes have occurred on the basis of congressional action. The period beginning in 1965 has been noteworthy as well for
major institutional adjustments in the executive branch of government.
While the Administration on Aging, created under the original Older
Americans Act, has not become the central point for overall leadership and
coordination as hoped for by some of its advocates, the agency has
administered a substantial number of grant programs and has been the
primary impetus for the creation in all states of an office or commission on
the aging to serve as a funnel for the grant money.[3] In the early 1970s a
Federal Council on the Aging, consisting of fifteen members appointed by
the president, was set up for the purpose of reviewing and evaluating federal
policies in the field and advising the president. And on the basis of a
recommendation of the 1971 White House Conference on Aging, the
president authorized establishment of a cabinet-level committee on aging in
his Domestic Council.

The changes sketched above are by no means exhaustive of federal
government initiatives, let alone ones at the state and local levels. Any
comprehensive listing of such changes would require a monograph in itself.

Admittedly, all this activity—federal, state, and local—has fallen substantially short of that required to lift all aged persons into decent,
healthful, and meaningful living conditions. Poverty-level incomes are still
substantially greater among the aged than in the general population, and it
should be borne in mind that, without a major redistribution of incomes in
the nation (which is unlikely), roughly a quarter of all aged persons will
remain deprived and disadvantaged.[4]

Still, the change over the past decade, while short of the absolute need,
has been considerable. How is the change to be accounted for and what are
its larger implications? Though the problem seldom has been posed quite
this way by journalists and publicists, their commentaries on old-age
political activity often have offered an implicit answer. In various accounts in
the press, the impression is conveyed that public officials have taken action

simply because old people have become more conscious of their collective self-identity and more insistent on a response to their demands.[5] This explanation seems inadequate, although growing self-awareness and articulateness among old people do have political importance. Despite their restiveness and cohesiveness, old people still might have been ignored; American history, after all, abounds in cases of vocal, socially visible movements which failed for extended periods to achieve even their minimum political objectives—one thinks of the American labor movement in the nineteenth century. What has been lacking in press accounts is any serious consideration of possible "triggering" mechanisms or the emergence of social structures that intervene between the mass of the elderly and the official decision-makers. It will be the primary purpose of the present work to probe for such significant intervening factors.

This issue has relevance beyond the somewhat limited sphere of old-age politics. In the past quarter-century several leading political scientists, among them Robert Dahl, V. O. Key, Nelson Polsby, and Bernard Berelson, have taken note of evidence indicating widespread apathy in the American electorate and an absence of mass consensus as to how abstract constitutional principles are to be applied in concrete cases. (Many voters, for example, would deny the right of freedom of speech to dissident and allegedly "subversive" minorities.) Whereas an earlier generation of democratic political theorists were inclined to regard with grave apprehension any indications of mass political apathy, any evidence of lack of political knowledge or failure to grasp basic libertarian principles, the above-mentioned "modern theorists"—as they have been called in the literature—maintain that the health of a democratic order requires political sophistication and active participation only at the elite level of a democratic system. They define the proper role of the masses as consisting in a willingness to rally around the regime in crises and in acquiescing, in normal times, in the elite's policy determinations. Though "modern theorists" do continue to regard mass participation in national elections as having positive results, they are disinclined to grant the masses much of any between-elections political role. Indeed, some of them even insist that a significant level of mass apathy is functional from the standpoint of a democratic system's well-being; too high a level of political involvement, it is said, creates political instability.[6]

This attempt at reformulation raises problems, both normative and conceptual, and critics have not been slow in pointing them out. One line of attack has been that modern theorists fail to explain adequately the cases of basic change in the system—change initiated in the name of popular majorities and, typically, opposed by elite spokesmen. As Jack L. Walker remarked in a widely quoted 1965 essay, "A Critique of the Elitist Theory of Democracy," modern theory is vulnerable by virtue of its inattention to the demonstrable influence of mass opinion and mass action:

> As rigid and inflexible as it is, the political system does produce new
> policies; new programs and schemes are approved; even basic procedural
> changes are made from time to time. The elitist theory of democracy looks
> for the principal sources of innovation in the competition among rival
> leaders and the clever maneuvering of political entrepreneurs, which, in
> its view, is the most distinctive aspect of a democratic system. Because
> so many political scientists have worn the theoretical blinders of the
> elitist theory, however, we have overlooked the importance of broadly-
> based social movements, arising from the public at large, as powerful
> agents of innovation and change. . . . Social movements (if they have
> been studied at all) have usually been pictured as threats to democracy, as
> manifestations of "political extremism."[7]

Secondly, modern theorists have been interpreted, though it may not
have been their intention, as suggesting that the proper focus of scholarly
political enquiry is "power"—how obtained, how wielded, by whom
wielded and to what ends—and that other aspects of the political process,
while not to be ignored, merit less emphasis. Though the stress on the
related concepts of "power" and "decision-making" represents an advance
over the earlier "positional" and "reputations" approaches, in which the
existence of power relationships is imputed without being empirically
demonstrated, it has had the unfortunate result of deflecting attention from
what goes on prior to the decision stage. All too little is known empirically of
the process by which proposals attract the attention of decision-makers and
come to be defined as "serious" policy options—the process, in other
words, of agenda-building. This phenomenon has for the most part passed
unremarked even among those political scientists who have devoted major
attention to the behavior of interest groups and who might have been
expected to stress the importance of agendas as a major focus of group
pressure.

These matters are a major theme of a highly suggestive, though rather
neglected, work by political scientists Roger Cobb and Charles Elder on
participation in American politics.[8] Cobb and Elder suggest that the success
of those advocating new government programs whose acceptance would
affect large numbers in the population depends on two conditions: the
advocates must first expand the issues they have raised so that significant
numbers of onlookers become involved in the struggle; then they must get
their ideas placed on the public agenda and thus have them defined as
"serious" policy options.

The authors deal at length with "the dynamics of how the expansion of
issues to larger publics acts as a prelude to formal agenda consideration."[9]
They maintain that such expansion depends fundamentally on the degree to
which the leaders of the interest groups active on the issue succeed in

expanding the issue's scope, intensity, and visibility. Without such issue expansion, the proposal is unlikely to impress decision-makers as a matter of compelling importance and one worthy of their serious concern. To achieve the desired transformation, Cobb and Elder maintain that the issue, among other things, must be (1) defined or redefined as ambiguously as possible; (2) promoted in ways that seem relevant to "possible onlookers who become cognizant of the controversy" and whose involvement in the struggle helps enlarge its scope and thus enhance the likelihood of success; and (3) articulated through the skillful manipulation of symbols and made appealing to the mass media of communication.[10] In advancing the proposition that mass participation is fundamental to issue-expansion on matters of broadly defined social concern, Cobb and Elder take issue with the normative views of modern theorists at the same time as they avoid the trap that besets traditional democratic theory—namely, that a successful democratic polity requires citizens who have both a sustained interest in political issues and a coherent, internally consistent view of political fundamentals. Cobb and Elder neither demean the average citizen's political sagacity nor demand that he be a modern day Plato or Jefferson.

If we bear in mind the stated objective of explaining the proliferation of old-age agencies and programs in recent years, the Cobb-Elder formulation has an obvious intuitive appeal. Moreover, the suggestiveness of their argument should become even more apparent if one also takes into account the earlier period of old-age activism in America—a period when the expenditure of effort by activists was comparable but the results achieved far less impressive. For comparison's sake, then, I propose to deal with the old-age pension movement of the period 1922–35. The announced goal of this movement was to replace the traditional local government efforts to alleviate old-age dependency—focused around the infamous county poor-house system—with a program of state and national government cash payments designed to give the elderly the income necessary to provide for their own health and welfare.

As will become more apparent later on, this movement was by no means all of a piece; many sharp policy differences existed among its adherents, and these helped to sap resources and were a factor in its ultimate collapse. But notwithstanding the points of disagreement, the movement led in the twenties and thirties by such people as Isaac Rubinow, John Andrews, Paul Douglas, Elizabeth Brandeis, and—most vocal and colorful of all—Abraham Epstein was not lacking in dedication and expertise. Their combined efforts did manage to arouse public concern with the old-age dependency problem and were instrumental in winning at least a measure of governmental action, especially at the state levels after 1929. Yet, as I shall also argue in more detail later, the pension movement was at most only a qualified success and in many ways failed in its basic objectives. By no means all the states passed pension legislation and, among those that did, appropriation levels were, typically, ludicrously inadequate; moreover applicants were often compelled to undergo degrading "means tests." After Roosevelt assumed office in 1933, he was not indifferent to the plight of the elderly, but his attitude, and that of the New Deal, departed in basic respects from what the pension forces had been advocating. FDR's attitude toward pension leaders varied from one of indifference to outright rebuff. The honor of being remembered as "the father of social security" is one generally bestowed on Edwin E. Witte, the man Roosevelt appointed in 1934 to head the Committee on Economic Security and under whose direction the Social Security Act was actually adopted.[11] The honor did not go to Abraham Epstein, who for more than a decade was the foremost leader of the pension movement and who, early in the thirties, had actually coined the term "social security." When in August 1935 FDR signed the act into law, Epstein and his allies were not among those invited to the well-attended signing ceremony.

In seeking to account for the very limited record of success of the pension movement—and bearing in mind the Cobb-Elder thesis—two propositions seem worthy of consideration: (1) the type of leader who arose to articulate movement demands was not fully compatible with the strategic "givens" of the period ("leader" here means the agitator-subject-matter-expert type who typified the movement); and (2) the symbols the leaders chose to employ were ones having only a limited appeal to larger publics and were manipulated in ways that did not arouse a high sense of urgency.

Assuming that the weight of evidence is in support of these propositions, the later chapters of the work will undertake to determine whether the greater relative success of what I choose to call the "modern senior movement" has resulted in part from greater shrewdness on the two points mentioned; in other words, whether the current movement has enjoyed a different and more relevant type of leadership and has employed symbols of greater mass appeal and inherent urgency.

A corollary is that the difference in success rates characterizing the two periods was a function of variations in the size and internal structure of the participating voluntary organizations. I shall explore the possibility that since the thirties there has been a shift away from groups composed almost exclusively of subject-matter experts and from organizations which were essentially an extension of the personality of one man, and the emergence in their stead of highly rationalized and internally specialized structures, several of them composed of the aged themselves, who seek social change through their own direct efforts and not, as before, through persons acting as surrogates. The change I am referring to was not total, since in both eras there were cross-cutting tendencies; a true old-age mass organization (the Townsend movement) was present in the earlier period, while groups like the Gerontological Society, composed of expert professionals and lacking a mass base, have been a factor in the more recent one. I am inclined to minimize the importance of these cross-cutting tendencies on the grounds that the Townsend movement came into existence too late to affect decisively the content or timing of the Social Security Act; and in the sixties and seventies the elite-professional associations, while important sources of advice and counsel, have only marginally influenced the course of public policy.

After consideration of how old-age groups have been influential at the public agenda stage, it would be appropriate to consider the decision stage. It is beyond this work's scope to attempt anything so unwieldy as a comprehensive treatment of decision processes surrounding all significant old-age legislation and executive orders. Rather, my aim will be to deal with decision-making selectively, focusing attention on particular developments believed to be representative of the larger whole. Particular stress will be placed on interest-group interventions, since this is both consistent with the overall theme of the work and a topic that has been somewhat neglected in earlier commentaries.

It appears that interest groups intervene in old-age policy not just separately and autonomously but also as recognized participants in an ongoing "policy system." As early as 1951, when the first edition of his highly regarded *Congress: Its Contemporary Role* appeared, Ernest Griffith noted the enormous latent potential of the aged as a political force. In his discussion of how public officials and private groups often coalesce to decide policy in various sectors of the federal government, Griffith observed that "there are four major groups with very great political power—business, agriculture, labor, veterans. A fifth group, the aged, is emerging on the horizon as one likely to be of similar stature."[12] In an essay published in 1972 my colleague Dale Vinyard presented evidence that by the late 1960s there had indeed emerged in Washington a semiautonomous system of power concerned with protecting and advancing the interests of older citizens, a system in which senior-citizen groups, while not yet as influential as their counterparts in policy systems elsewhere, had at least come to play a significant role.[13] The old-age pension groups of the 1930s essentially failed in their efforts to gain acceptance as partners in the emerging social security policy system of that period, and, as I shall show in more detail later, this was a factor in their subsequent decline. The question of how and to what degree old-age associations of the more recent period have managed to gain full policy-system status is therefore one of considerable moment and one to which I shall devote some attention.

The closing section of this work will summarize the findings presented and elaborate on their theoretical significance. I am interested in how the data relate to propositions that have been advanced in various fields of social theory—interest-group behavior, social movements, and policy systems theory—and the final chapters will address these topics.

The Early Politics of
Social Security

2 Pension Crusaders and the Social Security Act

Enactment of Social Security in 1935 was essentially the beginning of the national government's involvement in the problems of the dependent aged and the unemployed. In a fundamental departure from the view that old age and employment security are needs properly dealt with through individual effort and private charity (with emergency supplemental help from local government) the Roosevelt New Deal undertook to erect a structure of financial protection, the revenues for which would be generated from a tax on worker payrolls and employers. This statutory development was related to a long-standing social insurance and pension movement effort which emerged in this country beginning in 1922. It is appropriate, then, to investigate to what degree and in what ways the movement and legislation were causally related. As mentioned previously, an important objective will be to find out how the old-age dependency problem got on the national political agenda in the thirties and whether the Cobb-Elder formulation can be used in accounting for what transpired.

The Campaign for Old-Age Pensions in the 1920s

The movement for old-age pensions financed and administered by state government arose in the years immediately following World War I.[1] At all times the movement's adherents were few—never more than a few hundred in the entire country—a fact attributable on the one hand to the general public's indifference to the whole pension question (a prudent individual, it was believed, would somehow manage to provide for his retirement needs out of savings generated during his employment years) and on the other hand to the widely held belief among those informed on pension matters that a formal retirement program, where called for, was best handled through private industry without government involvement. Within the circle of social insurance activists there existed three quite distinct schools of thought, and the degree of dissension among them tended to increase as the twenties gave way to the thirties.

One school, which may be labeled the ''relief and charity'' tradition, was strongest among the early social workers such as Jane Addams and Paul

Kellogg, editor of *Survey*, and others who joined with them in founding the
National Conference of Charities and Corrections at about the time of
World War I. These people believed that the causes of financial need lay
with the individual and that the solution was normally to be found in his
rehabilitation. While essentially individualistic and voluntaristic in outlook,
this group did espouse the need for social insurance, especially old-age and
mothers' pensions, which to their minds did not too seriously infringe on
basic voluntarist principles. They generally favored the type of state pension
involving gratuitous public assistance out of the general treasury rather than
contributory insurance schemes. This tendency had no single organizational
focus, but many of its adherents were active in the National Social Welfare
Assembly.

A second group consisted of persons who had studied foreign systems and
made themselves experts in social insurance theory. Prior to World War I
their leading exponent was Isaac Rubinow, who first achieved prominence in
1912 with a series of highly publicized lectures at the New School of
Philosophy in New York. Rubinow remained an active campaigner in the
twenties and thirties, but by this time a younger man, Abraham Epstein,
had become the leading advocate for Rubinow's views. In 1927 Epstein
founded one of the leading pension reform groups the American Association
for Old Age Security (AAOAS), and for the remainder of his career served as
its executive secretary.

The "social insurance experts" were not fundamentally imbued with the
individualistic outlook that typified the "relief and charity" school. By
proposing to spread the costs of old-age pensions and unemployment
insurance among both workers and employers and, they hoped, the
government, and by stressing that benefits should be regarded as a matter of
right, the members of this school sought to alleviate financial distress and
overcome the invidious overtones of the government dole. Moreover, they
regarded social insurance not merely as a way of protecting individuals but as
a means of readjusting the national product, perhaps not with absolute
equity but justly enough for national vitality; left unregulated, the capitalis-
tic system was not sufficiently responsive to meet the income needs of all
workers, especially manual workers.[2]

The third major tendency among the social insurance activists consisted of
persons who believed that changes could best be achieved under collective
bargaining, through which organized labor, business, and public-minded
reformers and officials would design reforms basic enough to prevent, and
not merely mitigate, the causes of hazards to industrial workers. They
believed that employers should be required by the state to create reserve
funds under mutual insurance companies (the essence of the so-called
"Wisconsin plan"). While the main emphasis was on the risk of unemployment, it was clear that the same basic approach could be applied to the

closely related matter of old-age security. The American Association for
Labor Legislation (AALL), founded by University of Chicago professor John
Commons in the early 1900s and for most of its organizational existence
headed by Commons's protégé, John Andrews, embodied this school of
thinking nationally.

In probing for possible linkages between the 1935 Social Security Act and
prior pension-group activity, several lines of inquiry suggest themselves. In
the first place, one can examine the group identifications of those individuals in the Committee on Economic Security known to have participated in drafting the bill. Secondly, in view of the fact that President
Roosevelt is known to have had strong convictions on the matter and was
personally involved in shaping the bill, FDR's own prior experience can be
surveyed. Finally, one can review the salient aspects of the act itself in order
to detect possible parallels between it and what major groups had been
demanding.

Edwin Witte's detailed account of the passage of the Social Security Act is
useful in identifying those individuals serving the Committee on Economic
Security who were most directly involved in drawing up the old-age sections
of the administration's bill. Pursuant to the president's Executive Order
6757 of June 29, 1934, establishing the CES, a Technical Board on Economic
Security, consisting of "qualified representatives from various departments
and agencies of the Federal government," was constituted. The Technical
Board was subsequently subdivided into five functioning committees,
including a five-member committee charged with investigating old-age
security. Of the five members, four were listed in *Who's Who in America*,
and it is noteworthy that two of these four, including the chairman, Murray
Latimer, identified themselves as members of the American Association for
Labor Legislation.

Executive Order 6757 also provided for the recruiting of a CES staff,
which was similarly subdivided as to subject matter. University of California
Law School professor Barbara Armstrong, whose 1932 book, *Insuring the
Essentials*, was highly regarded by CES executive director Witte, was named
director of staff studies in the aging field. Assisting her were Professor
J. Douglas Brown of Princeton and the aforementioned Murray Latimer.
Latimer and Brown listed themselves in *Who's Who* as AALL members, and
it is clear that Barbara Armstrong, while not listed in *Who's Who*, was more
than casually aware of the activities of AALL and AAOAS; these two groups
are mentioned favorably in her 1932 work and are central to her treatment of
"The Old Age Security Movement."[3] In addition, both Arthur Altmeyer,
assistant secretary of labor and the person designated by Labor Secretary
Frances Perkins to draw up the blue-print for CES, and Edwin Witte, chosen
by Altmeyer and Perkins for the post of CES executive director, were likewise
members of AALL.

While it is conceivable that this striking pattern of AALL involvement
could have been simply an incidental aspect of these individuals' concern
with social legislation, it is more likely that the collective efforts of these two
bodies (AALL and AAOAS) significantly affected their thinking. As Lloyd
F. Pierce has remarked, "From 1927 to 1934 the Eagles, Epstein's AAOAS
and the AALL were most active in creating great national interest in old age
pension legislation."[4] The effect of reform-group involvement on Edwin
Witte may serve as an illustration. Theron Schlabach notes that one of the
factors in the 1934 decision to name Witte to the key post of CES executive
director was that he, almost alone among social insurance activists, was
about equally close to the rival Epstein and Andrews camps. "Reflecting his
affinity with Andrews's group," Schlabach observes, "Witte favored [non-
contributory] old age pensions, but not very vociferously. Despite the
fissure, he maintained a personal friendship with Epstein, and along with
Commons accepted what proved to be a completely figurative position as a
member of Epstein's Advisory Council."[5] Though he was more actively
involved in AALL than in AAOAS, Witte had been a friend of Epstein for
years. Witte's ability to draw upon the resources of several often mutually
contentious groups appealed to those in the Labor Department; Arthur
Altmeyer has since remarked that Witte was able to "assemble and
focus . . . the best thinking available within the very short period of less
than six months."[6]

Witte also appears to have had close ties with a third group favoring social
insurance legislation, the American Public Welfare Association, and this
group, too, may have helped to shape his views both before and after his
coming to Washington.[7]

If staff personnel on the Committee for Economic Security tended to have
backgrounds in one faction of the social insurance movement—the American Association for Labor Legislation—it was not necessarily the case that
this faction also succeeded in getting its preferences written into the actual
bill. For a variety of reasons, some of them relating to Franklin Roosevelt's
personal inclinations, others to the particular form which the national crisis
took in the thirties, the AALL was largely unsuccessful in securing national
validation for its unique views. The AALL was continuing as late as 1934 to
espouse company reserves rather than compulsory contributory insurance as
the basic protection against unemployment and, in the field of old-age
security, was insisting on state pensions financed directly out of general
revenues. Franklin Roosevelt's lack of sympathy with this approach had
become apparent as early as 1930 when the AALL had endeavored to get the
state of New York to adopt its model bill, "An American Plan for
Unemployment Reserve Funds." FDR, as governor, had blocked its passage.[8]

The New Deal's social insurance bill did bear a certain resemblance to the principles championed over the years by Abraham Epstein. It was not an accident that in giving the proposal the novel title of "social security" the committee was adopting the term coined by Epstein and in 1933 made a part of his organization's name, which at this point became American Association for Social Security (AASS). Epstein had adopted this term to denote an approach to social legislation in which categorical aid programs based on the premise of governmental relief—aid to the blind, aid to the indigent, and so on—would be coupled in a legislative package with programs based on the principles of contributory insurance—unemployment insurance, old-age insurance, health insurance. The administration's bill also paralleled Epstein in insisting that benefits under the old-age and unemployment categories be regarded as a matter of right rather than be made dependent on the recipient's passing a means test to prove need. In his long struggle Epstein had helped give currency to these ideas and to legitimize them as "reasonable" options, thereby helping to overcome FDR's early anxieties that the public would reject such an approach as too "radical" and "socialistic."

Are Franklin Roosevelt's own strong convictions regarding social security, manifested at several points while the bill was being drafted by the CES, similarly traceable in some fundamental way to prior interest-group agitation, especially to activity by Epstein's group?[9] Roosevelt was at no time a member of any of the leading pension organizations, but his awareness of their agitation is suggested by his endorsement of old-age pensions during his 1928 campaign for governor of New York and by his call for a New York State commission on old-age security immediately after taking office. Early in his years in Albany FDR was obliged to weigh the relative merits of the rival pension-group forces, since the legislative committee created in 1929 at his behest was chaired by Senator Murray Mastick, whom the AALL had converted into an enthusiastic advocate of its program.[10] After giving the matter considerable thought, Roosevelt signed into law the Mastick committee pension bill, but he did so reluctantly, announcing that he would have preferred an act built upon compulsory contributory principles.

It was not accidental that FDR increasingly accepted compulsory contributory insurance as the proper way of providing for state old-age pensions. The AAOAS, whose national headquarters was in New York City, saw to it that its views were presented to the governor in forceful terms. As soon as he was elected governor but before he assumed office, Roosevelt received a visit from Epstein, Rabbi Stephen S. Wise, and three other AAOAS directors. It was Rabbi Wise, the highly esteemed leader of Reform Judaism and a crusader for numerous causes, who seems to have been especially important in getting the governor's ear on the matter. Wise had been involved in the AAOAS from the very beginning, warmly accepting Epstein's invitation to him in January 1927 to sit on the yet-to-be-created organization's executive committee; Wise agreed and even requested that his wife Louise be included.[11] In advance of a 1929 blitz of the state legislature in behalf of old-age pensions Wise discussed his testimony before the legislative committee with the governor. According to Freidel's account, Roosevelt received as much in the exchange as he gave, since after the hearings were over he thanked Wise for his "splendid piece of work before the committee" and expressed the wish that the rabbi "could come up here once a week regularly to give me courage and enthusiasm."[12]

About a year later, but at a time when his views on social insurance still had not yet fully crystallized, Roosevelt came in touch with a second person, Paul Douglas, who also was closely identified with Epstein and the AAOAS. Douglas was introduced to the governor through their mutual friend Frances Perkins, and he accepted an assignment to draw up the agenda for the January 1931 eastern governors' meeting called by FDR to consider state responses to the national economic emergency. The two men, in the context of discussions on social insurance, developed a fundamental rapport; in the words of one observer, "they hit it off at once and the governor quickly digested the facts the professor presented."[13] While not an official AAOAS spokesman like Wise, Douglas did share its basic outlook.

Franklin Roosevelt thus did not come to his conclusions on the urgency of social insurance suddenly, at the time of his June 1934 message creating the Committee on Economic Security. Rather, his thinking matured gradually and can be traced back several years. Without denying that the views he finally reached on this issue were to some degree his own unmediated response to an emergent social problem, the record suggests they were also conditioned by the demands of pension reformers, especially as brought to focus by persons identified with AAOAS. In a larger sense, too, the pension and social-legislation forces had succeeded by the early thirties in finding a place for their policy proposals on the agendas of state and national governments. They did not, however, succeed in gaining a very high or very secure place on such agendas, and this seems to have been a factor in the pension reformers' being blocked in subsequent efforts to wield direct political power.

Frustration at the Level of Direct Political Intervention

It is not by accident that parallels exist between what the social insurance activists had been demanding and the subsequent actions of many states and, later, the national government. Between 1923 and 1933 fully twenty-five state legislatures enacted pension laws of one kind or another, and though several of them were invalidated by gubernatorial veto or court action the fact remains that by the end of 1932 approximately 100,000 persons were in receipt of old-age security, a little over half of whom were in

New York State.[14] And it is also true that in the period from 1930 to 1933 the amount of money appropriated to pay for these state benefits increased more than twenty-fivefold.

But the pension crusaders were not so naive as to believe that all this amounted to much in terms of genuine accomplishment, considering the magnitude of the need. As historian Clark Chambers makes clear, many of the laws were so weak as to be virtually meaningless. He writes that, by 1931 and 1932,

> the AAOAS [Epstein's group] and its allies had consented to one dis-
> tasteful compromise after another. The Association and its allies had
> consented to long residency and high age qualifications, to the applica-
> tion of degrading means tests, to niggardly schedules of payment, to
> the principle of noncontributory insurance or pension arrangements.
> Not one of these compromises was agreed to cheerfully.[15]

As the Depression deepened it became increasingly apparent to movement leaders that further pressure on state legislatures was essentially futile, since in the face of a rapidly shrinking tax-resource base the states were reluctant to consider even the most paltry pension scheme.[16]

It was logical that at this juncture the social insurance activists should turn their attention to Washington, hoping that they might secure from the national government a grant-in-aid program, involving federal standards to insure state-to-state uniformity, and that this might make it possible for the states to act more aggressively, without bankrupting their treasuries. In 1932 and again a year later the so-called Dill-Connery bill, embodying Abraham Epstein's 1927 proposal that the federal government subsidize one-third of state old-age pensions, was introduced in Congress. Though reported on favorably by House and Senate committees and even passing the House in spring of 1934, the bill died in both sessions and was not viewed as likely of success later. Similarly, the 1933 Wagner-Lewis unemployment insurance proposal, which reflected AALL thinking essentially, also failed of passage despite an initial flurry of enthusiasm. Having thus been thwarted in efforts at direct legislative intervention, the pension reformers at this point channeled their energies in more indirect ways, hoping to realize their aims by influencing the administration's newly created Committee on Economic Security.

Here, too, the results proved highly disappointing for them. The reformers would have preferred that Roosevelt act on their concerns immediately, but his approach was leisurely. Though the 1932 Democratic platform had appealed for old-age pension legislation through state action, FDR waited fourteen months after his inauguration, and his June 6, 1934, message on income maintenance and old-age security, creating the CES, amounted to a plea for delay and leisurely study. And it was another two months beyond this before Edwin E. Witte arrived in Washington to take up his duties as CES executive director.[17] Witte initially made gestures toward the social insurance activists, though more on the basis of personal inclination, apparently, than because of any encouragement on this point from his superiors, Roosevelt and Labor Secretary Frances Perkins. The important November 1934 Conference on Economic Security, planned by Witte as a means of generating increased public awareness and support for his work, was postponed several weeks and relocated from Washington to New York City in order that Abraham Epstein, who had been ill and was unable to travel, might attend it and address the delegates.[18]

But this direct pension-movement involvement was more pro forma than genuine, Epstein being considered a force to be feared more than a valuable source of advice and counsel. As Witte's biographer remarks:

> Witte and his staff had taken care to consult with Epstein on the subject upon which his credentials were the soundest, old age security, and had included him as a speaker at the November conference. Because of his dogmatism, however, they had quite deliberately kept him out of their inner counsels. Epstein felt the exclusion very keenly.[19]

The CES chose to ignore two of Epstein's major precepts: the utter depravity of the Wisconsin plan for unemployment compensation and the need to subsidize social insurance from the general treasury in order to redistribute wealth.[20] On both issues the committee reached for the more conservative, probusiness option. Moreover, the CES came down for a system of social insurance which mixed national and state government administration, whereas by this time Epstein and the others were inclined to favor a purely national plan as the only way to insure adequate appropriation levels.[21] Epstein tried to get Congress to reverse the administration on these key points. At one point, for example, his American Association for Social Security rounded up twenty-four prominent advocates for unemployment insurance to urge the Senate Finance Committee to adopt Epstein's scheme of subsidizing the unemployment fund with general treasury monies. Edwin Witte was called on by the committee to counter these arguments, and he succeeded in doing so to the members' satisfaction.[22] It is little wonder, then, that Epstein should have attacked the social security bill before Congress and, in revising his 1933 work, *Insecurity*, should have added a ninety-page chapter titled, "The Failure of the Social Security Act to Meet the Problem of Insecurity."[23] Some of Epstein's allies, Isaac Rubinow for one, were not so inclined to criticize the act, deeming it a long step forward and the best that was then attainable. But none of them claimed that the act was in any way the direct outgrowth of their joint efforts.

At the signing ceremony for the Social Security Act in August 1935 the pension movement participants were notable for their absence; of their number there was only Frank E. Hering of the Fraternal Order of Eagles, and he was there, so it was explained in a press account, at the invitation of Senator Guffy and not (apparently) of FDR. (To anticipate somewhat the discussion in a later chapter, it bears mentioning that in 1965, on the occasions of President Johnson's signing of the Medicare law and a few days later of the Older Americans Act, the leading advocates of these measures from outside government were not only present but were accorded generous praise by LBJ—far different from the comparable case in 1935.)[24] How is it, then, that the old-age pension movement, having managed to draw attention to a social need and to get its concerns placed on the agendas of state and national governments, had such difficulty in gaining direct access to lawmakers and in getting its proposals defined as significant policy options?

Underlying Causes of Pension Movement Frustration

It is not surprising, considering his deep personal investment in the movement, that Abraham Epstein should have assessed its efforts favorably and explained its shortcomings as the consequence of various outside forces. He maintained that the absence in this country of a true radical and socialist movement on the European model, and the existence of implacable opposition efforts, together explained why progress toward social insurance was so slow in the United States. Epstein wrote:

> ... the movement for social legislation in the United States has remained
> to this day more in the nature of a philanthropic reform movement
> than an economic struggle between more or less equally powerful forces.
> Whatever progress has been accomplished has been due entirely to the
> small groups of individuals, banded together in private associations,
> who fought more or less militantly against universal overwhelming op-
> position. This fact accounts not only for the very slow and piecemeal
> achievements of our social legislation, but also for the emasculation of
> measures between their introduction and their passage.[25]

While there is no disputing Epstein's point that external factors contributed to the tardy and incomplete record of movement successes, it is
also the case that factors internal to the movement were quite important.
Historian Roy Lubove notes that "the legislative achievement before 1929
was nowhere commensurate with the intensive drive led by the Eagles and
Epstein" and goes on to give as one of the two main contributing factors to
this lack of achievement "the bitter controversy which erupted between
Epstein, on the one hand, and the Eagles and Andrews on the other."[26] The
quarrel was initially a personal one between Epstein and his supervisor at the
Eagles, Frank E. Hering, resulting finally in Epstein's 1923 dismissal from
the Eagles' staff. Later on, it evolved into a continuing doctrinal controversy

over the willingness of the Eagles and John Andrews's AALL to compromise on local optional state pension laws and, after 1930, over the proper approach to unemployment compensation.[27] Epstein's decision in 1927 to found the American Association for Old Age Security (AAOAS) alarmed his erstwhile movement colleagues. No matter what the new group's fate, John Andrews wrote to a fellow activist at the time, the result would prove harmful to the movement:

> If Epstein's movement is not strikingly successful or effective and fades away in the course of a year or two, it will do considerable harm both to our Association and to the old age pension movement. If . . . it becomes a really effective national membership organization it will divert from our Association a certain amount of interest and certain financial support that any duplicating organization is bound to do.[28]

As it became increasingly clear that AAOAS was to survive, the AALL explored new ways of coping with the menace its existence represented. Efforts were made to co-opt Epstein by giving him office space in the AALL's New York City headquarters, which came to naught when John Andrews realized that such a move might offend the Eagles and the United Mine Workers, with both of which his group had close ties. "I also had in mind," Andrews remarked in a letter to Hering, "the apparent danger that Epstein would suddenly at some juncture come out for a contributory plan of old age pensions which I know all three of our organizations [AALL, Eagles, Mine Workers] would consider unwise."[29]

The growing interorganizational rivalry, while not entirely preventing collaboration on shared concerns, was a real problem when it came to the framing of actual laws. Increasingly, in the 1929–33 period, Epstein's group identified itself with the so-called Ohio plan, involving abandonment of employer-controlled reserves and the substitution of pooled funds under state control, while Andrews's AALL pushed the Wisconsin plan, entailing employer reserve accounts in a state unemployment reserve fund. The difficulties were augmented in 1933 when Epstein's group enlarged its aims, since the difference of opinion between the two bodies now encompassed virtually all areas of AALL interest and not, as before, simply the issue of old-age pensions. The eventual defection of prominent social reformers like William Leiserson and Paul Douglas, and of major financial contributors such as Dorothy Douglas, to the upstart group was a major blow to AALL. The old-age pension movement was thus no exception to the rule that protracted factional strife tends to frustrate efforts to broaden the base of public support and thereby hampers efforts to achieve what Cobb and Elder describe as "issue expansion."

And there were other intramovement problems as well. As the authors of *Participation in American Politics* make clear, a reform effort's success tends to be heavily dependent on the types of symbols used and the forcefulness with which they are projected. The symbols employed, Cobb and Elder remark, should be highly abstract and ambiguous in order that "everyone can find a cause in the campaign that he likes and can identify with." In addition, the symbols should make the cause seem socially significant, that is, "concerned with the basic welfare of most people or a substantial segment of the populace."[30] The authors go on to mention other symbolic characteristics contributing to issue expansion, but these illustrate their general point. With this point in mind it is worthwhile to compare the relative potency of pension movement symbols and those employed by their conservative, antisocial legislation opponents. For this purpose the contents of one representative movement journal, the AAOAS house organ, *Old Age Security Herald*, were examined for a four-year period (1930–33). Since for the purposes of rebuttal the editors of the *Herald* gave considerable space to the views of their opposition, it was possible from this source to compare the kinds of symbolism employed on both sides.

The single, overriding symbol employed in AAOAS statements—one used for its strong negative valence—was the country poorhouse as an institution. The following headlines selected from various issues of the journal are illustrative: "Poorhouses Like Prisons," "Poorhouse Derogatory of Dignity," "Fit Only for Criminals," "He Prefers Death to Poorhouse," "Pensions Cheaper than Poorhouses." No other symbol remotely approaches this one in terms of frequency. Of course, the positive case for old-age pensions is made from time to time in the *Herald;* one number for example, contains a lengthy article maintaining that pensions are economical, administratively practical, contributory to old-age self-respect, and so forth.[31] But though rich in logic and data, the article is lean symbolically.

The symbolism of the opposition was broader in content. There is the image of the farsighted Founding Fathers of the republic shrewdly placing firm checks on the tendency of popularly elected legislative bodies to make extravagant use of tax resources. Also, there is the "opening wedge" image, seen as a dangerous step toward socialism. Finally, one finds the image of the "prudent citizen" wisely providing for his own retirement out of savings and not relying on wasteful government handouts. One National Association of Manufacturers spokesman voices opposition to old-age pensions "because the many virtues of the American people are threatened by such legislation. Our integrity, good habits, thrift and industry will go by the boards as soon as the Legislation is adopted."[32] An editorial in the *Hartford Times* (Connecticut), which the *Herald* quoted, affirms that such laws "paralyze the will to self-support and take away the inducement to build up a modest estate."[33] Indeed, the opponents of pensions call up almost every facet of the traditional American creed, making vivid use of such symbols as prudence, "higher" constitutional morality, self-reliance, thrift, and free enterprise. As the editor of the *Herald*, Abraham Epstein quoted these appeals in order to ridicule them and expose their use as a way of cloaking allegedly self-interested economic motives. Yet, there is no escaping the fact that Epstein's own propaganda made use of a narrow spectrum of symbolism, while that of his opposition had something in it for everyone.

Moreover, though the *Herald*'s emphasis on the evils of the county poorhouse presumably evoked a sympathetic response from its humanely inclined readers, there was notably little effort to reinforce this theme with appeals to defend cherished American institutions. One is reminded of the contrasting case of the temperance movement, whose adherents crusaded during the same period against the evils of the "saloon." The highly successful Anti-Saloon League made it a point in its propaganda to link the saloon with the evils of drunkenness and debauchery, the saloon occupying a place in its imagery roughly equivalent to the place of the poorhouse in the pension movement's symbolism. But the former movement by no means stopped here; it hammered away on the theme that drinking had deleterious consequences for the family, the church, the community and, the very fiber of American society.[34]

It is particularly interesting that the pension movement was deficient in images and symbols designed to evoke a positive response from the labor movement. It would have been difficult under the best of circumstances to generate labor support for pension legislation, considering that the American Federation of Labor under William Green's gentle leadership had recently assumed a new posture, shifting from militance to respectability, and in so doing working out a modus vivendi with business interests that ruled out most crusades for liberal causes. Nevertheless, at its 1929 Toronto convention the federation, in a sharp deviation from the voluntarism favored by Green's predecessor, Samuel Gompers, had explicitly endorsed the need for state-level pension legislation.[35] Epstein was aware of this development, and from time to time the *Herald* made references to evidence of growing labor support for its goals.[36] But this never became more than a minor theme.

The characteristic internal structure of the prosocial insurance groups also seems to have exacerbated the difficulty of issue expansion. The groups active on the pension issue in the twenties were of the caucus type, a form of organization which James Q. Wilson defines as one "in which one or a few leaders carry out the work of the organization, supported by funds or other kinds of support contributed by persons who rarely, if at all, are brought together in meetings or are otherwise asked to concert their actions in cooperative ventures."[37]

There seems to have been little thought given to the possible strategic advantages of transforming the pension groups into mass organizations and in so doing both enlarging the size of their attentive publics and enhancing the possibility of direct political action. In the course of a lengthy 1928 work on old-age matters Abraham Epstein had occasion to identify the kinds of people who recently had joined with him in founding AAOAS. Among the categories of participants he listed churchmen, businessmen, labor leaders, manufacturers, and workmen; significantly, he made no mention of direct participation by the elderly.[38] It apparently did not occur to Epstein or to his allies in the Eagles, the AALL, or the American Public Welfare Association to seize on the growing distress among America's old people—a development all of them knew about and emphasized—as a basis of political mobilization. Historian Clark Chambers was later to remark on this as a problem: "The failure of the pension forces to stir up the aged themselves to political action" was one circumstance which "conspired to minimize its influence."[39]

A decision to create mass organizations also might have enabled many labor union retirees to become involved in the pension movement, and as a result the linkages between pension and labor movements might have been strengthened. The establishment in the 1960s of the National Council of Senior Citizens would make it clear that a mass-based organization of this type was eminently viable. And as early as the 1930s the remarkable growth of the Townsend movement demonstrated that the aged, even then, could be mobilized in their own behalf.

The Townsend movement has not played a part in this account, not for any lack of intrinsic importance, but because the Townsend forces did not figure prominently in the events leading up to enactment of Social Security. Though one analyst has advanced a contrary view of the matter,[40] there is general consensus that the Townsend movement, which was unofficially launched with the founding of the first Townsend Club in 1934, came too late to decisively effect the course of legislative development. It is even doubtful that there is much substance to the view that the movement was instrumental in accelerating FDR's social security timetable, although in the 1934 elections several Townsend-endorsed candidates got into Congress and were highly vocal. When the movement's founder, Francis E. Townsend, with much fanfare visited Washington in 1935, Roosevelt refused his request for a meeting, an indication of the administration's strict hands-off policy.

Even if the movement had arrived on the scene earlier, it is doubtful that Franklin Roosevelt would have acquiesced in its demands. The Townsend organization—originally designated "Old Age and Revolving Pensions, Ltd." and after 1936 renamed "Townsend National Recovery Plan, Inc."—proposed a scheme to pay $200 per month (a very large sum by then-current standards) to all persons over sixty years who would agree to renounce gainful employment. More than just a pension proposal, the plan aimed to end the Depression by giving buying power to the elderly masses. While the movement's leader condemned socialism and sought to justify his plan as a method of making the traditional profit system work, he still was viewed by those in the political mainstream as demagogic and dangerous. The fact that revenues to support the plan were to be financed out of a tax on business transactions also tended to alarm moderate opinion, since this seemed to involve a vast enlargement in the scope of federal regulatory power.[41] The movement also suffered from serious structural deficiencies and the organizational ineptitude of its founder and leader.

For all of this, however, the Townsend movement did achieve remarkable grass-roots strength and in the words of Arthur Schlesinger, Jr., was "the most striking political phenomenon of 1935."[42] With virtually no support from putative opinion leaders in the country and with scant media publicity, the Townsend movement mushroomed into a mass crusade with a dues-paying membership numbering in the hundreds of thousands. In part, this vast support may have been attributable to the grandiose promises made by its founder, promises whose very extravagance contributed to their unfeasibility. What is more significant for present purposes, however, is that Dr. Townsend might well have evoked a large response even if he had not promised so much so soon—even if his proposals had been more "reasonable." The aged were an increasingly frustrated and disadvantaged group in the thirties, and many of them had been so since before the Depression.

In conclusion, one's assessment of the old-age pension movement and its efforts to influence the shape and content of social security legislation must vary, depending on what particular branch of it one is considering. The Townsend movement and the American Association for Labor Legislation helped influence the climate of public opinion in such a way as to increase the acceptance of the old-age pension concept, but they seem to have been relatively unsuccessful in gaining validation for their specific policy recommendations. For different reasons, AALL's Wisconsin plan for pensions financed out of employer reserve funds established in each state, did not prove broadly appealing, any more than did the Townsend scheme of pump-priming the economy by old-age pensions financed out of a business transactions tax. On the other hand, Abraham Epstein's concepts did find a place on the national public policy agenda, and he had the satisfaction of seeing many of his ideas enacted into law in 1935 and also (as will be noted in the following chapter) in the important 1939 amendments.

What Epstein failed to achieve, and this was largely responsible for the bitterness he felt, was genuine political access—"access" meaning the ability of a group or individual to affect, modify, or in some way shape the actions of a public official or lawmaker. Cobb and Elder state that the analysis of "access" is not a central purpose of their book, though on the other hand they remark that "it is not necessarily irrelevant to our concerns."[43] For a thoroughgoing treatment of this concept one may turn to David B. Truman's work, *The Governmental Process*. Truman remarks that of the various factors affecting the degree of group access "perhaps the most basic is the position of the group or its spokesman in the social structure"; handicaps in social status tend fundamentally to diminish group power over decision-makers.[44] In the case of Epstein's AASS in the 1930s one has a group advocating a cause—social insurance in a form which entailed heavy subsidies out of the national treasury—which was not only politically controversial but whose full-scale acceptance would have posed a serious threat to numerous vested interests in American society, business interests particularly. Franklin Roosevelt, during his first term of office, was faced with a Congress still quite conservative in many respects, and it was this political orientation, and the cluster of organized groups representing it, that FDR obviously had in mind in opting for the "conservative" options under social security. The social status of AASS was low in much the same sense given by Truman to the status of organized labor in the early years of the twentieth century;[45] in both cases the result was a frustrating sense of exclusion from policy formation on the part of the involved activists.

It is an interesting question why Epstein managed to gain access to Franklin Roosevelt as governor of New York and yet appears to have been denied it once FDR entered the White House. One plausible explanation has to do with the extent to which Epstein was in control of specialized information which Roosevelt considered valuable. In 1928–30, when Epstein was one of the few recognized experts on social insurance in the country and FDR was trying to formulate his views, the information provided by AAOAS was regarded as a valued resource; four years later, when FDR had gained a surer feel of the political implications of social insurance and when Epstein was no longer the exclusive possessor of expert knowledge, Roosevelt was in a position to listen to other advisors more sympathetic to his political thinking. Edwin E. Witte's biographer has referred to Witte as a "cautious reformer," and it is suggestive that it was to Witte that FDR should turn in 1934. In a scholarly essay Jack Nagel has argued that the manipulation of information is a crucial factor in group power,[46] and it follows that variations in the degree of group access will be a function of differences in the degree to which the group represents a monopoly of relevant information.

3 The Dismal Years

The national organizations active in the social security field at this time were not financially robust ones, but it still would have appeared to a viewer in the year 1935 that they were fixtures of the political scene and would quite probably survive. The American Association for Labor Legislation had been in existence for twenty-seven years and the American Association for Social Security had existed for eight. Though the Townsend organization was much newer, an observer might well have concluded that, given its expanding national membership and militant spirit, it too was destined to endure. Other groups, like the Eagles, the Mine Workers and the American Public Welfare Association, which had involved themselves in social security as an important secondary objective, could also be expected to continue lending their support.

As it happened, however, none of these expectations was fulfilled. By 1944 the AASS and AALL had passed out of existence, the Townsend National Recovery Plan was in an advanced state of organizational decay, and the more peripheral groups seemed little concerned with the course of social security policy. And it would be well into the decade of the fifties before new national groups would emerge to replace those that had disappeared or turned their attention elsewhere.

The question of why the pension movement should have declined so precipitously will be treated in this chapter, but the disappearance of national groups espousing the old-age cause raises a more fundamental issue, which will be the primary focus here. The question is, in what ways and to what degree did the absence of sustained interest-group involvement affect the course of old-age public policy in the 1940s? If, as has been argued in the preceding chapter, the pension movement had a significant, albeit highly indirect, impact on the Social Security Act, it follows that the absence of such a social force in the forties should have had certain consequences— either in the form of slower-than-expected legislative refinement and amendment of the act or in lesser substantive changes than deemed necessary, or in both.

The Decline of the Pension Movement

In some respects the waning of the two most prominent old-age advocacy organizations in the decade after 1935 was an outgrowth of pathologies already apparent in earlier years. Mutual distrust and policy differences continued. Lloyd F. Pierce, an authority on the history of AALL, remarks that in its conflict with AASS this group "dissipated much of its energy and lost some of its more influential members as well as some of its important financial contributors."[1] Presumably, AASS was similarly affected by the struggle. The continuance of the Great Depression also worked a severe hardship. The depression's effects had been felt earlier, but the absence of any prospect for quick recovery after 1935 tended to discourage both leaders and supporters. Staffs were slashed sharply and appeals for money took on an increasingly strident tone. A 1940 statement in the AASS newsletter affirmed bluntly, "The movement for social security for the American people is passing through a most critical hour.... We [in AASS] are now threatened with a complete blackout! Our financial need is now more desperate than at any time in our history! Our activities may come to a complete halt just when they are needed more than ever."[2] AASS income for 1940 was $19,000, down 50 percent from a few years before.

But the collapse of the two groups also stemmed from factors that could not have been forseen in 1935. The untimely death of Abraham Epstein at the age of fifty in 1942 was a crippling blow to an association he had come to embody, just as John B. Andrews's demise a year later deprived his association of crucial leadership. Even these events might not have been ultimately devastating if in years previous the two groups had managed to identify with goals broadly supported among the membership. In fact, however, many former supporters had left the fold and many of those remaining were unhappy. A glimpse of how Abraham Epstein had come to be regarded is offered in the following account published at the time of his death in the AASS official house organ:

> In 1934 began the greatest tragedy in Epstein's life and one which was ultimately to hasten his death.... Epstein attacked the [Social Security] Act as a regressive and dangerous measure.... People reviled him, friends deserted him, *half of the members of the association resigned....* Others went further and accused him of being in the pay of the Republican Party during the 1936 Presidential campaign. "Those were bitter fights," said he at his testimonial dinner. "They were no minor fights; they were basic fights which took away my sleep, my desire for food, some of the most productive years of my life; *for it was not easy to be fighting with my own friends, and nobody cherishes being called a 'sellout'.* "[3] [Emphasis added.]

The enactment of the 1939 amendments to the Social Security Act were in some respects a vindication of Epstein's views—the acceptance, for example, of the principle that recipients' needs should be considered in his social security benefit level, the substantial reductions in the "excessively large" reserves in the social security trust fund, and so forth—yet this victory did not bring his old friends flooding back into the fold.[4]

In the early 1940s Epstein became embroiled in a dispute with organized labor, in prior years one of the largest sources of revenue for his association. Another contributing factor in the demise of his organization may have been the continued coolness manifested by the chairman of the Social Security Board, Arthur Altmeyer. Altmeyer cooperated with AASS when it suited his purposes, but his relationship to Epstein seems to have been a "correct" and distant one.[5]

The Townsend organization began to fall to pieces in 1936 when Dr. Townsend agreed to participate in an abortive third-party presidential campaign along with Father Charles Coughlin and Gerald L. K. Smith. In the same year he broke with the man who in fact was the cofounder of the movement (and its organizational brains), Robert Earl Clements, and Townsend never succeeded in finding a suitable replacement. Followers also became increasingly discouraged when it became apparent that the Townsend plan had no realistic chance of adoption by Congress. The "plan" in its original form was introduced in the 1935 congressional session as H.R. 3977. Though by this time there were several members of the House who had been elected with Townsend support, the bill found little support among floor leaders after being reported out of committee. Three years later in hopes of attracting greater congressional support an alternative "plan" was drawn up (H.R. 2), but it still represented no concessions to the social insurance approach favored by those in the political mainstream, and it died in committee. After 1938 the Townsend program no longer aroused much interest on Capitol Hill.[6]

With the decline and fall of the three organizations for which old-age pensions were a primary focus, it was scarcely surprising that the other involved associations, for which pensions had always been somewhat secondary, should turn their attention elsewhere.

As a result of these developments those in the administration and in Congress who hoped to enlarge and perfect the social security statute worked in the absence of organized old-age clientele group support. The purpose of the following section will be to determine what, if any, were the consequences of this lack. The treatment of social security politics in the 1940s will be quite selective since the intent is not to present a history of social security but to access, as best one can, the significance of one particular variable in the legislative process.

What Reformers Demanded

If the purpose of social security was, as its architects had intended, to provide protection as a matter of right for the American worker in his retirement, then the program as it stood after the 1939 amendments left a good deal to be desired. By 1950 over twenty million workers would remain ineligible for monthly benefit payments under the Old Age and Survivors Insurance (OASI) provision of the Social Security Act. Given this limited range of OASI benefits, another program, Old Age Assistance—stigmatized by many as a "dole" and requiring a means test to determine eligibility—continued to be massive: there would be only 2.1 million OASI beneficiaries in 1950, compared to the 2.8 million still drawing OAA benefits.

Moreover, monthly payment levels for workers eligible for OASI coverage would remain virtually static during these years—the average primary benefit remaining fixed at $23 for the 1940-49 period—and this meant a drastic decrease in buying power, considering the factor of inflation. A Social Security Administration study of 377 randomly selected OASI beneficiaries in Philadelphia and Baltimore, which compared income from all sources in 1941 to that in 1949, would forcefully underscore the extent of the distress. A clear majority of the retirees surveyed had suffered a decline in real earnings over the period in question. "Three-fourths of the 237 aged beneficiary groups whose composition remained unchanged . . . had less real income in the 1949 survey year," the study revealed. "Nine-tenths of the 105 aged beneficiaries who has lost a spouse between 1941 and 1949 had less real income in the second year than the couple had in the first."[7] Furthermore, the report went on to stress, the initial 1941 coverage had been anything but adequate by then-current living standards: "If in the first survey year [the aged] had received only their retirement income, three-fifths of the aged beneficiaries . . . would have had less than the cost of a maintenance level of living. In 1941 the cost of maintenance level of living for a single old person living alone in Philadelphia or Baltimore was about $450."[8] With a diminution in real income in the intervening years, many retirees presumably were having even greater difficulty reaching a "maintenance" level of living, though exact figures on this point were unfortunately lacking at the time the study was published.

Aware of the millions of workers who were either not covered at all or were receiving benefits inadequate to even a very modest level of need, informed voices were heard as early as the beginning of the 1940s calling for further substantial enlargements in the basic program. In its *Seventh Annual Report* for the 1941 fiscal year the Social Security Board went on record favoring extension of OASI benefits to agricultural labor, domestic service, public employment, service for nonprofit institutions, and self-employment. It drew attention to the fact that, as of 1941, only about 42 percent of wives of primary beneficiaries over sixty-five were entitled to coverage. Also mentioned was the need for enlarged monthly payments. Subsequent annual reports made the same plea in increasingly forceful terms. As World War II drew to a close board chairman Arthur Altmeyer, in a series of articles in the official *Social Security Bulletin*, offered detailed evidence of the distress caused by the failure of OASI to cover many categories of workers. He wrote of the need to "round out" Social Security in "terms of the groups it should cover and the groups in the population to which it should afford protection."[9]

Closely parallel views were set forth at about the same time by the major labor federations, the AFL and CIO. Though the American Federation of Labor had not played a leading role in enacting the 1935 Social Security Act (according to one observer the federation was concerned with how the program might affect the benefit programs long maintained by some of its affiliates), by the early forties the federation's views had shifted decisively toward support. In part the shift grew out of a need to counter criticism on the Social Security front from the upstart CIO.[10] As early as 1941 the AFL executive council went on record in favor of extending OASI to cover all workers not then included, and about the same time President William Green came out for higher old-age insurance benefits and supplementary allowances for dependents. Shortly thereafter the AFL appointed Nelson Cruikshank as its first Director of Social Insurance Activities; working through the AFL's Social Security Committee, Cruikshank maintained close relationships with the federation's legislative department and with labor's friends in Congress.[11] The CIO was also active in this field. The position of both labor federations in favor of expanded coverage and enlarged benefit levels, as well as a higher payroll tax to finance it, was often noted in press accounts at the time.

It should occasion no great surprise that the initial response to these demands on the part of federal officials and lawmakers was to quietly shelve them; with the Second World War in progress no domestic reform legislation was receiving more than a polite nod in official Washington. As the war drew to a close, however, the prospects for new domestic initiatives brightened. In 1946 Congress, heeding the demands of a vocal and highly energetic coalition of organized labor and liberal interest groups (the "lib-lab lobby"), passed the Employment Act of 1946.[12] The advocates of enlarged Social Security coverage must have felt that the atmosphere also was propitious for action they had long recommended.

Immediate Postwar Developments

The issue of Social Security affected the lives of such a large segment of the population that reform proposals relating to it elicited a response from the president, congressional leaders, and national party conventions. But what was said and done on the matter could not have made the reform advocates very happy. Although in his January 1946 State of the Union message, President Harry Truman called for higher benefit-levels and inclusion of many additional workers under OASI, he did not follow this up, as he did for issues of major importance, with special messages later on. During the first session of the Eightieth Congress, in 1947, he again referred to the Social Security issue, but in general terms and without much urgency. And the same was true of his handling of it later in 1947 when he delivered his first economic message to Congress. Congressional leaders likewise seemed to believe that some legislative action was called for but that Social Security could wait until other matters were taken care of. Toward the close of World War II the House appointed a Special Committee on Post-War Economic Policy and Planning, and among the numerous recommendations the committee made was one to expand OASI coverage and liberalize benefits. But the proposal was sidetracked in Congress, and instead the lawmakers voted to delay for another year any increase in the Social Security payroll tax—an apparent concession to workers' desire for continued high take-home pay. The action of platform writers for the two major political parties showed a similar lack of concern. The 1944 Democratic platform failed even to mention Social Security in listing needed legislation, despite the fact that the platform that year was specifically aimed at anticipating postwar domestic needs. This actually amounted to dropping a plank from the 1940 Democratic platform that called for expansion of OASI, and it was not until four years later (1948) that the proposal was reintroduced. The Republican platform writers were more consistent in what they had to say on the matter, proposing in 1940, 1944, and 1948 that OASI coverage be expanded to include "groups and classes not now covered." But in the first two of those election years the language was guarded; in the words of the 1940 platform, expansion was to occur "wherever practicable."

Thus Social Security Administration officials found themselves in the difficult position of having to confront acute distress among their old-age clientele for which they were unable to attract much official interest or concern. This may have been a factor in the SSA's attempt to expand, by administrative interpretation, the range of occupational groups covered by OASI. Early in its existence in the late 1930s the old Social Security Board had ruled that newspaper and magazine vendors were entitled to coverage as "employees." Subsequently, in the mid-1940s, the SSB rendered a judgment later confirmed in rulings by the U.S. Supreme Court, which extended the concept of "employee" to include approximately 750,000 "independent contractors" consisting of salesmen, insurance agents, miners, and loggers.[13] Congress's response to this action was revealing. Faced with what it chose to view as a challenge to its legislative prerogatives, the Eightieth Congress responded swiftly, voting to repeal the unlegislated expansions of

Social Security coverage in what was termed the "status quo resolution" and later to override President Truman's veto of the repeal legislation. While this is not to be construed as evidence of any basic congressional unhappiness with the Social Security system as such—indeed several congressional leaders used the occasion to call for a reaffirmation and broadening of the system[14]—the action does substantiate one's impression that the issue lacked urgency for the Congress.

Further Delays in 1948

In 1947 the Senate Finance Committee appointed an Advisory Council on Social Security, the authorizing resolution being cosponsored by Eugene Millikan, Republican, and Walter George, Democrat—the chairman and ranking minority member, respectively, on the committee. This bipartisan sponsorship was indicative of an emerging consensus on the social security reform matter. The advisory council's report, issued early the following year, made a strong case for massively enlarging Social Security expansion and backed up its recommendations with voluminous data.[15] Similarly, the House Ways and Means Committee, acting on the basis of a four-month study by one of its subcommittees, around the same time voted out a bill embodying a proposed expansion of the federal program.[16] The White House, too, began to manifest a degree of interest. In mid-1947 President Truman abandoned his attempts at conciliation with the Republican-controlled Eightieth Congress and instead, in the words of an analyst, adopted a strategy of "unequivocal demands for action on a variety of social and economic questions and sharp reaction to even the most limited Congressional attacks on Administrative programs."[17] With the 1948 elections impending, the president's advisers urged him to concentrate on the Democratic coalition—labor, liberals, urban minorities—by moving toward the position of Henry Wallace and thus to preempt the Republicans and Wallace's Progressive party on social reform legislation. In his 1948 State of the Union address Truman spoke up for significant improvement in OASI. Under the rubric of developing and protecting the nation's human resources, Truman emphasized that the existing system "has gaps and inconsistencies, it is only half-finished."[18] In a subsequent special message on social security Truman called for an increase in OASI benefits of at least 50 percent, extension of coverage to an additional 20 million workers, and a raise in the base of wages on which the contributory tax is collected.

But if a consensus was emerging that significant steps were required, the leisurely atmosphere persisted. By spring 1948 Congress had before it committee-endorsed bills, blue-ribbon panel recommendations, and a host of supportive data which could have provided a basis for new legislation, at least of a stopgap character. Instead, the lawmakers adjourned for the summer and for the upcoming presidential nominating conventions with Social Security matters still pending.

A Minimally Adequate Statute

With his upset victory in the November 1948 election behind him, President Truman early the following year introduced draft legislation on Social Security, the provisions of which essentially paralleled those made for close to a decade by the Social Security Administration (formerly SSB). The bill provided for extension of coverage to self-employed workers, farm laborers, independent contractors, and state and local government employees, and also for increases in the level of benefits and in the contributory tax base. Eligibility requirements also were liberalized. Congress thereupon held hearings on the proposal, and support was voiced by spokesmen for a wide variety or groups, even business groups like the U.S. Chamber of Commerce.[19] A slightly scaled-down version of the bill was approved by overwhelming margins in both houses, and the Social Security Amendment of 1950 was signed into law in the summer of that year.

In the view of many, what got through was decidedly modest both in terms of coverage and levels of benefits. In discussing the then-pending bill before the Senate Finance Committee in February 1950, Harvard economist Sumner Schlichter observed that the measure would bring under Social Security only about half of the jobs not yet covered.[20] Congressional leaders were aware of the remaining gaps but rationalized their decision to exclude certain occupational groups on the ground that spokesmen for these groups had not demanded coverage. The failure to include farm workers employed less than sixty days per year—mostly day laborers and migrant workers—was a case in point; another was the specific exclusion of many professional workers. Moreover, the authorized increase in monthly benefits of 77.5 percent (from $26 to $46.15) does not seem particularly impressive in light of changes in price levels over the previous decade. According to the Bureau of Labor Statistics' Consumer Price Index the cost of living between 1941 and 1951 rose 77 percent, from an index number of 62.9 to 111.0.[21] Since OASI benefits had risen scarcely at all over the decade, it would appear that the amendments barely made up for the cost of living rise and involved no increase in real income. It will be recalled that an average retiree living in a major metropolitan city in 1941 had a combined income from all sources that did not even reach a ''maintenance'' living standard. Retirees situated in smaller communities may have fared somewhat better, but they could not have been much better-off. These gaps and deficiencies were readily apparent at the time, and it would take a decade or more of further struggle before anything approaching universal worker-coverage under social insurance was to be achieved in the United States.

Conclusion

It is my contention that if there had existed in Washington one or more politically self-conscious and aggressive aging organizations in the 1940s—organizations with a mass constituency of retirees—it might not have taken five years after World War II to get significant social security amendments passed, nor would the final legislative product have been so modest. This is admittedly an arguable point, but I believe the weight of evidence supports it.

For purposes of analogy the case of California may be introduced. In the early 1940s a vigorous advocate for old-age pensions, George McClain, began to emerge as a significant force in the state's politics. Though California had long been noted for old-age pension activism, by Town-sendites and the Ham and Eggs Organization particularly, it was not until McClain entered the picture and created his "Citizens Committee for Old Age Pensions" that the state's aged had a spokesman who combined an ability to adopt politically feasible goals with a shrewd "feel" for effective lobbying. McClain was never reluctant to use the political power he derived from the support of California's senior citizens, who backed his efforts by the hundred of thousands. He became both widely revered and fiercely hated as a consequence. Though not without faults as a tactician and organizer—for example, he tended to foster a dangerous dependency relationship between himself and his old-age constituents—McClain knew how to build a pressure-group structure and to turn it forcefully toward the achievement of policy goals. The fact that the state old-age pension expenditures in California soared from $68 million in fiscal 1940–41 to $223 million in 1950–51 and to $375 million in 1968–69 has been attributed in at least two scholarly studies to the effectiveness of the state old-age lobby, of which McClain's organization was the leading component.[22]

Obviously, the political environment in Washington differed greatly from that in California, and even a man of McClain's considerable skills would likely have found the going rougher in the nation's capital than in Sacramento. Old-age activists had not been as vocal in Washington over the years as they had been in California, and the aged nationally are not as readily mobilizable as in California where a large proportion of them are transplants, uprooted from their original home states and thrown back in many cases on local and state resources. California governors have been known to be elected or defeated on the basis of their stand on old-age pensions; the same has not been true of U.S. presidents. But notwithstanding the differences in political climate, one can not reject the hypothesis that if a McClain-type organization had existed in Washington in the 1940s it probably would have enjoyed substantial success.

It might be objected that the delay in congressional action did not result from the absence of external-clientele group pressure but from the political deadlock between the president and Congress, with social security reform being one among several legislative victims. I feel this view tends to overlook the fact that the issue in question was not essentially a party-line matter, even though Harry Truman tried to make it appear as such in his 1948 reelection campaign. It would be hard to demonstrate that on this issue there was any greater degree of support on the part of northern, urban Democrats than among Republicans and southern Democrats. The usual cleavages on domestic reform legislation did not apply in the Social Security area, and thus the problem seems to have been not so much deadlock between antagonistic forces as a lack of real urgency anywhere in the legislative process.

2

Movement Origins:
Social Supports and
Structures

4 Birth of the Senior Movement

Analysts until quite recently have commonly discounted the possibility that the aging might become a political force in American society or lend support to politically effective old-age pressure groups. The author of a 1969 article in the official journal of the American Gerontological Society observed that during the entire period from before the passage of the 1935 Social Security Act through at least the early 1960s the nation lacked "the necessary conditions for the formation and maintenance of [aged] interest groups," and that as a consequence old-age political movements were, and presumably would continue to be, "handicapped from their very inception."[1] The views of most writers who addressed aging matters in the 1950s were similar in tone. Abraham Holtzman, the author of the definitive study of the Townsend movement of the 1930s, maintained in a 1954 essay that, as a result of changes begun by the New Deal, "socio-political conditions have been so altered" and the major political institutions have become so responsive, that it is extremely unlikely that the aging will once again "resort in large numbers to independent political action."[2] Another observer, Angus Campbell of the Survey Research Center at the University of Michigan, maintained on the basis of 1950s survey data that older people had not, and in all likelihood would not, "become a self-conscious political group with a sense of common interest and a capacity to move as a group."[3]

Yet, looking at the situation from the perspective of the 1970s, it is apparent that the decade of the fifties was prelude, not to a period of quiescence, but to a time of marked activism among the aging, involving the emergence in the sixties of politically influential, mass-based organizations and interest groups. It is not suggested, of course, that recent events have exactly contradicted the analyses put forth by the aforementioned writers; spokesmen for the aging, for example, have not functioned "independently" of the established two-party system, and to this extent Abraham Holtzman's 1954 assessment remains valid. Nevertheless, what has been seen recently does at least point in a different direction from the one predicted, and for this reason a reassessment of the 1950s seems to be in order.

It can be assumed that political interest-groups do not spring fully formed out of a political vacuum but are instead typically preceded by periods of gestation. Moreover, when a series of groups, all pointing in the same political direction, appear to spring into life at about the same time, or when long-existing ones fundamentally alter their goals in similar ways, there is reason to suspect that all are responding to some common underlying motivation. In the case of the aging a clue to the identity of this common element may be found in the remarks of Arnold M. Rose, a sociologist on the faculty of the University of Minnesota, who was among the persons addressing the Fourteenth Annual Conference on Aging at the University of Michigan in June 1961. In the course of his address Rose explicitly "parted company" with the rather pessimistic views of his fellow panelist Angus Campbell, one of the analysts mentioned above. Rose contended that at the time of the conference there was already in existence "a dynamic movement of aging consciousness that has developed in the last five years and that promises to sweep aside the traditional [inhibiting] factors that Campbell so well analyzes." Without suggesting that the aged groups had yet achieved the degree of cohesion or sophistication characteristic of some mature political movements, he nevertheless underlined the fact that "there is a great increase in the number of voluntary associations for the elderly, and some of these are taking on the function of acting as pressure groups to work for legislation for the benefit of the aging, even while they retain other functions such as providing social and recreational outlets for their members." Rose offered the challenging and suggestive opinion that what had been happening in the 1950s amounted to the continuance in another form and under different leadership of the Townsend movement of the thirties, the earlier movement having failed to develop into a full-scale social movement for a number of reasons including the discrediting of some of its leaders and the distractions created by World War II. "Such a full-scale social movement," he suggested, "did get under way in the late 1950s, although not under the aegis of a single organization."[4]

Though Rose was to develop the sociological implications of this insight in other writings, neither he nor other writers have undertaken to establish possible linkages between the diffuse social movement of the fifties and the politically aggressive, organized senior-citizens groups of the sixties and seventies. Since evidence of such a linkage would strengthen my argument regarding the importance of senior citizens as an autonomous political force, there is ample reason for investigating the point.

Difficulty of Mobilizing the Aged

Attempts to organize aged persons for any purpose—sociability, mutual benefit, recreation, political pressure—are marked by frustration, and this was probably an important reason why John Andrews, Abraham Epstein, and most other pension activists of the twenties and thirties made little effort to bring their numbers to bear in pension crusades. Several factors underlie the problem. First, far more of the aging suffer mental and physical handicaps than do younger persons. For those who are becoming mentally senile, any kind of organizational work is, of course, practically out of the question. Although senior citizens in a social movement may not abruptly cease to participate when their health and mental agility begin to deteriorate, the quality of their participation inevitably declines, and this tends to hamper the larger effort of which they are a part. A closely related consequence of physical impairment is the very high rate of membership turnover that typifies all organized senior-citizen efforts. In the case of senior clubs, for example, surveys reveal that membership turnover—resulting from death, illness, disabling injury—averages a staggering 25 percent annually.[5]

Second, compounding the purely physical factors is the widespread lack of income and organizational experience among older persons. Studies have shown that financial problems are an inhibiting factor to individual participation in groups regardless of age level, and that among retired persons, many of them uncertain as to how long they will have to stretch their savings, the reluctance to pay dues to an organization or otherwise make a long-term commitment is especially marked. In a culture that teaches its members that economic and health problems are rightfully to be met through individual effort, attempts to meet problems collectively through united action are typically viewed with suspicion, and this tends to further frustrate group efforts. Even in cases where the older person was accustomed in prior years to participation in voluntary associations, the thought of doing this on an age-graded basis scarcely presents itself as an option. Younger persons do not typically group together on the basis of age, and this attitude tends to carry over into later years, with frustrating consequences for senior-citizen organizers.[6]

Public Agency Efforts to Reach the Aging

In view of these interlocking factors, it is scarcely surprising that the initial push toward what later was to become a true social movement should come not from the aged themselves but from governmental agencies and officials whose work obliged them to deal regularly with an aging clientele.

On the basis of a report presented by his staff committee on the aging, Oscar Ewing, head of the Federal Security Agency during the later Truman years, convened in 1950 a National Conference on Aging. Though the conference did not achieve any dramatic results or generate a large measure of publicity, the 816 delegates in attendance did give explicit attention to the problems of aging persons and helped to legitimize this topic as a focus of public concern—something that had not been done before. The conference's long-term impact may have owed something to the fact that it occurred not, as in the 1930s, during a period of profound economic crisis which called for "emergency" programs for various needy groups, but during a time of relative prosperity when it had become clear that certain population categories had not automatically benefited from the return of economic normalcy. Moreover, the timing of the conference was politically opportune, since the Truman administration's Social Security advisors were then casting about for a strategy to overcome congressional hostility to the president's national health program, decisively defeated in its comprehensive form in the 1949 session of Congress. By narrowing the coverage of the program to the aged alone, chances for enactment could be greatly enhanced: as one analyst has noted, "the aged, like children and the disabled, commanded public sympathy. They were one of the few population groupings about whom one could not say that the members should take care of their financial-medical problems by earning and saving more money."[7] During the summer following the conference, Ewing announced a broad new legislative proposal to provide sixty days of hospital care per year to the 7 million aged Social Security beneficiaries, and a short time later the "aged approach" received the president's official endorsement.

The emphasis on the aged as a public policy priority did not significantly abate with the advent of the Eisenhower administration in 1953. Consistent with the new president's overall political preferences, however, the administration's approach was to encourage activity by the states rather than the federal government, and to deemphasize proposals for sweeping new measures in the area of health care, which Mr. Eisenhower saw as entailing the risk of "socialized medicine." Especially important in the effort to encourage state efforts was the work of Clark Tibbetts, head of the Federal Security Agency's staff committee on aging, and of Sidney Spector, a staff member of the Council of State Governments. At about the same time, the Conference of State Governors sponsored a comprehensive study; the results, released in 1955, recommended that the states undertake a broad program of action for the elderly—in employment, welfare, housing, and so forth. The emphasis on federal-state joint planning characteristic of this period found expression in two major conferences on aging, one in September 1952, attended by federal officials and representatives of fifteen states, and another in 1956 in which forty-one states were represented. By 1955 twenty states had created permanent councils or commissions, and an additional seventeen had established temporary study groups, on aging problems. Since most of these bodies employed full-time staffs, a cadre of knowledgeable professionals was emerging in state capitals across the country.[8]

The changed climate of opinion reflected in these governmental initiatives was also mirrored in the work of scholars and practitioners. The number of articles and special periodicals dealing with aging matters grew explosively; as many articles are listed in the standard geriatrics-gerontology index for the six-year period ending in 1955 as in the entire forty-eight years preceding. Likewise, under the heading "Older Persons" in the *Congressional Record*, the number of entries increased from six in 1953 to a full column in 1955 and one and one-half columns in both 1956 and 1957.[9]

Significance of Senior Centers

Had the emergent interest in the aging remained, as it was at the outset, the expression of concern by social workers and expert professionals with a newly identified dependent group in the population, the long-term effects might have been modest. But one important aspect of governmental interest was the realization that senior citizens must be located, visited, and brought to an understanding of efforts being made to assist them. One effect of this effort, probably not wholly anticipated, was to give the elderly an unprecedented consciousness of their collective needs and political opportunities.

Except in the rather atypical retirement community, most senior citizens in these years did not cluster together in well-defined neighborhoods or social settings where their concerns routinely became matters of interest to elected representatives. As is typical of most disadvantaged minorities, the aging were largely "invisible."[10] In keeping with the growing official concern with the aged, officials of both government and private social welfare agencies came more and more to emphasize the value of "senior centers" and other formal structures where older persons could come together, both for professional advice and for mutual reinforcement and sociability.

The first known centers for older persons came into being only in the early 1940s, in the form of New York City's Hodson and Sironich centers. News of them, conveyed by word of mouth, writings, and speeches, prompted a sustained organizing effort; a survey completed in 1961 by the National Council on the Aging found 218 senior-citizen centers in existence—the definition of a center being the presence of at least one full-time staff person. There were in addition two thousand "aged group services units," often designated as clubs, which had an ongoing existence but lacked staff.[11]

Relative to the total aging population, the rate of senior-citizen participation in these clubs and centers has never been large. Surveys conducted in various states and communities during the mid-1950s found that membership rates ranged between 1 and 3 percent of eligible persons; in 1960 one informed observer, Robert J. Havighurst, estimated that nationwide about 2 percent of the elderly, or 250,000 persons, were members of senior clubs.[12]

Though small in terms of absolute numbers, the elderly, through such associations, were beginning to make an impression by virtue of their commitment and group cohesion.

The core of the club movement was the senior center which, as a consequence of its relatively greater resources and superior staffing, had a capacity for autonomy and long-term survival that the old Townsend clubs had conspicuously lacked. The purposes of the senior centers were diverse, though recreation, self-help, and sociability were among the central concerns. Political activism was almost never among the goals initially set forth, and in this respect, too, they were different from their Townsend forerunners. And because they spoke day in, day out to the needs of their elderly constituents and not simply to a millennial dream of seeing Dr. Townsend's "plan" adopted, the senior centers manifested an impressive capacity for long-term survival.

The degree to which the centers are, or ought to be, the focus of mass-based political action by the aged has long been a major concern of the movement's leaders. To eschew altogether a concern with public-policy matters clearly would serve no useful purpose, and the leaders have not attempted any such thing. One of the goals found to prevail among most centers surveyed by the National Council on the Aging was "to serve as one vital force that will alert and educate the community to change its own attitudes toward older people, and move the community to create and develop appropriate services to meet their needs."[13] Though a few centers did try to prohibit outright discussion of social and political issues, the vast majority opted for a conception of the senior center as a forum through which education, information, and debate on current public issues might be presented. The leaders have sought to encourage the elderly to "more effectively exercise their rights as citizens to participate in political activity . . . [and] to act with enlightened self-interest to attain fair and decent living conditions" but at the same time to avoid fostering the "development of older people as a political power grouping over-concerned with their own welfare."[14]

Whatever these ambiguous formulations may have meant to those who phrased them, they probably did not allow for senior centers to become staging areas for age-based mass pressure by and for the elderly. Indeed the staff professionals assigned to the various clubs by and large have resisted direct political involvement. Reflecting the apolitical stance of the National Committee (later Council) on the Aging, to which many of them looked for policy cues, and mirroring as well the wishes of local donors (private and public) on whom the clubs were dependent financially, the tendency among staff personnel was to encourage avoidance of controversial actions. At the 1961 conference on aging at the University of Michigan mentioned above, Charles Odell, head of the large United Auto Workers' retired

workers organization, protested against the widespread practice of prohibiting older people from discussing candidates and political issues in clubs and
centers set up for them, and went on to point out that it frequently was the
same professional and community leaders who were urging activity and
participation by older people and then discouraging their concern with social
issues and political affairs.[15]

Yet the very process of bringing the aged into age-bracketed local
associations during an era of rising governmental concern with the needs of
senior citizens inevitably had far-reaching consequences, ones exceeding the
apparent intentions of those instrumental in getting the senior centers
launched. In an important study of such centers published in 1969, James E.
Trela undertook to compare systematically four groups of senior citizens,
totalling 709 individuals, in the Cleveland area: the first group consisted of
those with no group memberships of any kind; the second, those with senior-
center or other old-age memberships only; the third, persons involved only
in groups with widely diverse ages ("mixed generational groups"); the
fourth, those with both senior-citizen and mixed-generational-group involvements. Trela's study had some striking conclusions. His data revealed,
for example, that the degree of participation by the elderly in sociopolitical
discussions was significantly related to the intensity of their involvement in a
senior center: "Whereas only three per cent of those who had not
participated recently had ever discussed politics at the center, this was true of
almost one-fifth of those who had attended more than five times during the
preceding three months . . . [and, moreover,] members were increasingly
likely to discuss taxes, inflation, and riots and demonstrations, and the more
often they attended the center, the more likely they were to have these
discussions."[16]

Trela's findings also revealed that those elderly who were not members of
any voluntary association and were therefore isolated from group influence
were least likely to have engaged in political activities. The next in order of
increasing political activity were those with exclusively mixed-generational
memberships, followed by those with exclusively senior-citizen group
association. In the highest category of engagement in some form of political
activity, *almost double the rate of those in the lowest group,* were those
having both senior-citizen and mixed-membership involvements. It was also
discovered that involvement in a national organization with political
objectives relevant to senior citizens has a pronounced impact on an
individual's level of personal political involvement and that the tendency to
join such a national body is significantly related to the person's prior type of
local group identification. Thus, whereas none of the exclusively mixed-
generational participants were identified with a politically active national
senior-citizens organization, five of those with exclusive old-age memberships and ten of those with both old-age and mixed-generational member-

ships were so involved. Among those in the latter two categories, the persons with both types of group memberships were substantially more likely to engage in two or more political activities (60 percent) than was true of those in the group with only senior-center membership (40 percent). Although the small sizes of the cells in this part of his analysis made it impossible for Trela to reach any firm conclusions about the joint effects of age structures and group political goals, he could at least conclude that "while affiliation with age peers represents a form of separation from the larger society and may indicate withdrawal into one's own age status: nevertheless, when compared to mixed generational patterns of association this form of affiliation does not dampen and indeed appears to stimulate political involvement."[17]

Trela's findings are supported by Arnold M. Rose's study of old-age-club involvement in Minneapolis-St. Paul. In the early 1960s, Rose interviewed 108 elderly persons who were active in any of three local old-age clubs and compared their responses with 94 senior citizens lacking age-group consciousness or club involvement, as identified in a survey of the general Twin Cities population. In terms of the usual indices used to measure socioeconomic status—sex, educational level, subjective identification of class—there was no significant difference between the two samples. Considering the lack of differences on these dimensions, Rose remarked that "aging group consciousness is not the same kind of participation as most others which have been shown for the general population to be correlated with education and other indices of class."[18] Yet, comparing the behavior and attitudes of the two samples, substantial differences were found to exist. The conversation of the aging-group-conscious sample when they were with people of their own age was shown to differ from that of the nonaging-group-conscious sample, and in a direction suggesting a more focused concern among the former with old-age problems and needs. The former talked more about health and medical care (25 percent versus 2 percent) and about other problems of old age (16 percent to 5 percent), and by similarly wide margins they were less likely to gossip about past events, personal or general.

Underlying the differences in what the two groups chose to discuss with their peers, Rose found substantial disparities in attitudes. In response to the question, "Do you believe that older people ought to organize to demand their rights?" 68 percent of the aging-group-conscious sample replied in the affirmative whereas only 39 percent of the other, nonaging-conscious sample did so. When the question was put, "Do you think older people ought to be more active in politics?" the corresponding affirmative percentages were 74 and 48. Further questioning provided evidence of a rather marked "minority group" sentiment among the old-age-conscious respondents.[19]

Rose's findings are ambiguous on the question of whether the attitudinal differences resulted from a respondent's involvement or noninvolvement in a senior club. But the most plausible inference was that the measured disparities were not simply a result of preexisting differences between the organizationally involved and noninvolved samples and that, instead, club involvement itself had helped to mold attitudes in a more activist, politically self-conscious direction. The findings thus provided empirical support for the view advanced in a 1953 essay by Milton Barron to the effect that the aged, especially those who are significantly involved with their age-peers, are coming to define themselves as a ''quasi-minority'' group.[20] This is not the same thing as saying, however, that the aging possessed, or would ever possess, the degree of cohesiveness needed to forge themselves into a highly unified political force, accompanied by independent political action, bloc voting, and so forth. As will become more apparent later on, the senior movement from its inception has been a fragile entity with many older persons refusing to actively identify with its central tenets or in some cases even be aware of its existence. But, as is the case with social movements generally, it was not essential for the senior movement to gain well-nigh universal acceptance among potential constituents in order to have significant societal impact.

Organized Labor

If the ''senior consciousness'' movement found some of its initial expression through senior centers, it also was articulated through a reorientation of priorities among existing organizations. Several national voluntary organizations, the American Legion, for example, created in the fifties units devoted to older constituents' needs. By all odds the most important reorientation occurred in the trade union movement. A decade later—in the late sixties—a number of industrial unions would establish regular departments for older workers. The machinists would do so, as would the electrical workers, steelworkers, communications workers, garment workers, and others; some unions would even amend their constitutions to more sharply focus on this concern. But these actions were only possible by virtue of what went before.

Already in the fifties unions were responding to retiree needs, typically by enlarging the mandates of existing staff units. Union education staffs, for example, were expanded to include the problems of soon-to-retire workers. In 1956–57 Professor Woodrow Hunter of the University of Michigan's Division of Gerontology set up a preretirement education program for the Upholsterers International Union, and about the same time the University of Chicago's Labor and Industrial Relations Center introduced a course on preretirement in which a number of union staff representatives participated. In the case of the United Auto Workers the initial response seems to have been through the Recreational Department, which as early as 1953 established ''drop in'' centers for UAW retirees.[21]

Of all the actions taken by union leaders in the fifties probably none was quite so important as the vote by delegates to the United Auto Workers' 1957 constitutional convention to adopt Resolution 17. This resolution provided for the creation of a special department within the international union to direct and coordinate efforts in the retiree area, and it designated a per capita tax of union members amounting to one cent of local dues and one cent of international dues—a financing arrangement still used in 1974. (Additional funds began coming in after 1966, when voluntary membership dues on the part of UAW retirees were provided for.) The special assistant to the undersecretary of labor, Charles Odell, was called from Washington to head the new unit, the Older and Retired Workers Department. Under Odell and, later, Andrew Brown, who succeeded him in 1966, the department made rapid progress in implementing the intent of Resolution 17 for a strong grass-roots organization. By 1968 there were 359 local union retired-worker chapters, 18 regional retired-worker councils (one in each of the 18 UAW regions) and a total of 69,143 dues-paying retired members. (All these figures would double by 1974, by which time the union would be spending almost $2 million annually in this one program area.)[22]

Resolution 17 did not define any political role for the new department, nor was one stated or implied in the new director's job description. But the enthusiasm engendered among union retirees by the Medicare crusade made such a role obligatory. With the enthusiastic endorsement of UAW president Walter Reuther and his brothers Roy and Victor, Charles Odell presided over the expenditure in the 1958-65 period of three to four hundred thousand dollars on the Medicare struggle, some of it in the form of direct payments to the National Council of Senior Citizens and some of it in staff time and printing costs that were written off by the UAW. Though he had been recruited on the basis of his credentials as an administrator informed on aging, Odell now found himself in the position of a politician-broker—on the one hand articulating UAW legislative demands in the course of frequent trips to Washington and, on the other, endeavoring to reconcile internal organizational stresses brought on in part by the department's direct political interventions. The director often found it a frustrating existence, especially since he had not come up through the UAW ranks and was not regarded as a full-fledged "union man." He later remarked:

> Without meaning to become a political power within the Union, I had become one! Senators, Congressmen, Administration officials, Governors, Mayors, State legislators, and leaders of voluntary organizations were all calling me for help and support and money. I was forced to make commitments and decisions on my own which should have been made, or so they thought, by elected officials of the Union, or at least by the "palace guard" of Administrative Assistants at Solidarity House [the UAW's international headquarters].[23]

Adding to Odell's troubles was the fact that the retiree leadership in Detroit regarded his Washington journeys with misgivings; it was resented that he was not always on tap when day-to-day decisions in the area of "retiree affairs" were asked for. Some of them also resented the director's refusal to go along with their demand to be paid for their "volunteer" work. Though Odell had high praise for the UAW top leadership at the time he left the organization in 1966, it is clear that an inability to reconcile all these conflicting demands and expectations was a factor in his departure.

None of this is intended to diminish Odell's stature as a leader of the senior movement—a matter to be treated in some detail below. It does underscore the fact, however, that, as is typical of nominal "leaders" when major groundswells of opinion occur among their constituents, Odell was a follower as well. Though by no means disapproving of the militant mood among his retiree constituents—and indeed welcoming it—Odell neverthe-less had to accommodate himself to this force; it was not something that he himself (or for that matter any other UAW official) deliberately brought into being. The support for the Medicare cause among officials in other unions may be similarly related to rank-and-file enthusiasm with which they had to come to terms, but there is unfortunately no data on this point.

Less Structured Manifestations of the Movement

More important than the movement's more structured and formalized facets at this stage was the emergence at the mass level of something difficult to pin down precisely but portentous in its long-term implications. There arose a set of attitudes and expectations which approximated an "ideology," if one uses that term to connote a sense of collective self-awareness, a well-defined sense of grievance, and a vision of a better future realizable through struggle and commitment. And emerging out of this "ideology," there was group effort—spontaneous, fluid, innovative, and impulsive for the most part—and a leadership skilled at directing the group and articulating the ideology. I have already touched on this point in discussing attitude changes associated with senior-center participation and with labor-union retiree groups. But this development is so compelling as to justify further consideration, and for this reason I shall now take up the interrelated matters of ideology, leadership, and collective political expression.

Ideology

In the absence of survey data based on interviews with a valid sample of the old-age population, there is no way of knowing how widespread was the sense of injustice which characterized the attitudes and behavior of the more vocal senior citizens in the 1950s. They may have been no more than a small minority of the total. But their significance lay not in absolute numbers but in a sense of commitment and of being in the vanguard of social change. Various observers commented on this trend, though without always agreeing on which factors were most crucial in causing it. In a 1960 essay Arnold Rose focused primarily on economic and service needs:

> The needs and interests that are unique to older persons around which [old age] voluntary associations have formed include: special needs for economic assistance, housing, and the full range of welfare assistance; the need to take care of the characteristic health care problems of the older years; the need for special training and orientation to meet the problems of aging; the need to organize politically in order to protect themselves as a group. . . . it can fairly be said that until recently elderly people in American society could be regarded as a category rather than as a social group . . . [but the forces at work] are increasingly transforming them into a social group and as a result old people will increasingly form and participate in voluntary associations.[24]

Other observers, in particular political scientists Robert and Leona Rienow, were inclined to lay greater stress on nonmaterial factors. Analyzing the remarks of senior-citizen witnesses before the 1959 McNamara subcommittee, the Rienows did concede that the aging were suffering from "penury and untended illness" and that this in turn contributed to premature retirement from the work force and general alienation. Yet they insisted that it was lack of fulfillment rather than physical lack that was most fundamental in this distress: "The overriding reason for unrest among the senior citizens is not the lack of health or money. What our retired olders yearn for more than anything else is involvement. They are crushed with the feeling of no longer being wanted, useful or important to others. They have been stripped of their value—and so of their dignity as human beings." Reinforcing this feeling was a fairly widespread belief that the country had fallen into alien hands: "The senior citizen worries about abstractions, such as the frightful turn affairs are taking in the hands of the incompetent younger set. He worries by the hour about 'young people's morals and religion' . . . 'about the way the country is being run' or 'the way the city is being mismanaged.'" These senior citizens, outraged by trends in the larger society which they regarded as abhorrent, were in a mood of incipient rebellion: "'We are not discards!' angrily shouted a retired gentleman at the [McNamara] committee hearings, and the room mutteringly answered him: 'It hurts more than anything to be ignored!' . . . 'My family neglects me—as if I were dead already' . . . 'I am made to feel that I am contributing nothing. Why keep on living?'" The Rienows were convinced, though again the evidence was necessarily impressionistic, that "the army of the aged is redoubtable and disquieting . . . [and that] the absolute and proportionate number of its members is growing fast."[25]

Leadership

Unlike in the 1930s when the charismatic Dr. Francis E. Townsend emerged to voice elderly citizens' grievances, the senior movement of the 1950s did not produce a single dominant spokesman. Instead there were numerous leaders, their messages varying somewhat on the basis of temperament and particular circumstances but all pointing in a common direction. One such leader was Ethel Percy Andrus. According to the official account of her decision to found the American Association of Retired Persons, Andrus had a dual purpose in mind: on the one hand she "knew the greatest fear of retirees concerned what would happen to them in case of illness or accident" (a concern suggesting the need for making available reasonably priced insurance protection against such risks); on the other hand she "knew there were things people needed far more which they could not even ask for—such as a new way of feeling about themselves, a new role to play in the society they'd helped build, a new framework in which they could find ways to help themselves and each other."[26] The solution to this latter need, she maintained, lay in tapping the "leadership potential, experience and wisdom of older citizens" and bringing it to bear on societal institutions and in this way overcoming not only the neglect of the elderly but benefiting the nation as well.[27]

Slightly different in tone, yet not essentially so in substance, was the outlook of another typical leader of the 1950s, Charles Odell. The head of the UAW retired workers' organization insisted that

> there cannot be adequate social progress made in behalf of the aged unless they themselves are actively enlisted in the cause . . . . Those of us who represent what [Abraham] Holtzman calls "respectable organizations" therefore have a responsibility not only to maintain our respectability but to become ever more respectful of the innate good sense and responsiveness of an educated, politically alert and informed senior citizenry . . . . We are in a real sense pioneering in a new and relatively unexplored area.[28]

As was true of Ethel Andrus, Odell was aware of a profound restiveness among many of the elderly and shared her belief that disciplined intervention in the legislative process was an important avenue toward overcoming injustice.

Both of these leaders were instrumental in founding organizations of the elderly, but it should not be thought that their views were essentially organizational expressions. Andrus and Odell reached beyond their own dues-paying constituencies, and in forums, conferences, and assemblies of all kinds sought to express the grievances and aspirations of the elderly in general.

Even by the early 1970s the movement was to retain a good deal of this popular, unstructured character. There emerged in these years the much-publicized "Gray Panthers," an activist group brought together in Phila-delphia under the charismatic leadership of sixty-seven-year-old Margaret ("Maggie") Kuhn. With funds provided from the United Presbyterian Church and the United Church of Christ, the nondenominational Gray Panthers first gained attention in 1970 by taking to the streets with banners and picket signs to protest nursing-home abuses. More recently the organiza-tion has broadened its goals to cover such matters as the need for easier loan terms for the elderly, increased social security benefits, improved health care, and matters that transcend age—war, peace, poverty, penal reform, and so forth. The group soon claimed a national membership of six hundred and had chapters in several major cities. As late as 1973 it was still without professional staff, and Maggie Kuhn made it clear that there was no intent to create a structured organization. "We do have a steering committee," she told a reporter in 1972, "and we've adopted a statement of purpose—the Panther Manifesto. But a lot of people who have come out of a bureaucracy can't understand why we don't have membership cards and a formal office and letterheads."[29] The Gray Panthers is not a lobbying group in the strict sense, but its existence presumably is a factor in the continuing pressure for improved governmental old-age benefits and protections.

Group Solidarity and Political Involvement

On the basis of an ideology and under the guidance of shrewd leaders, the aged began to coalesce in the fifties on behalf of social change. It would be an exaggeration to say that they were unified or monolithic; what *was* achieved was a degree of common purpose, especially in 1958, 1959, and 1960 as the Medicare struggle warmed up and the 1961 White House Conference on Aging drew near. Professor Rose caught the essence of it:

> One of the early manifestations of [aging group-solidarity] is for them to join some kind of recreational or other expressive association in which they can interact almost exclusively with persons of similar age. . . . *A social worker may have helped to get the club started, but the elderly some-times take it over and the social psychological transformation toward group pride is theirs.* . . . The next phase occurs when they begin to talk over their common problems in a constructive way. Probably elderly have been complaining for some time. . . . But recently some have come to talk about such problems not only with reference to themselves as individuals, but with an awareness that these things occur to them as a social group. [Finally] they begin to talk in terms of taking social action, not merely individual action, to correct the situation.[30] [Emphasis added.]

Since this increasing assertiveness occurred mostly in local communities remote from the gaze of the national media, the seemingly "spontaneous" eruptions of senior-citizen sentiment usually came as a surprise, occasionally as a shock, to national officials and lawmakers. When Nelson Cruikshank and Andrew Biemiller of the AFL-CIO sought a sponsor for their senior-citizens health care bill in 1956, they were turned down by all three top-ranking Democratic members of the House Ways and Means Committee, presumably because there was no political mileage to be gained from sponsorship of the bill. Finally they got the fourth-ranking member, Aimé J. Forand of Rhode Island, to introduce the bill, but not without considerable misgivings on his part. Shortly after Forand's initiative became known, however, a reporter from the *Providence Journal* discovered that the bill had aroused great enthusiasm among senior citizens in Rhode Island, and Forand, surprised, became far more interested in the bill and optimistic about its prospects.[31]

An apparently "spontaneous" elderly upsurge also had a major impact on members of the McNamara Subcommittee on the Problems of the Aged and Aging in the course of hearings held in various communities. The subcommittee's initial hearings were held in Washington, but late in 1959 and in 1960 it went on the road, hearing testimony in Pittsburgh, San Francisco, Charleston (West Virginia), Grand Rapids, Miami, and Detroit. So long as the hearings had been confined to the nation's capital, there was only modest press coverage and senior-citizen interest. But, as noted by Richard Harris, interest picked up considerably once the hearings went on the road:

> "We knew we had a popular issue, but we didn't realize it would be that popular," one of McNamara's staff men recalled later. "The Senator's policy of conducting the hearings was unique as far as I know. After listening to experts on both sides, he simply opened up the micro-phones to anyone in the room who wanted to have his say. Well, the old folks lined up by the dozen every place we went.... For the first time we had these people telling what life was like for them—and letting us know that they were more than a lot of statistics. The upshot was that the hearings got headlines and front page stories every place we went. This gave the Medicare movement its first big push on the national scene."[32]

If the outpouring of senior sentiment came as a surprise to subcommittee members, it presumably was a shock to leaders of the American Medical Association, whose anti-Medicare propaganda had insisted that the proposal lacked support among its intended beneficiaries.[33]

In its final report to the Senate, the subcommittee strongly endorsed Medicare, something not expected at the outset. James L. Sundquist, a leading political analyst, is convinced that this endorsement had a decisive influence on Democratic congressional sentiment.[34] Among the more important factors contributing to this change, were the expressions from the elderly. At one point in the hearings, Senator McNamara remarked that "we are—more and more—becoming convinced that our older citizens resent bitterly the minority status that other Americans are imposing on them." The subcommittee report devoted some attention to the expressed views of these citizens.[35]

Conclusion

The present findings can best be interpreted by reference to the theoretical literature on social movements. In an important 1929 work whose influence can still be seen in recent writings, sociologists Carl A. Dawson and Warren Gettys observed that the typical social movement passes through four phases in the course of its evolution.[36] Though the first of these, the "stage of social unrest," marked by "random and erratic behavior," seems to have no very precise parallel in the senior-movement case, and the last one, the "institutional stage," is not presently apparent, the two middle stages to which the authors allude are strikingly illustrated in the movement's history to date. Immediately following the period of social unrest there comes what the authors characterize as the "popular stage." For the movement of the elderly it seems appropriate to view this as having encompassed both the Townsend effort of the thirties and, following a ten-year hiatus, the "senior-citizens movement" of the 1950s. (Since the third stage, that of "formal organization," did not commence until the 1960s, discussion of it may be deferred for the moment.)

The mood of the "popular stage" of a social movement is summed up by Dawson and Gettys in the following terms:

> The unrest which had developed as a reaction to the general situation first becomes well coordinated in [a] tentative objective. . . . This objective, as yet nebulous and temporary, [serves] to focus the attention and to become for the group the representation of an object of action and an outlet for its restlessness. Social movements in general are characterized at this stage by the tendency of those participating in them to formulate some ideal end which is sufficiently remote as to have a more or less universal appeal.[37]

The authors thus distinguish between the "tentative objective"—a reasonably concrete aim achievable in the short run—and an "ideal end"—a more diffuse goal whose achievement will require protracted struggle and will be realized, if ever, only in the long run. For the senior movement in the 1950s, the tentative objective was embodied in agitation for government-assisted medical care for the aged.

The "ideal ends" that I have considered in discussing ideology and leadership would involve a fundamental restructuring of American norms and values such that old people would come to be accepted, not as a dependent and needy group, but one recognized as having a vital social contribution to make. In place of a society fixated on youthful vigor, beauty, and imagination, there would emerge one in which the elderly's wisdom, experience, and reflectiveness would count for just as much.

Each of the four stages identified by Dawson and Gettys has its characteristic type of leader, and in the "popular stage" the leadership is "characteristically of the prophet and reformer types." Their characterization of the "prophet" could well have been written with Francis E. Townsend in mind:

> The prophet feels a sense of possession. He has a sense that he has a special and separate knowledge on the matter. He speaks with a sense of authority. He is a revealer of a message, a new philosophy of life. He uses the sense of authority to make articulate the hopes and wishes of the people and to add weight and prestige to their direction.[38]

The leaders who emerged in the 1950s diverged sharply from the "prophetic" pattern and tended decidedly toward the "reformer." Whereas Townsend, in his messianic zeal, had bolted the party system to join in a third-party effort in the 1936 election, the leaders of the senior movement in the 1950s insisted on working with both political parties. The Townsend plan of the thirties was regarded as extremely radical and was branded as fiscally unsound by policymakers, both Republican and Democratic, whereas the senior-citizen leaders of the fifties identified themselves with objectives that were marked by their political feasibility. Townsend was a platform orator with a charismatic appeal; the reformers of the later period relied more on reasoned persuasion and the inherent logic of their case.

5 Senior Citizens for Kennedy

with Peter A. Corning

Over the relatively brief period of four years—1956 to 1960—a series of developments occurred at the national level which, taken together, marked the genesis of sustained official concern with old-age matters. In the Department of Health, Education, and Welfare a new unit was created, the Special Staff on Aging, which later was to metamorphose into the Administration on Aging—the primary focus for senior-citizen matters in the executive branch. There was significant discussion of aging matters in both House and Senate, including the Forand "hospital care for the aged" debate which presaged the later struggle to enact Medicare. The presidential wings of both major parties were beginning to manifest interest, and without question the most significant age-related action in this area was the creation of the "Senior Citizens for Kennedy" project in the 1960 Kennedy-Johnson presidential campaign. In view of the major impact which this last-named operation was to have on the thinking and behavior of national party leaders, it seems worthwhile devoting the present chapter to a consideration of its origins, three-month lifespan, and effect on subsequent party behavior.

Origins

As has been pointed out above, as well as in works by other authors, there was no old people's organization with sufficient numbers, geographical dispersion, or money to engage in national-level political action subsequent to the short-lived Townsend movement in the late 1930s.[1] In the absence of continued pressure-group activity, the problems of the aged were relatively neglected, there being no major piece of legislation relating to the aged enacted by Congress during this period, other than periodic amendments to the Social Security Act. The aged were a relatively disadvantaged group in American society and had a number of distinct socioeconomic problems which set them apart from younger voters and which were potentially a focus for pressure-group activity and governmental response.

The data and analysis in this chapter are based on Peter A. Corning, "Senior Citizens for Kennedy: An Effector of a Political Subsystem" (Master's thesis, New York University, 1969).

By the latter part of the decade of the fifties there was some basis for thinking of the "aged vote" as a distinct entity which could be appealed to separately from other voting blocs. As has been noted previously, there were a number of events in the 1950s, beginning with the 1950 National Conference on Aging, which drew attention to the problems of the aged and stimulated an ongoing concern with these problems within the Federal Security Agency. The legislative and executive initiatives of the 1956–60 period in particular created the possibility that substantial numbers of elderly people might now be transformed into a self-conscious political force with its own formal structures, goals, and autonomous leadership, and with some capacity to influence election outcomes.[2]

Yet the initial attitude which prevailed among national party leaders on this point was decidedly apathetic. Republican leaders tended to take the aged vote for granted, while Democrats tended to be skeptical about the possibility of converting many of the aged voters away from their traditional Republican loyalties. Ever since the 1948 election, a majority of elderly voters (the average was 55 per cent) had cast their ballots for the Republican candidate,[3] and some experts on voting behavior cautioned that there was little likelihood that this pattern would change significantly, at least over the short run. The view of Angus Campbell on the matter, already alluded to in the previous chapter, gave scholarly and empirical support to the view predominant among practicing politicians. The aged would be a difficult group to move from habitual voting patterns, Campbell warned, observing that there was some basis for the notion that voters generally became more conservative with age. It was widely believed among prominent Democratic leaders that an effort to win over older voters would be like fighting "human nature."[4]

However, the subject of voting behavior is a complex one, and there are reasons why any such unequivocal assumption should be qualified. In *The American Party System and the American People*, Fred I. Greenstein identifies three bases for a person's vote—party, personalities, and issues. Party is by far the strongest basis for voting, and issues is the least important one; only about 12 percent of voters have an issue-based description of the two parties.[5] Yet, notwithstanding the lesser importance of issues as compared to party loyalty, voting patterns and alignments do change over time. People also cross party lines on occasion. As Warren Miller puts it, "Although a person's educational background or his religion or his party identification seldom undergo any change between two elections, some of his partisan attitudes toward the affairs of politics do change in response to new events and new situations."[6] In a major work devoted to the matter of voters who bolt their traditional party loyalties in a given election, V. O. Key took the position that clear-cut issues directly affecting a particular group do have an impact on voting behavior. He identified what he called "switchers" as crucial variables in any particular election, and asserted, "Those who switch do so to support governmental policies or outlooks with which they agree."[7] Other authorities on voting have made similar observations.

These statements do not contradict those of Campbell, of course; it may well be, as he suggested, that it is relatively more difficult to make "switchers" out of older voters. But the implication of the above statements is that this can be done (as subsequent events confirmed) and that there are rational elements in voter behavior. Accordingly, it is our contention that the traditional preference of elderly voters for the Republicans was based, at least in part, on a rational perception of self-interest. Rather than assume on the basis of raw survey data that aged voters are by nature more Republican and "conservative" in their voting preferences than the general public, one might better probe for issues that might have served to bind most older voters in the GOP camp and that made this tie in large part a matter of perceived self-interest rather than mere sentiment and tradition. For in the postwar years there were two specific "bread-and-butter" issues of relatively greater importance to elderly voters, both of which worked to the disadvantage of the Democratic party. During the New Deal–Fair Deal era, the Democratic party came to be associated, first, with high taxes and, later, with inflation. Because the elderly had lower incomes than the rest of the population (and often lived on fixed incomes), they were acutely affected by these two economic realities. Indeed, the association of the Democratic party with high taxes and inflation in the minds of elderly voters was confirmed in the Survey Research Center's own polls, as Campbell conceded.[8] Conversely, the Republican's posture of balanced-budget conservatism had a logical attraction for elderly voters.

Second, it is understandable why the social-welfare programs enacted by the Democrats failed to blunt the Republican advantage on these issues. While Social Security and Old Age Assistance did put more money into the hands of the elderly, benefit levels were far from adequate. Social Security benefits did not begin until 1940, and throughout the next two decades benefits remained low and lagged behind increases in the cost of living. By the same token, public assistance benefits were inadequate to maintain a modest level of living, and many states contrived to exclude from welfare rolls many citizens who were technically qualified for assistance.[9] Finally, Campbell himself pointed out the anomaly that aged voters, though conservative on taxes, were surprisingly liberal about government social-welfare programs, which suggested to him that elderly voters might be appealed to on social-welfare issues with some success.[10]

If, in fact, the preference of elderly voters for the Republican party contained a strong element of perceived self-interest, one might expect that a change in that perception would yield some change in the voting patterns of the elderly, all other things being equal. Indeed, an important thesis of this chapter will be that such a correlated change of perception and voting patterns did take place, though it was one that occurred gradually and was blanketed by other factors in the 1960 election.

The process of change in the perception of the Democratic party held by elderly voters began during the 1950s, when the Democrats were out of power. According to two informants, private polls for the AFL-CIO's Committee on Political Education early in 1960 showed, as might be expected, that the Democratic party had lost some of its stigma as the party of high taxes and inflation.[11] But more important, the Democrats espoused a major social-welfare proposal of direct and significant benefit to elderly voters—what later came to be known as "Medicare." This measure gradually became a "cutting-edge issue," in the parlance of the political operatives. That is, it fulfilled the three requisites set forth in *The American Voter* for an issue to be able to influence a person's voting decision: (1) the issue was "cognized" by a great many elderly voters; (2) it aroused at least a "minimal intensity of feeling"; and (3) it was accompanied (ultimately) by a perception on the part of a number of elderly voters that the Democratic party better represented their position on this issue.[12]

However, in the early months of 1960, it was by no means clear that Medicare would be a major political issue and that it would be possible for the Democratic party to mount a fruitful appeal to elderly voters. As late as early spring of 1960, key Democrats were dubious, if not contemptuous, of the idea of featuring Medicare in a special appeal to elderly voters. James C. O'Brien, the head of the United Steelworkers Retired Workers Department, recalls trying to persuade his friends in the party to undertake a "senior citizens" campaign appeal as early as 1959, but to no avail. Charles E. Odell, O'Brien's counterpart among UAW retirees, likewise was unsuccessful in his attempts through Michigan's Democratic national committeeman, Neil Staebler, to spur the Democratic National Committee to set up a senior citizens division. And when Lizabeth Bamberger (assistant director of the AFL-CIO's influential Social Security Department) discussed campaign strategy with a member of the National Committee's staff early in 1960 and urged him to focus attention on the Medicare issue, her suggestion evoked derision.[13]

In the ensuing months, however, there was a significant shift in the political climate, both with regard to the Medicare issue and the political importance of the elderly. First, the House Ways and Means Committee began holding protracted executive sessions on the medical-care issue early in the spring. In the first two weeks of April the Senate Subcommittee on the Problems of the Aged and Aging conducted public hearings on the problems of the elderly, particularly their medical problems.[14] In addition, state-level conferences on the problems of the aged in preparation for the

White House Conference on Aging (scheduled for January 1961) were beginning to stir interest and publicity in many states, while a large, pro-Medicare rally in Detroit by UAW retirees and another by retired needle-trades workers in New York's Madison Square Garden both attracted national publicity.[15] Finally, when all the major Democratic presidential contenders and, belatedly, the Republican front-runner (Richard Nixon) espoused some form of medical assistance for the elderly, it was clear that the climate had changed. Indeed, by June 1960, *Business Week* spoke of a "national stirring" on the problems of the aged,[16] while the *New York Times* referred to health care for the aged as "the number one domestic issue" of the presidential campaign.[17]

Sensing the change in public mood, a few strategically placed Democrats, primarily those involved with the problems of the aged, began to meet in Washington in the spring of 1960.[18] The participants, who were aware that most of the planning for the upcoming 1961 White House Conference on Aging (as well as planning for other official programs) was occurring without direct elderly involvement, were interested in finding ways in which older people might express themselves in government decision-making. A second objective, subordinate at first but increasingly central as time passed, was the need to exert pressure on the Democratic party to make an appeal to the elderly in the upcoming national election. The participants in these conversations included James C. O'Brien, Charles E. Odell, Lizabeth Bamberger, Harold Sheppard (an industrial sociologist formerly on the Wayne State University faculty and at the time research director of the McNamara Senate subcommittee on aging problems), and Blue Carstenson (chairman of the technical staff of the White House Conference on Aging and for five years previously [1954–59] an organizer of senior centers in California). All of these diverse personalities were expansive and progressive, and none were bureaucratic in outlook. Their emphasis on the need to increase senior-citizen participation in federal old-age policymaking was directly in line with the stress on participation which characterized the senior movement generally.

By early summer of 1960 the number of people involved in these strategy sessions was enlarged, with the focus of attention shifting to the upcoming Democratic national convention. From the staff of the Subcommittee on the Problems of the Aged and Aging there was Sidney Spector, who joined his close associate Harold Sheppard. From the staff of the liberal senator James Murray there was William Reidy. From the Democratic National Committee there were Wade Jones and Mary Gresham. The ranks of those identified with organized labor were swelled by the addition of Hyman Bookbinder of the AFL-CIO's legislative department and Katherine Ellickson from the same federation's Social Security Department. There was also Joy Elmer Morgan, the president of a splinter retiree group called Senior Citizens of

America; a professor from American University and a representative of the National Committee on the Aging, whose exact identities informants requested not be revealed, were also members.[19] This enlarged group met on July 14 while the Democratic convention was under way in Los Angeles. After lengthy discussion, the members agreed to press for a volunteer special-interest appeal to elderly voters in the coming campaign under the aegis of the Democratic National Committee's "citizens" effort. It was decided that Carstenson, by then a member of the DNC staff, would draft a memorandum proposing such an appeal to the DNC chairman who would take charge after the convention.

Meanwhile, O'Brien was detailed to enlist the support of COPE and various labor unions, including his own. He found COPE's leaders, James McDevitt and Alexander Barkan, receptive; they agreed to commit a portion of COPE's campaign war chest to a special-interest appeal to elderly voters.[20] O'Brien also was successful in his appeals for support among the unions, enlisting the aid of his own steelworkers union and of the United Auto Workers and the International Ladies Garment Workers Union, all of which had large retired workers' organizations.

Moreover, O'Brien, in company with Carstenson, went to talk with the Democratic Advisory Council's Committee on Social Security to try to enlist its support. Because the Council was composed of a number of prominent Democrats it was felt that support from that body might help persuade the leadership of the Democratic National Committee. But, as it turned out, the Council was decidedly uneasy about such an undertaking, being concerned on the one hand lest political exploitation of the issue lead to another upheaval among the elderly similar to the Townsend movement in the 1930s and, on the other, wondering if aged voters were not too set in their ways to switch their party allegiance. The upshot of the meeting was that the Council would neither aid nor oppose such an appeal.

After John F. Kennedy received the Democratic nomination in Los Angeles, his supporters took charge of the DNC and began organizing the campaign.[21] The candidate's brother Robert served as campaign manager, but day-to-day operational control devolved upon Lawrence F. O'Brien, who moved into the DNC. Therefore, Dr. Carstenson sought the approval of O'Brien for a senior-citizens appeal; a memorandum was sent to O'Brien within a week after the convention. However, the memorandum got no response, and Carstenson's attempts to talk with O'Brien in person were rebuffed with the explanation that O'Brien was too busy. Evidently, O'Brien's initial response to the idea had been unfavorable.

Carstenson thereupon decided to attempt a more indirect approach. He sought out the aid of James C. O'Brien of the Steelworkers, who agreed to call a friend on Senator Kennedy's congressional staff, Ralph Dungan. Dungan had been handling the problems of the aged for the senator and was politically sensitive to this group as, indeed, was Senator Kennedy himself.

Dungan's efforts to secure a hearing were successful, and on August 15 Carstenson and James O'Brien met at the DNC with Lawrence O'Brien, Dungan, and Richard Donahue, another Kennedy staff aide. Lawrence O'Brien was skeptical, doubting that the aged could be moved from their traditional conservatism by the Medicare issue. But if labor were willing to support it, and since it would involve a relatively small financial investment by the DNC (the original budget request was for $85,625), he would not veto the idea. So, with two and one-half months remaining until election day, Senior Citizens for Kennedy became a part of the Democratic campaign effort.

Functions

In recent years, political scientists have been moving toward a definition of the functions and structures of American political parties which is derived from the systems approach to the study of political life. The present discussion will be focused on what is denoted as "manifest functions" in the sociology literature, although in the course of research considerable evidence emerged that Senior Citizens for Kennedy filled many of the "latent functions" as well.

As far as the all-important electoral function is concerned, there would seem to be a consensus among students of the subject that a political party's primary contribution to the political system, at least in this country, is to aggregate support for a particular set of authorities, of whom the most important by far is the president; indeed, the building of both diffuse and specific support is the essence of the election campaign process. In its role as a campaign organization, then, the party functions as an *effector*— communicating to the voters the various *outputs* of the party, which are shaped in a way that, it is hoped, will induce the voters to support the party and its candidates at the polls.

On closer examination it becomes evident that the two major parties are in fact composed of a number of subsystems: the national committees; congressional party organs; state and local party organizations; the nuclear organizations of particular state and local candidates; in the case of the Democrats, the AFL-CIO and its numerous subsystems (particularly COPE); and, in the Republican case, the political arm of the American Medical Association, the American Medical Political Action Committee (AMPAC). In a presidential election campaign, each of the party's subsystems becomes an effector, working to a greater or lesser extent (depending upon the particular circumstances) in cooperation with the other party subsystems. In addition, specialized effectors may be created for the duration of the campaign, in order to communicate specialized outputs to a particular segment of the electorate or to perform some other specialized activity.

One such specialized effector was Senior Citizens for Kennedy, and its manifest function was to create and disseminate specialized outputs designed to generate support for John F. Kennedy and the Democratic party among elderly voters. These outputs were designed primarily to fulfill the third condition set forth in *The American Voter* (see above, p. 59) for an issue to have an influence on a voter's partisan choice. That is, the outputs of Senior Citizens for Kennedy were designed to differentiate the two presidential candidates and the two parties in terms of those issues which were of concern to elderly voters, particularly the issue of medical care. With the preceding as background, we will consider the structure of Senior Citizens for Kennedy, both with respect to its relationship to the Democratic party (and the campaign effort as a whole) and with respect to its own internal organization.

Structure

The basic structure and organizational linkages of Senior Citizens for Kennedy can best be understood in relation to the overarching Democratic volunteer organization in the 1960 campaign called "Citizens for Kennedy."[22] As had been the case in previous elections, at the outset of the 1960 campaign the DNC created a temporary "front" organization to coordinate and serve as an umbrella for the dozen-odd special-interest appeals planned for the campaign—Lawyers for Kennedy, Businessmen for Kennedy, Farmers for Kennedy, Viva Kennedy, and Senior Citizens for Kennedy. This umbrella organization was controlled, funded, and supported logistically by the DNC. (For example, telephone calls were paid for by the DNC, and "creative work" on publicity materials was provided by the DNC's publicity and radio-TV departments.) In essence, the task of Citizens for Kennedy and each of its units was to establish a network of local volunteer organizations around the country to serve for the campaign's duration in an effector role.

At the national level, the overall citizens organization was headed by Byron White (a Kennedy intimate) and was headquartered in an office building in downtown Washington, as were the headquarters staffs of each special-interest appeal; each staff was assigned a large cubicle on the main floor of this building. Although the appeals were housed together, each was essentially a separate operation with its own personnel, communications channels, and organizational linkages, budget, campaign materials and strategies.

In the case of Senior Citizens for Kennedy, the staff consisted of fourteen people, headed by Carstenson from the DNC staff, and including two other

DNC staff members, two people on loan from organized labor, one Senate and one House staffer, four volunteers, and secretarial help. Essentially, then, this was a paid professional, not a volunteer, headquarters staff. In theory, there was a division of labor among staff members, with the leadership core being assigned different clusters of states to coordinate, while Carstenson handled dealings with the DNC, booked the figurehead chairman, retiring congressman Aimé J. Forand (D., R.I.), for speaking tours (and accompanied him), and handled a number of special projects. In practice, however, the division of labor was only loosely adhered to.

As for the structure at the local level, this was determined by the structural linkages of Senior Citizens for Kennedy. As a part of the larger Citizens for Kennedy operation, local senior-citizens units were to be coordinated with the overall Citizens effort and, wherever practicable, housed in the local Citizens for Kennedy headquarters.

Since the entire Citizens for Kennedy operation was meant to supplement the regular party organization and serve as a personal campaign organization for the presidential candidate, local senior-citizens units would ordinarily operate outside the established party structure and would focus their energies in an undivided effort to help elect the presidential candidate. The effort was to be centered upon the nine industrial states that were considered crucial to the success of the presidential candidate (New York, Pennsylvania, California, Michigan, Texas, Illinois, Ohio, New Jersey, and Massachusetts).[23] Instead of paralleling the state, county, and precinct organizations of the regular party the emphasis was to be upon large cities, key counties with large concentrations of elderly voters, and direct contacts with senior citizens through their unions, golden-age clubs, and so forth. The reason for this concentration of effort, of course, was that the electoral college system has the effect of focusing the presidential campaign struggle in a few key states with large blocs of electoral votes and competitive parties (that is, states in which marginal increments in the distribution of the votes might have a disproportionate impact on the outcome of the election).

Finally, just as the headquarters staff of Senior Citizens for Kennedy was distinct from the staffs of other volunteer appeals, each local senior-citizens unit was to be organized, financed, and managed independently of other local campaign appeals, preferably with a prominent public figure as a chairman and with skilled political organizers as ''coordinators.''

In practice, of course, the local structure varied with the local political topography, with the personalities involved, and with happenstance.[24] One important determinant of the local structure was the activity of organized labor. The retired railroad employees organization (the National Association of Railroad Veteran Employees) and the retired workers organizations of three major unions, the United Auto Workers, the United Steelworkers and the International Ladies Garment Workers, comprising several hundred thousand members in a dozen states, became major loci of activity—providing organizers, clerical help, and volunteer manpower, and organizing rallies and other activities on behalf of local Senior Citizens for Kennedy units, in addition to proselytizing among their own membership. In several localities, union retirees were coincident with the Senior Citizens for Kennedy organization, and perhaps one-half of the total manpower for the senior-citizens operation was provided by these and other unions. Although figures for the other unions proved unobtainable, the UAW, which made the largest single contribution, had eighteen full-time staff people working on the senior-citizens campaign and several thousand rank-and-file volunteers.[25] On the other hand, in at least two states (California and Florida) nonunion old people's organizations provided a major share of the manpower for local units of Senior Citizens for Kennedy.

Indeed, there was no such thing as a typical local unit. The degree of structuring varied widely from one state to another, with Pennsylvania, New York, and California at one extreme, all having highly formalized command structures (state chairmen, regional coordinators, and organizers for the larger urban areas); at the other extreme were Kansas and Ohio, neither of which had so much as an official state chairman, and New Jersey, with no organizations as such, only a single UAW man traveling throughout the state addressing old people's clubs. In Michigan, Senior Citizens for Kennedy was merged with a state-wide Senior Citizens for Senator McNamara operation whose headquarters were in Detroit. A former staff member of the Senate Subcommittee on the Problems of the Aged, Dr. Harold Sheppard, headed the operation, and he was assisted by a large infusion of money, campaign literature, and personnel from the Older and Retired Workers Department of the UAW.

According to the final report of Senior Citizens for Kennedy, local senior-citizens units were set up in forty states and informal efforts were made in five others.[26] The report also stated that in several key states units were organized down to the county level; in addition to the forty-eight in Ohio, there were twenty-three in New York, sixteen in Pennsylvania, fifty-eight in Minnesota, one hundred in North Carolina, twenty in California, eighteen in Utah, twenty-one in Michigan, and twenty-three in Illinois. Altogether, according to the final report, Senior Citizens for Kennedy recruited about 17,500 volunteer workers, including 490 state and county chairmen and 65 coordinators and other behind-the-scenes staff.[27]

Furthermore, the railroad retirees organization and the three major union retiree organizations which participated in Senior Citizens for Kennedy (Steelworkers, Auto Workers, and ILGWU) retained their autonomy throughout the campaign, and their relationship to the national headquarters of Senior Citizens for Kennedy was one of voluntary cooperation between equals. Because the labor organizations operated independently of each other (with the exception of their cooperation for one major rally in Cleveland), they did not come into conflict.

On the other hand, the headquarters staff did have a modicum of structure and cohesiveness: it was small; most staff members were paid; and, since no one treated the organization as a permanent arrangement or a career ladder, competitiveness and friction were minimized and a high degree of cooperation was attained. Moreover, one cannot underestimate the motivational value of being a participant in a cooperative enterprise of great social and political importance—with a quick payoff to boot. By the same token, the "cause" of winning Medicare for the aged was also an important motivational factor, both at headquarters and on the local level. Of course, the possibility of obtaining jobs in the future Kennedy administration provided an additional incentive for one or two headquarters staffers, while the participants from organized labor were motivated by the political objectives of their organizations, in addition to the other motives mentioned above. Consequently, headquarters staff was able to achieve a considerable degree of coherence and a relatively high level of output during its brief existence.

Specific Activities

Essentially, the specific activities of the national headquarters can be classified under five major headings:

1. Recruitment. This included seeking out suitable leadership types for the roles of state chairmen, coordinators, and other volunteer leaders.

2. Supporting activities. Of particular importance was the creation and channeling of campaign materials, especially printed flyers, spots produced for radio and TV, and visual aids for use in presentations before senior-citizen clubs.

3. Generation of media publicity. Involved here was the drafting of press releases, exploitation of the publicity value of Congressman Aimé Forand (the Senior Citizens for Kennedy chairman and author of the Forand Bill in the House), and the drawing together of a handful of illustrious physicians for a figurehead board of "medical advisors."

4. Support of the presidential candidate's personal campaign effort. Whenever Senator Kennedy was scheduled to talk about the problems of the aged or the Medicare issue on TV or at an important gathering, headquarters passed the word to elderly voters in the area.

5. Lobbying and educational work within the party. Senior Citizens for Kennedy urged Democratic congressmen to make use of DNC-produced senior-citizens literature in their own reelection campaigns and also worked within the party structure to gain a higher priority in the campaign for old-age concerns.

A survey of the way that Senior Citizens for Kennedy units functioned at the state and local levels indicates that activities there were broadly analogous to those at national headquarters, although there were, of course, variations from one area to another.

One of the most unorthodox, if not to say unclassifiable, facets of the senior-citizen operation was a special project aimed at neutralizing a powerful generator of pro-Nixon propaganda in California. In that state George McLain, head of the hundred-thousand-strong California Institute of Social Welfare and a regular radio speaker with an audience estimated at one million listeners, was using his influence on behalf of the Republican effort. The genesis in the 1940s of McLain's California movement has been alluded to previously (Chapter 3). In the 1950's McLain began trying to build a national organization, and as the 1960 campaign approached he contacted one of Senator Kennedy's top staff aides to propose that he be made the national chairman of the planned senior-citizens appeal. When, following some sober thinking, the Kennedy managers decided to turn McLain down, he turned to the Nixon camp, and, when the campaign began, his newspaper took a favorable line toward Nixon. Then, in October, he revealed in his newspaper that Nixon had helped him obtain a FHA mortgage loan for his $4.5 million senior-citizens housing project in Fresno, California.[28]

When McLain began publishing pro-Nixon propaganda, the Kennedy managers decided that steps should be taken to counteract it, and a strategy was worked out which Dr. Carstenson was delegated to execute. Working through an intermediary in California's Democratic headquarters, Carstenson relayed a message to McLain to the effect that Senator Kennedy was greatly distressed by McLain's posture and, if he were elected, might cancel McLain's FHA loan unless McLain were willing to give the Kennedy organization some immediate behind-the-scenes assistance. What Carstenson proposed was that, without making a public about-face, McLain should merely lend his mailing list to the Kennedy people so that they could send out some of their own pro-Kennedy propaganda to McLain's followers. In addition, McLain would be asked to print a letter to the editor from Senator Kennedy in an election-eve edition of his newspaper. After some hesitation, McLain agreed to cooperate, and, when Carstenson flew out to Los Angeles a short time later in company with Congressman Forand, a meeting was set up with the intermediary to work out the details.

Effectiveness

In assessing the effectiveness of Senior Citizens for Kennedy it will be useful to consider the matter from two standpoints. First, viewing the operation as an exercise in communications, one may examine the outputs of the presidential campaign organization as "messages" to the voters in the 1960 election. Although such messages are shaped so as to induce the voters to behave in a certain way, their effects are inherently limited, considering that most voters already have had significant "preprogramming" from numerous previous inputs—childhood learning, parental influences, socioeconomic background, and so forth. There is the additional problem of entropy. Volunteer campaign organizations do not have previously established channels of communications to many voters, nor are the voters automatically receptive to the campaign outputs. And the effort to establish channels of communication for the duration of the campaign is hampered by shortages of time, money, personnel and motivation, and by the confusion characteristic of most ad hoc operations. The effects of the Senior Citizens for Kennedy on the 1960 election must be evaluated in relation to these limitations.

Second, one may examine the operation in terms of its immediate and long-term consequences for the Democratic party and the party's allies in the labor movement.

Effect on 1960 Election

The first and most compelling point about the electoral impact of Senior Citizens for Kennedy is that, regardless of whether one relies on the postelection Gallup Poll or on the data compiled by the Survey Research Center at the University of Michigan, the shift of elderly voters from Republican to Democratic between 1956 and 1960 was *less* than the percentage for the electorate as a whole. Between 1956 and 1960 there was an aggregate shift among all voters of plus 7.7 percent from the Democrats and minus 7.9 percent for the Republicans, with an additional .2 percent going into the "other" category. This was .7 percent more for the Democrats than the 7.0 percent increase in Democratic voting among persons sixty years and older as revealed in the Gallup figures, and was 6.39 percent more than the same elderly voter shift as revealed by the SRC data.[29]

More important, the aged as a group were less supportive of the Democrats in 1960 than any other age group—according to SRC's figures, by 4 percent. In view of the expectation that party loyalties will be more intense among elderly voters, this is not surprising. But significantly, this was in marked contrast to the pattern in 1956, when, according to SRC, the percentage of the aged who voted for the Democrats was higher than the percentage from any other group.[30] In other words, the Democrats did less well among the elderly, in terms of percentages, in 1960 than in 1956, despite the fact that there was no senior-citizens operation in 1956 and no such operation on the GOP side in 1956 or 1960.

There is a seeming paradox in the election returns relating to the aged vote in 1960, however, which needs to be explained. In 1956 there were approximately 14.53 million elderly, of whom 11.04 million (or 76 percent) voted; in 1960, there were approximately 16.56 million elderly, of whom 13.08 million (or 79 percent) voted.[31] That is, there was an absolute increase of 2.4 million elderly voters. By applying the percentages (according to Gallup and SRC) that voted Democratic to the number of elderly who actually voted, we find that Gallup shows a net increase of 1.69 million elderly voting Democratic, while the SRC also shows a net increase of 831,000 votes. However, the point is that, according to SRC, a much larger proportion of the 2 million more elderly and the 3 percent (or 2.4 million) larger turnout in the 1960 election went into the GOP column (1.5 million versus 831,000)—which reversed the normal pattern of a higher turnout favoring the Democrats.

Even if, for the sake of argument, we were to assume that the absolute increase in the number of elderly voting Democratic in 1960 represented conversions from the Republican party and, furthermore, that all of these supposed conversions were attributable to the efforts of Senior Citizens for Kennedy (which is most unlikely)—even with these generous assumptions we are still forced to conclude that Senior Citizens for Kennedy was not very effective, at least in converting elderly voters.

Taking the Senior Citizens for Kennedy staffers' own rough, and probably overgenerous, estimate of how many elderly they reached (between 5 and 6 million) and matching it against the increased number of elderly who voted Democratic, we must conclude that even under the optimum set of assumptions, Senior Citizens for Kennedy only succeeded in converting one out of every 2.8 to 3.38 people reached (using Gallup's figure of a 1.69 million increase in the number of elderly voting Democratic) or one out of every 6.02 to 7.22 (using SRC's figure of 831,000 more Democratic voters among the elderly). Under any less favorable set of assumptions, moreover, the conversion figure might be one out of every 100, 500, or 1,000 people reached. And, in all probability, these assumptions are far too generous.

The inherent limitations of a volunteer operation such as Senior Citizens for Kennedy may account for this poor showing. In addition, the impact of this particular operation may have been partly neutralized by the actions of the Republican presidential candidate. On the all-important medical-care issue, Nixon had two advantages over Kennedy. First, Nixon belatedly endorsed and prompted a liberal Republican health-care proposal aimed specifically at low-income elderly, to be paid for out of the general revenues. Though it involved a means test and state administration, its benefit package was actually more liberal than the Social Security-based proposal of the Democratic candidate. And Nixon, of course, played up this advantage. Second, the Congress had just enacted a new program called Kerr-Mills that was designed to finance some health care for the aged under the public assistance system. This new program enabled the Republican candidate to point out that steps to meet the problem were already being undertaken by the incumbent Republican administration, and GOP spokesmen, notably HEW secretary Arthur Flemming, spent a considerable amount of time talking about the new program during the election campaign.[32]

As students of voting behavior have concluded, external events and the actions of the presidential candidates themselves are probably far more important in the campaign—especially in these days of mass television— than the efforts of a volunteer campaign organization.[33] Indeed, Senior Citizens for Kennedy seems to bear out Lazarsfeld's conclusion that the principal accomplishments of such appeals are (1) activation and (2) reinforcement, rather than (3) conversion, though we have no data with which to measure possible activation and reinforcement directly.[34]

There were, however, a few local exceptions to the generally poor results of the senior-citizens appeal as a conversion mechanism. In their final report, the Senior Citizens for Kennedy staff pointed to several "key precincts" with high percentages of elderly voters where their campaign efforts did produce favorable results—in Florida (especially Miami), in McKeesport, Pennsylvania, in several communities in Los Angeles County, California, and in certain senior-citizens precincts of New York City. All these communities substantially increased their previous Democratic majorities among senior citizens, and in the senior-citizens areas of Miami Beach, a notably impressive case, the vote went six to one for Kennedy.[35]

Presumably there was some cause-effect relationship between the exceptional effort made by Senior Citizens for Kennedy in these areas and the favorable results obtained at the polls. As far as can be ascertained, the influence of the senior-citizens operation represented the single most significant difference from the influences at work in other areas with equally high proportions of elderly voters. The conclusion to be drawn from these exceptions is that a highly motivated, efficiently managed, volunteer campaign effort *can* make some difference, all other things being equal. This conforms with the conclusion of Edward C. Banfield and James Q. Wilson that between 5 and 10 percent can be added to a party's vote by a well-managed "grass-roots" volunteer effort.[36]

Effects on Party Leaders

As a persuader of elderly voters, Senior Citizens for Kennedy was certainly not dramatically successful. However, as a persuader of Democratic politicians, there is reason to believe that it was; and, in the long view, that success may have been more important. As noted earlier, Senior Citizens for Kennedy had a significant educational influence within the party, and the testimony above has been corroborated in numerous conversations with Democratic politicians at all levels.[37] In postmortem discussions by Mr. Kennedy's personal campaign managers, their conclusion was that it had been desirable for the party to continue to court elderly voters; as Myer Feldman put it: "We had to keep trying."

In spite of its apparent failure to move great numbers of elderly voters, Senior Citizens for Kennedy had convinced top-level Democratic politicians that the basic hypothesis upon which the operation was organized had been correct. Elderly voters could be appealed to, like the farm vote or the Negro vote, on the basis of their own separate identity and self-interest.

Subsequent events testified strongly to this intraparty success. In 1961 President Kennedy was to assist in the formation of the National Council of Senior Citizens for Health Care Through Social Security (later, simply "National Council of Senior Citizens" or NCSC) and within a few months the Democratic National Committee would be subsidizing the efforts of the new group to create a network of senior-citizens groups and a permanent channel of communication to elderly voters. Then, in the 1962 mid-term election, the DNC would launch a massive campaign effort built around the Medicare issue, with a heavy emphasis on appealing to elderly voters and with NCSC as a significant vehicle in the effort. In a subsequent chapter we will have occasion to deal in some detail with the NCSC's founding and subsequent growth. Here it is enough to point out that there was an essential continuity between it and Senior Citizens for Kennedy. Aimé Forand served as chairman of the new group and Blue Carstenson was its executive director from 1961 to 1963, both of these roles being analogous to those they had earlier filled in the 1960 campaign effort. There were many other such carryovers and, indeed, the entire top leadership groups of the two organizations were almost identical.

In the 1964 presidential campaign, likewise, there was another senior-citizens operation, this time called Senior Citizens for Johnson-Humphrey. Former skeptics in the party organization, such as Lawrence O'Brien, were won over; in the *Democratic Campaign Manual 1964* (popularly known as the O'Brien Manual) senior citizens were included in the chapter on "Special Group Activities" along with youth, farm, labor, veterans, business, and professional groups.[38] In the presidential election 59 percent of the elderly voted Democratic, according to Gallup, or 1.8 percent *above* the shift for all age groups. If Campbell et al. are correct in their assertion that it is relatively harder to move elderly voters than younger ones, then this shift is doubly significant; it would seem to bear out the assertion made earlier in this chapter that, under the impact of new issues and a changing perception of the Democratic party, a gradual but significant shift took place in the voting pattern among the elderly—a change that was quite probably already under way in 1960 but had not had measurable electoral consequences.

The long-term impact of the 1960 effort has been apparent in more recent Democratic campaigns. In the 1966 off-year elections President Johnson made a particular effort to woo elderly voters, with promises to increase Social Security benefits. And in 1968 Vice-President Humphrey's campaign staff used promises of expanded Medicare and increased Social Security benefits in what had by now become the customary campaign effort among elderly voters. The vice-president also spoke before groups of elderly voters on both coasts.

It would appear, then, that Senior Citizens for Kennedy set in motion a train of events that was to alter significantly attitudes among Democratic politicians and make courtship of the elderly a permanent element of Democratic electoral strategy. As a consequence of the 1960 experiment an appreciation of the aged as a distinct voter group became, in the words of a well-placed informant, a "part of the orthodoxy" of the party.[39] As the director of a senior center in New York City observed:

> Ten years ago [i.e., mid-1950s] we couldn't get politicians from the major parties to come to talk to our people. They weren't interested. . . . But in 1960, things began to change. They began to make an effort to come when invited. And today [1966] we frequently have to literally throw them out when they come—as they frequently do—uninvited, to campaign and distribute literature. Politicians now realize that the elderly represent a large number of voters, that they do vote, and that they have needs and desires.[40]

In conclusion, Senior Citizens for Kennedy represented a critical juncture in the history of old-age political activism. At the same time, this unique operation also has theoretical value for political science because it enhances our understanding of volunteer appeals in political campaigns. Though such appeals have been considered at length in several systematic works in political science, most impressively in V. O. Key's *Parties, Politics and Pressure Groups*, there have been relatively few efforts to test empirically the propositions offered in them.

Broadly speaking, the present data are consistent with Key's interpretations.[41] As Key suggested is typical of such efforts: (*a*) the senior-citizens organization was jerry-built; (*b*) the lines of authority were hazy; (*c*) it was managed through the DNC as an "unacknowledged subsidiary," a principal duty of which was the distribution of propaganda materials created by the DNC; (*d*) it did serve as a vehicle for prominent people (in the aging, medical, and political worlds) to support the presidential candidate and work in the campaign; (*e*) Senior Citizens for Kennedy became an adjunct campaign organization in many districts, supplementing regular party organizations rather than working within them; (*f*) there were in fact problems of coordination with various other parts of the campaign organization and with local party organizations; (*g*) the operation did provide a vehicle for "plain citizens" to work in the campaign; (*h*) Senior Citizens for Kennedy was used to make a more pointed appeal to elderly voters; and finally (*i*) much of the literature was probably not distributed, as Key believed.

There is, however, one sense in which Senior Citizens for Kennedy did not seem to conform to Key's discussion, though this involves not so much a contradiction as a possible needed modification of his thinking. Key wondered if the principal *objective* of volunteer appeals in political campaigns was not to "bestir the faithful." In order to account for the present findings, one might modify his conclusion to this extent: the principal *effect* of the senior-citizens operation was probably to bestir the faithful, although the initial *objective* of the organization had been to convert the elderly voters to the Democratic party.

Finally, it would seem that Senior Citizens for Kennedy fulfilled certain functions which are not on Key's list, but which could be added: (*a*) the operation served as an instrument of education within the party ranks; (*b*) it was a vehicle for the concerted participation of a major interest-group (and kept the group insulated from the regular party); (*c*) it served as a feedback mechanism for the attitudes of elderly voters; (*d*) it acted, to a limited degree, as a lobbyist within the campaign organization on behalf of the Medicare issue and the aging vote; (*e*) it conducted a variety of activities in direct support of the presidential candidate's personal campaign; and, most important, (*f*) it served as a mechanism for "reality testing"—it was used to test the hypothesis entertained by it organizers and others in the Democratic party that elderly voters could be appealed to as a separate group with separate interests. On this final point it succeeded to the extent of convincing the new president of the United States and the hierarchy of the party. In sum, such appeals may represent a cutting edge of political change and political innovation.

6 Old Age Politicization: An Etiological Analysis

The present work has thus far been organized chronologically. The discussion has stressed the increased political activity among the aged and their allies at various stages, with emphasis on how the behavior of governmental officials has conditioned the strategy of old-age spokesmen. The chronology will be extended subsequently into the 1960s and '70s as the public policy breakthroughs of that era are analyzed. But before moving in this direction it will be helpful to shift somewhat the focus of discussion in order to consider basic societal changes, not confined to any one decade or limited time-span although growing more pronounced in the past twenty years, which have impinged directly on the aging population and which have helped to transform it into something more than a mere statistical aggregate.

Robert Salisbury has asserted that groups become politicized when any one of several "socially disruptive factors," of which he lists technological innovation first in order, disturbs a "putative equilibrium among social groups." He goes on to say that the resulting "disequilibrium will evoke a response from the disadvantaged sectors as they seek to restore a viable balance [and] a principal way of doing so is by organizing a formal association [i.e., interest group]."[1] Writing somewhat earlier, David B. Truman advanced essentially the same argument. He suggested that the causes of the multiplication and expansion of organized groups "lie in the increased complexity of techniques for dealing with the environment, in the specializations that these involve, and in the associated disturbances of the manifold expectations that guide individual behavior in a complex and interdependent society.[2] The general perspective suggested by Salisbury and Truman, emphasizing interest-group formation as arising out of a felt need to restore homeostasis following disruptive societal events, would seem to have value in accounting for the recent growth of senior-citizen activism. In the case of elderly Americans as a grouping, one may be confronting a situation in which technological change and the increasing complexity of mechanisms for coping with change have impinged on the group with great

This chapter draws heavily on Nancy Gina Bermeo, "Aged Activism: Causes, Effects, and Future Trends" (Honors thesis, Mount Holyoke College, 1973).

force and quite possibly with significant results both for aging individuals and groups of the aged.

In the present chapter, therefore, we will endeavor to do two things essentially: first, to explore the character and extent of societal disturbances affecting the aged and the extent to which these have produced mass frustration and political unrest among them; second, to determine whether these same disturbances may have affected the larger society's perception of the aged and its receptivity toward political demands advanced in their behalf. We will defer for the following chapter the treatment of how all this has affected the larger national senior-citizen organizations.

Technology and the Breakdown of Agrarian Culture

In nineteenth-century agrarian society the family, bonded together by ties that were economic as well as emotional, functioned as a working unit. Large, three-generational families were economically advantageous, since the number of man-hours required to produce the goods necessary for their survival was relatively large and the presence of grandparents had a positive effect on the economic security of the entire unit. Because of a high mortality rate the presence of unhealthy grandparents who could contribute little to family maintenance was uncommon. Aged individuals had a secure status within the extended family system.[3]

Technological advancement, by both prolonging life and fostering a highly dynamic economic order with built-in obsolescence of methods and skills, has shattered the old agrarian equilibrium and helped to create a situation in which old people are frequently regarded by their offspring as a burden. The former equilibrium between aging parents and children has been upset, and the extended family of nineteenth-century America has given way to the present two-generation "nuclear" family. While the data presented in table 6.1 are somewhat restricted as to time period, they reveal a decided long-term trend toward older persons living apart.

The effects of this disintegration of the three-generation family unit are both numerous and profound. Among other things, it has contributed to the mushrooming growth of the nursing home industry. While it is true that many elderly persons have been placed in such homes on the basis of clear physical and mental indications, it is also true that other factors than these are often determinative; one survey revealed that 50 percent of the elderly in "costly" nursing institutions are there for nonmedical reasons.[4] Younger family members are increasingly unable or unwilling to house, feed, and care for their aged members within their own homes, and the effect of this has been a kind of "subsidized segregation" in nursing homes and retirement villages. The disturbance in the equilibrium of the extended family system increasingly appears to be alienating the aged from the

Table 6.1 Decline of the Three-Generation Family

Year	Persons 65 and Over Living with Household-head Offspring (%)	Persons 65 and Over Living with Household-head Relatives (%) Not Their Offspring
1940	26.2	8.6
1950	15.5	5.3
1960	12.3	5.1
1970	9.2	3.7

Source: *U.S. Census of Population*, table titled "Persons in Households by Relationship to Head," for the census years mentioned.

family that once gave them security and cared for them in their infirmity. A little later we shall consider the political consequences of this development.

Technological advancement has also disturbed the equilibrium between the aged and the labor force. The need to exclude by formal rules the elderly person from the work force, regardless of his health, education, and experience, has arisen only since industrialization.[5] In less populated agrarian societies an individual could work as long as his physical strength endured, and with the high mortality rate the nonproductive years during which he had to rely on other sources of income were minimal. Younger people typically did not look upon such persons as threats to their jobs.

In an age of advanced technology this state of affairs has been disturbed in two important respects. In the first place, acquired skills become obsolete and the aged, many of whom find the learning of new skills difficult, are frequently regarded (often irrationally) as inhibitors of "progress." Second, medical science has increased longevity and thus the number of theoretically employable older persons; the increased number of employable aged produces pressures on the number of available jobs and heightens the potential for rivalry between generations.

The increased economic isolation and the related alienation from the family unit—both of them consequences of technological change—have tended, for the first time in history, to set the aged apart as a distinct population grouping. Is it possible that the elderly, having become a distinctive grouping in the population, additionally have experienced mass frustrations and that such frustrations have been an important factor in the mobilizing of their latent political potential? The question is worth pursuing.

Frustration and Political Mobilization

Inflation has played a major role in provoking an increased sense of frustration among older Americans; like the other elements discussed below, this factor is not new, but it is newly intense. Many aged persons feel the adverse effects of inflation more than other segments of the population because their livelihood is largely dependent on savings and fixed-income pensions. They are the only age group in which poverty is actually increasing.[6] Whereas in 1961 the median income for families headed by aged individuals was 51 percent of that for families headed by nonaged individuals, in 1967 the median income decreased to 46 percent and by 1970 to 44 percent.[7]

Moreover, savings and pensions provide frail security in today's inflationary economy; savings decrease in purchasing power and pension plans often fail to adjust to cost-of-living increases. Many private pension plans fail to dispense any payments at all. The Department of Labor estimates that one-third to one-half of those who expect to be covered by their employer's pension plan eventually find out that they are not. Prior to enactment of recent federal legislation, the government was prevented by law from "interfering in the management of any welfare or benefit pension plan," and private pension funds operated independently and often unjustly.[8]

Because private pension plans are inadequate, the majority of the nation's retirees are forced to rely on Social Security as their main source of income. But the Social Security system does not insure the economic well-being of our nation's elderly. As of June 1972, Social Security provided an average annual income of only $2,500 for a retired couple and $1,596 for a single individual—leaving more than 4.7 million elderly (or approximately one-fourth of the aged population) below the poverty line. Poverty is especially great among certain segments of the aged population: 50 percent of all aged widows, 48 percent of all aged nonwhites, and 88 percent of all aged black females are classified as poor. A recent survey revealed that: (1) 10 million elderly individuals have incomes of less than $75 per week to meet all living expenses; (2) 2 million elderly couples subsist on combined weekly incomes of only $50, and (3) half of all the aged living alone have less than $30 a week to cover all expenses. The precarious economic situation of these and other marginally poor elderly Americans is greatly exacerbated by rising inflation.[9]

Another element provoking politicization is the rising cost of medical care. In 1967 the per capita medical cost for all age groups was $147. By 1971 it had risen to $345, and by 1980 it is expected to reach $814. The cost of a hospital bed has risen more than 63 percent since 1960. The aged feel the effects of soaring medical costs more than any other segment of the population, both because their health care expenditures are more than three and one-half times greater than those of younger segments of the population, and because their medical costs begin to rise as their incomes start to decline. Though the elderly make up only 10 percent of the population, they constitute 25 percent of all "hospital users" and pay 27 percent of all health care expenditures. And ironically, Medicare and other related programs designed precisely to alleviate this burden of expense are becoming increasingly costly and ineffective. As medical costs have increased, Medicare coverage has declined relatively: in 1969, for instance, Medicare covered 45 percent of an average medical bill, whereas by 1970 it covered 43 percent, and in 1973 only 41.5 percent.[10]

By increasing longevity, technological development has increased the number of individuals requiring health care. Today, for example, more than 86 percent of the nation's elderly (more than 17 million individuals) have "some kind of chronic condition" requiring periodic medical care.[11] Since Medicare coverage is declining and the need for health care is increasing, higher medical costs have a greater effect on a greater number of people than ever before. Just as the increasingly heavy burden of medical costs prompted the mobilization of masses of aged citizens in the early sixties, newly expensive health care continues to promote the politicization of the aged today.

Yet another new element having a deleterious effect on the well-being of the aged is the deterioration of mass transit systems. For physical and economic reasons, elderly citizens are frequently unable to operate private automobiles. Yet public transportation is often too costly, too inaccessible, or too dangerous to afford them substantial mobility. Aside from reinforcing the loneliness and isolation that typify the lives of so many aged citizens, the lack of mobility resulting from inadequate means of transportation aggravates many other gerontological problems; it is likely, for example, that isolation from food stores and medical facilities exacerbates the health problems of many elderly individuals. That inadequate public transportation contributes to the politicization is suggested by the fact that the elderly delegates to the 1971 White House Conference on Aging, in part reflecting the previously expressed demands of old age mass-membership bodies, cited transportation as the third major concern of the nation's senior citizens, exceeded only in importance by income maintenance and health needs.

A fourth element fostering the expansion of aged interest groups has been the steep rise in the local property tax. Dr. Wilbur Cohen, former HEW secretary and one of the country's leading authorities on old-age problems, insists that "the tax problem" fosters most of the "political discontent" among the elderly.[12] In placing taxes ahead of all other sources of frustration, Cohen may have somewhat exaggerated the importance of this problem. But the fact remains that taxes have risen at an unprecedented rate in recent years. In the brief interval between 1967 and 1970, for example, local property taxes rose an average of 35 percent. Rising property taxes affect the fixed-income aged more than any other segment of the population. The Senate Special Committee on Aging recently reported that large percentages of the nation's elderly are spending a staggering 20 to 40 percent of their income on local property tax. The report revealed that in the state of Wisconsin alone 8,000 elderly individuals earning less than $1,000 annually paid a full 30% of their income in local property tax. Ironically these and other aged citizens derive little (if any) benefit from the public school system which these taxes finance. Thus, for the 12 to 14 million elderly homeowners in the United States, spiraling property taxes represent an increasingly costly and fruitless expense. Prior to 1964, home ownership among the aged had been rising, but in recent years the proportion of old people who own homes has decreased markedly—a change partially attributable to municipal levies on their residences.[13]

Tax problems also have a deleterious effect on the security of home renters, because tenants usually absorb the tax burden of landlords. In New York City, for example, the average elderly tenant spends more than one-third of his income on rent if the dwelling is rent-controlled and one-half of his income on rent if he resides in a non-rent-controlled hotel. Not surprisingly, landlords justify rent hikes as a legitimate response to rising property taxes. For the country as a whole, well over 90 percent of all property taxes on housing are borne by occupants.[14]

As was stated before, the number of aged individuals residing with members of their immediate family has decreased sharply in recent years. This implies that an increased number of elderly individuals must finance (at least in part) an increased number of separate dwellings and, thus, that higher property taxes adversely affect the aged more than ever before. Moreover, the vast majority of aged interest-group members reside where property taxes are highest, that is in urbanized areas, and it is therefore not surprising that old-age interest groups cite tax reform as one of their major legislative goals.

Closely related to the rise in the property tax has been an increase in the number of ill-housed elderly. In the early sixties the Social Security Administration estimated that 26 percent of the aged population resided in "substandard" housing, whereas a decade later the proportion had increased to 30 percent (6.5 million persons), and this despite marked prosperity in the economy generally. The decline in the proportion of the elderly residing in safe and decent housing has occurred in the face of an increasing investment of their personal incomes in this area of need: by 1970, housing costs consumed approximately 33 percent of the average senior citizen's income, up from 22.4 percent twenty years previously. Notwithstanding the high proportion of ill-housed elderly, the federal government in the decade from 1962 to 1972 constructed only 350,000 units specifically for the elderly. Though many aged individuals are eligible for residence in "general housing" projects, they frequently fail to apply, thinking they might be unsafe in such projects. Seeking solutions to these and other problems, aged interest groups are united in demanding that the government be more responsive to the unique housing needs of the elderly.[15]

One could go on at length enumerating the national economic trends which have worked a particular hardship on the elderly, but for present purposes it will be sufficient to mention only one more. This is the recent and rapid expansion of nursing institutions (now a $2.5 billion industry) and the well-publicized abuses involved in their approach to health needs. Nursing homes in this country now house more than 1 million aged individuals, the number of patients having increased 14 percent in the 1966–71 period alone.[16] Along with the growth of the industry has come increased publicity concerning nursing home scandals. Ralph Nader, David Pryor, George McGovern, and numerous other public figures have surveyed the industry and decried its abuses publicly. Aside from informing the general public, this publicity has stimulated concern and apprehension on the part of the elderly themselves. The disintegration of the multigenerational family, the increase in the number of "invalid" aged and the corresponding increase in the availability of long-term care facilities has meant that an unprecedented number of individuals will have direct contact with the nursing home industry. Moreover, the nature of this contact is anything but salutary in many cases. For example, a recent survey revealed that 54.4 percent of the "healthy" persons admitted to old-age institutions die within their first year there.[17] Believing that this high mortality rate is at least partially a result of neglect and carelessness, senior-citizen leaders across the nation are lobbying for legislation to improve nursing home standards and to provide viable alternatives to nursing home care.

Recalling the previously quoted passage from David B. Truman's work, how have the "new elements" discussed above disturbed the "manifold expectations" of the nation's aged population? The following hypothetical case study may facilitate our analysis. Although its subject, Sarah Smith, bears no intentional resemblance to any specific person, her problems are by no means atypical and her dilemma can serve to illustrate the disturbed expectations of the aged in general.[18]

Sarah Smith is the sixty-eight-year-old widow of a Pittsburgh steelworker. She resides in a house which was purchased in 1935 for $4,200. The house is located in a recently "urbanized" area where taxes have been climbing gradually for years. Last year Mrs. Smith paid $750 in property taxes and was assessed $260 for sewer work. Her total income in only $2,000.[19]

Though she worked as a waitress for fifteen years, Mrs. Smith receives no pension and no Social Security benefits for her own earnings and must subsist exclusively on her husband's modest company pension and Social Security benefits.[20] She and her husband had expected to have security in their retirement. They had paid off the mortgage years ago and had set

"emergency" funds aside in their savings account. When Medicare was
enacted they thought they might eventually spend their emergency savings
on vacations. But when Mr. Smith became chronically ill, the family savings
were expended and Mrs. Smith had to go into debt: Title XVIII of the
Medicare program pays extended-care benefits only for the "acutely ill." For
the Smiths and for thousands of other aged individuals Medicare benefits
were "retroactively denied because the patient [did] not meet the written
definitions for being acutely ill, even though he [needed] extensive nursing
care."[21]

Because of the financial problems brought on by her husband's death,
Mrs. Smith cannot afford to use the public transportation system. Unable to
shop at large supermarkets, she must pay high prices for food at the small
local grocers and gets little food value for her money. She also gets little
exercise because she is afraid to walk on her crime-ridden neighborhood
streets. Like four million other elderly individuals, Mrs. Smith has no
surviving relatives. And, like several million aged poor, she is unaware that
she qualifies for state and local supplements to her Social Security pension.[22]

The "Mrs. Smiths" of this country number in the hundreds of thousands
and, as her case illustrates, the expectations of many of the elderly are being
disturbed more radically than ever before. Most of today's aged were young
when Congress passed the Social Security Act in 1935 and have spent a large
number of their employed years contributing to a government program
which promised a measure of economic security in old age. They have thus
come to expect, in a way that their forebears did not, that government will
provide them with a certain immunity from economic hardship after
retirement. Furthermore, the enactment of Medicare legislation in the
mid-sixties has entailed the additional expectation of adequate health care
protection.

These rising expectations are especially susceptible to the disturbances
associated with inflation and the other new elements discussed in the
previous section. If we accept Truman's assertion that the growth of interest
groups is enhanced by "disturbances of the manifold expectations that
guide individual behavior," it follows that these "rising expectations" and
"increasing disturbances" contribute to the expansion of aged interest-
groups. Indeed, in the politicization of the aged we are witnessing
something akin to a "revolution of rising expectations." While the attitude
changes referred to impinge to some degree on all elderly Americans, the
"revolution"—as is typical of revolutions generally—has affected one
category of the aged population, namely the "slightly privileged," to an
especially marked degree. As revealed in a recent gerontological study, most
members of old-age interest groups are from the "slightly privileged"
classes.[23] Such persons are, on the one hand, more susceptible to "disturbances" than is true of high-income aged and , on the other, less inclined to

accept as inevitable the lesser estate that the low social-status elderly have had to confront throughout their lives. Thus, as Truman's theory predicts, they are more politicized than either of the other two groups.

For many aged individuals the new elements and disturbed expectations discussed above have combined to produce status anxiety, a term denoting a sense of anguish resulting from an incapacity to bring society's definition of one's "place" into line with one's own sense of self-worth. Status anxiety, according to one survey, is the main motive for older persons' enrollment in interest groups.[24] While factors like inflation and rising taxes have had a readily measurable adverse effect on senior citizens' economic status, social status has also been drastically affected by job market displacement and the enforced idleness of many able-bodied "young-aged" persons. Today's elderly were raised in an era when nonproductive activity was strongly stigmatized. Since they exist in an environment where "occupation" is still the overriding determinant of status, their often involuntary exclusion from the means of production tends to produce in them a sense of marginality. Their decline in status often results in feelings of worthlessness and anomie. A recent survey substantiates the point: nearly 25 percent of the older people in the United States feel that they are "unwanted," and an additional 22 percent feel that there is "nothing left to live for."[25]

Further tending to intensify status anxiety is the phenomenon of "agism." Although the social status of specific aged individuals varies according to their economic circumstances, the prestige and deference bestowed upon senior citizens as a group are comparatively low. A survey conducted by Joseph H. Bunzel of the University of Buffalo indicated that nearly half of the nation's population is afflicted with a mild neurosis called "gerontophobia," that is, the dread of old age.[26] The youth orientation of our society produces, according to psychiatrists, "severe mental anxiety" among many aged and near-aged individuals, "forcing a significant number to indentify themselves as considerably younger than they actually are."[27]

The marked expansion of aged interest-groups in recent years is thus partially attributable to a desire for meaningful activity and a concomitant desire for status. In addition to performing their well-publicized lobbying activities, these secondary associations serve as substitutes for the primary associations that furnished security and status for old persons in earlier generations. Senator Harrison Williams, a longtime member of the Senate Special Committee on Aging, puts the point well: "Political organization is the kind of antidote needed to overcome feelings of neglect and of not being useful or wanted—feelings derived from a society willing to assign status only for the pursuit of a gainful occupation."[28]

Elements of Old-Age Political Access

One important effect of technological advancement, as was noted, has been the emergence of a sense of rage and resentment among the elderly. Yet paradoxically, one suspects that the same dynamic forces that have helped to make the aged a "problem" for the larger society have also, in another sense, served to insure that old-age problems, once brought forcefully to the attention of policymakers, will receive sympathetic attention. This is not to suggest that old-age groups are invariably heeded or that the fundamental problems of elderly people are on their way to a solution in this country, but rather to underscore the point that the aging have proved a difficult group for officials to ignore or to "buy off" with purely symbolic concessions.

As a point of departure one should recall the discussion earlier in this chapter regarding the breakdown of the three-generation family. While it is true that the younger generation is often unwilling or unable to provide for the needs of aging parents, many of whom may reside in communities distant from them, it cannot be assumed that the younger generation is therefore indifferent to what happens to the elderly. While the aging are in one sense a "minority group"—bearing all the stereotypes and stigmas which this term connotes—it is also the case that all younger persons, assuming their lives do not end prematurely, will eventually become old. The aged are a unique minority whose ultimate membership will include the great majority of Americans, and this gives the aged something of an advantage relative to other minority groups. Moreover, the elderly constitute an "unrivaled minority," a politicized group which has no institutionalized and self-proclaimed political adversaries. It confronts no interest groups which continuously lobby against a wide range of its policy objectives in the way that road builders' groups, for example, are opposed by conservation groups, farm workers' groups by the organized farm owners, pro-abortion by antiabortion lobbies, and so forth. This is not to suggest that the aged function without opposition but merely to state that when they are opposed—as they were by the American Medical Association during the fight over Medicare—they are opposed on a temporary basis only and usually in a half-apologetic manner. In the Medicare case, for example, the AMA went to elaborate lengths to demonstrate that it was not "really" opposed to old folks, just to the socialistic schemes of which the elderly were sometimes "innocent dupes."[29] Because aged interest-groups have no institutionalized adversary, a political decision-maker can verbally support their general recommendations without automatically jeopardizing his popularity among other groups—a considerable advantage for such groups in the legislative struggle. This "unrivaled" position appears to be in part related to a general feeling that the aged are among the few deserving claimants for assistance out of tax revenues and that their disadvantaged status is a consequence of societal trends which are not of their making.

For similar reasons old-age interest groups possess a second important advantage, namely, an ability to form coalitions and alliances with large and well-organized occupational associations. The close, even symbiotic, link-ages between the National Educational Association and the National Retired Teachers Association, and between the AFL-CIO and the National Council of Senior Citizens, are only two examples of many that could be offered. A northern Democratic congressman or senator who might indulge in thoughts of rejecting the appeals of the NCSC, for example, will often think twice when it is called to his attention that this group is bound up with "Big Labor" and its substantial political clout on Capitol Hill.

Third, the senior citizens' lobby has a relatively easy time identifying itself with the "rules of the game"—meaning a society's pervasive but unorgan-ized expectations regarding the nature and limits of authority and the conduct of decision-makers. The rules of the game in American society include the values incorporated in the Bill of Rights, mass participation in the designation of leaders, semiegalitarian notions of material welfare, and a predilection for evolutionary rather than revolutionary political change.[30] Aging interest-groups, mindful of their strategic advantage in this area, boldly pushed through a "Declaration of Aging Rights" at the 1971 White House Conference on Aging. Paraphrasing the Declaration of Indepen-dence, the delegates proclaimed that the fundamental rights of "life, liberty and the pursuit of happiness" are inalienably possessed by all people "without regard for age." They followed this with a listing of ten old-age "rights."[31] While this particular document is of no great importance in itself, being only one among many resolutions passed at the White House conference, it does illustrate the ease with which old-age spokesmen can invoke fundamental constitutional values and justify their cause as synony-mous with the general good. All interest groups attempt in varying degrees to invoke the "rules of the game," but the aged, given unrivaled status and broad distribution throughout all strata of society, are in an especially favorable position to do so.

Finally, the structural differentiation of society—an important by-product of technological advancement—has enhanced old-age group political access by making the group leaders the possessors of sought-after expertise and specialized knowledge. The ability to provide technical information consti-tutes a special advantage for senior-citizen organizations, for it gives them the opportunity to command a certain deference among lawmakers and officials. The science of gerontology, which is rarely studied or even discussed on the undergraduate level, is not a particularly popular subject. While most, if not all legislators enter Congress with at least a vague knowledge of American foreign policy or civil rights legislation, few of them enter with knowledge about gerontology. It stands to reason that groups which attempt to influence legislators concerning well-known, much-studied issues are more likely to encounter opposition than groups which deal with more obscure subjects. Representing this latter case, old-age

associations have the advantage of being informants rather than only
supplicants and probably have less chance of encountering deep-seated
policy biases on their broad platform recommendations. Moreover, it seems
reasonable to suppose that such groups are in a position to provide
"political" information to decision-makers—information having to do with
the electoral costs and benefits of supporting proposed old-age legislation.
While it is true that lawmakers, being politicians, must have their own
"hometown" sources of political advice and counsel concerning grassroots
opinion on various subjects, it is also true that even in the political realm
information provided them by aging interest-groups may have significant
value.

In summary, we have suggested that the impact of technological advancement on the growth of the national senior-citizens lobby has been essentially
twofold: first, it has tended to set the aged apart for the first time from the
larger society and to generate frustrations which are the basis for mass
political action. In this sense the findings are quite consistent with the
Salisbury-Truman hypothesis advanced at the outset. Second, it has been
suggested that social disruptions have affected general public attitudes
toward the aged and have laid the foundation for substantial increases in
political access. The question of whether they are in a position to do this will
occupy our attention in the chapters to follow.

7 Emergence of Stable Voluntary Organizations

In the early Kennedy administration era groups nominally representing the elderly were not equipped organizationally to wage effective legislative campaigns, not even on issues like Medicare that vitally affected their constituents. As Theodore Lowi remarks, there was "no need to debate the social significance of the [Medicare] bill. . . . The only surprise in the Medicare case was the difficulty of passage. But that was due to stalemate, not between liberalism and conservatism, but between the unorganized and apathetic elderly and the intensely felt and highly organized trade union interests of the American Medical Association."[1] Yet, old age spokesmen at this time did not so much lack organization as such—senior groups did exist in Washington and up to a point were active—as they had difficulty in mobilizing the widely scattered pockets of local senior-citizen strength and in forging them into an effective national force. As the decade progressed, however, this problem was one that they increasingly learned to cope with.

Though some of the aging group emerging in this period were ephemeral, surviving precariously on the basis of work by a mere handful of activists, others manifested evidence of staying power. And it is the latter type which merits attention. How were these organizations able to get started? Once organized, where did they derive the resources, material and otherwise, necessary to their survival? How did they go about developing the talent and skill necessary to exert tangible political leverage?

These are intriguing questions in view of the long record of instability which, as noted in an earlier chapter, characterized the old-age associations of the 1930s and 40s. This earlier period witnessed the demise not only of the previously discussed AALL, AASS, and Townsend movement (as a genuine national force), but also of other old-age pension groups, such as the railroad retirees' National Pension Association (NPA) and the California pension movements of the early 1940s.[2]

An earlier version of this chapter appeared as "Old Age Associations in National Politics," *The Annals of the American Academy of Political and Social Science* (September 1974): 106–19.

National Groups Presently Active

While many groups interest themselves in aging matters from time to time, only a handful—ten at the present time—are both engaged in politics at the national level and more or less exclusively preoccupied with old-age problems.[3] Four of these are trade associations with a decidedly narrow policy focus: the American Association of Homes for the Aging, the American Nursing Home Association, the National Council of Health Care Services, and the National Association of State Units on Aging (NASUA). The four invest virtually all their efforts in national politics, trying to get more federal funds for their operations and seeking adjustments in the detailed official conditions under which they function. Another group, the American Gerontological Society, with about two thousands individual members and several affiliates, is a professional association. Still another, the National Council on the Aging (NCOA), is a loose confederation comprising specialists in the field and public and private social welfare agencies. A recent body, the National Caucus on the Black Aged, is a coalition of about 150 professionals attempting to bring to light the particular plight of the black elderly. Finally, and not least in importance, are the three mass-membership organizations: the National Council of Senior Citizens (NCSC), initially constituted in the early 1960s to campaign for Medicare but later broadened to include the whole gamut of senior-citizen concerns; the American Association of Retired Persons (AARP) and the National Retired Teachers Association (NRTA), which function in national affairs as one organization; and the National Association of Retired Federal Employees (NARFE).

Rather than attempt the unwieldy task of treating each of the ten organizations individually, I will select four of them that are known to manifest a particularly acute interest in legislative issues. The three mass-membership organizations mentioned (NCSC, NRTA-AARP, and NARFE) lend themselves well to this purpose, since their interventions in the national policy arena are backed up by at least the apparent support of hundreds of thousands of voters in all walks of life (the interventions of the other organizations are more easily dismissed as the expressions of special interests). I also propose to treat NCOA, since it likewise has a range of legislative concerns and, by virtue of its linkages to senior citizens throughout the country, has a quasi-mass-membership character. There is an obvious risk of oversimplification in this narrowing of the focus of discussion from ten groups to four but the advantages accruing from greater depth of analysis would seem to outweigh the risk.

In order that the analytical material to follow may be fully comprehended, it is first necessary to present certain basic data about the four groups, in particular their goals, internal structure, and organizational growth.

National Council of Senior Citizens

The NCSC had its origins in the 1960 Senior Citizens for Kennedy effort and in the burgeoning sentiment for Medicare which came to a focus at the 1961 White House Conference on Aging. Richard Harris has pinpointed the moment when the NCSC concept was first conceived:

> At the [1961] White House Conference on the Aging, [Congressman] Forand had got into a dicussion with several union leaders who were considering whether it was desirable to organize older people to work for Medicare. Some of the men he talked to opposed the idea on the grounds it would inevitably lead to a kind of Townsend Movement. Among those who held this position was Nelson Cruikshank, head of the AFL-CIO's Department of Social Security. . . . Then, in the summer of 1961, the two men who ran programs for retired workers in the AFL-CIO—Charles Odell of the United Auto Workers and James Cuff O'Brien of the United Steel Workers—decided to go ahead with the project on a part-time basis, despite the opposition of Cruikshank and other labor leaders. They persuaded their unions to put up small amounts of money and prevailed on Forand to lend his name as Chairman.[4]

The organization was formally launched at a founding convention in Detroit at which the United Auto Workers and other industrial unions were preeminently represented, though they sought to avoid the impression of dominating the proceedings. Crucial to the fledgling organization, in addition to union support, was aid from the Democratic National Committee, which construed the results of the 1960 election as evidence that elderly voters had become a significant "swing" vote.

In the NCSC's first five years of operation, roughly two-thirds of its income was generated from unions and the DNC, with the remainder coming from member dues.[5] Throughout this period union officials were becoming increasingly convinced of the strategic value of NCSC; even Nelson Cruikshank, once a skeptic, was in time persuaded to allocate AFL-CIO funds to its maintenance and later to assume a leadership role. Cruikshank is currently the president of NCSC. Though vocal and energetic in its support of the Medicare crusade, the NCSC was handicapped by limited funds and staff resources. "When I came down here," Executive Director William R. Hutton remarked to an interviewer in 1965, "the office was a dilapidated flat, the one secretary worked at the kitchen table and kept the press releases in the bathtub, and there was precious little in the way of funds. The AMA had all the money, and we had all the old people."[6] Typewriters were borrowed from the industrial union department of the AFL-CIO, and a part-time staff man was loaned by the UAW. Despite the meager resources of the organization, most (though not all) observers are convinced that NCSC did manage to play a significant role in the passage of Medicare.[7]

From a small, highly specialized organization whose early efforts were focused largely on a single legislative issue, the NCSC grew both in membership and political leverage following the decision in 1965 to expand its range of political goals. There are currently over 3,000 affiliated senior-citizen clubs throughout the country, with a combined membership of over 3 million. The national office estimates that the local clubs are distributed about equally into three categories: trade union retiree groups, religious and ethnic groups, and social welfare retirees. The 3 million membership figure includes many people who identify with NCSC only indirectly, and for this reason it bears mentioning that the number of directly contributing, dues-paying members—Gold Card members—is currently 250,000, an increase of more than 250 percent since 1971.

Although the national leaders have worked to expand their membership base beyond that of labor union retirees, and as a result the rolls now include a number of middle-class and nonunion-related persons, the leadership of NCSC is nevertheless securely in labor-union hands, particularly in the hands of the more politically aggressive and socially involved industrial unions. Of the fifty persons who in 1972 were serving on the organization's national board, only sixteen did not come from the union movement; among the four national vice-presidents, three were former union officials.[8] The current president (Cruikshank) and the executive director (Hutton) both have many years of union involvement. (As a visitor to the NCSC's 1971 national convention, the author was impressed by the degree to which these social background characteristics were reflected in the style and rhetoric of the leaders: they frequently addressed one another as "brother," and resolutions memorializing deceased labor officials abounded.) This union predominance in NCSC affairs has important implications for the organization's political behavior, as subsequent discussion will suggest.

National Retired Teachers Association-American Association of Retired Persons

If the origins of the National Council of Senior Citizens were in the first instance political, it may be said that the goals of the NRTA-AARP, though always including a political dimension, have tended to subordinate political goals to those of individual uplift and social betterment.[9] The National Retired Teachers Association was founded in 1947 by Dr. Ethel Percy Andrus, a prominent California educator and Los Angeles high school principal with close ties to the National Education Association. The initial goals did include such legislative goals as improved state teacher pensions and federal tax benefits for retired teachers, but Dr. Andrus was more directly concerned with efforts to improve the image and raise the relative status of retirees generally and to provide, through private enterprise, for their material needs. By 1955, eight years after its founding, the organization had attained a national membership of 20,000—a significant but not especially impressive number by national standards.

In that year, Dr. Andrus was introduced to a Poughkeepsie, New York, insurance agent, Leonard Davis, a man forty years her junior. Prior to their meeting, Davis, in consultation with Robert Decormier, then president of the New York State Retired Teachers Association, had persuaded a leading insurance underwriter, Continental Casualty Company, to write life insurance policies for 800 New York State retired teachers on an experimental basis, despite the then-prevalent view in the industry that retirees constituted poor actuarial risks. Dr. Andrus long had been convinced that the frustrations experienced by elderly persons across the country in obtaining life insurance constituted a major element in their frequent financial distress. In the course of a series of meetings, Dr. Andrus and Davis drew up an arrangement under which NRTA members nationwide would become eligible for the New York State type of benefits; as his part of the bargain, Davis agreed to invest $50,000 of his own capital, an investment, incidentally, which has paid off handsomely for him: the value of his NRTA-AARP related insurance holdings in a recent year (1972) was estimated at about $184 million.[10]

Once implemented, the Davis-Andrus plan proved immensely popular, with 5,000 NRTA members signing up to participate in the first few months. So great was the interest that retirees outside the teaching profession began to ask for such policies. Rather than turn these persons away as ineligible, Andrus and Davis took steps to found a new organization, the American Association of Retired Persons, which would have a far broader constituency than its parent body.

Chartered in 1958, the new group shared the staff and headquarters of NRTA but had its own board of directors and regional affiliates. AARP has prospered, not only through its ever-expanding membership, but also by virtue of the fact that the insurance operation—later expanded to include travel, pharmacy, and training services—returned a fixed percentage of premiums and fees to help meet NRTA-AARP operating expenses.

In view of its auspicious beginnings, it is scarcely surprising that combined dues-paying membership of NRTA-AARP easily makes it the largest organization of its kind in the country. It grew in size from a modest 150,000 in 1959 to about 1 million in 1969, to 6.02 million in late 1973, and to move than 9 million in 1975, making it one of the largest voluntary bodies in the country.

The organization's underlying perspective and social outlook have generally been closely linked to that of business enterprise, especially the insurance industry, with which the group has evolved a symbiotic relation-

ship. Illustrative of its underlying predispositions was the health care
proposal introduced by Dr. Andrus in the course of July 1959 Forand bill
hearings before the House Ways and Means Committee. The Andrus plan,
while not identical to that being offered by the American Medical Association, was not inconsistent with it. Dr. Andrus proposed the formation of a
"trusteeship" to initiate and administer the health insurance plan for the
elderly which she espoused. The trustees would include equal numbers of
representatives of health care ("such as AMA and AHA"), of business
("such as the U.S. Chamber of Commerce"), representatives of the aged
("such as NRTA and AARP") and representatives of labor (no illustrations
given). In administering the program, the trusteeship was to begin by
submitting specifications "to the insurance industry and/or Blue Cross and
Blue Shield for competition." After accepting the best bid or bids and
arranging for the collection of premiums, the trusteeship would then transfer
all premiums paid to the respective insurance company or companies.[11]
NRTA-AARP was not on record as opposing the Medicare measure passed by
Congress in 1965, but neither was it among the bill's active promotors. A
bias toward the industry management viewpoint on current issues is also
implicit in the fact that not a single former labor union official currently sits
on the AARP board of directors, whereas a number of former businessmen
do. However, in the early 1970s, with the office of executive director filled
by Bernard Nash, the organization worked to gain acceptance in official
Washington as a strictly nonpartisan body. The fact that its voice is now
heeded by leading Democrats as well as by Republicans suggests that these
efforts have met with a large degree of success.

National Association of Retired Federal Employees

Just as the specialized needs of government retirees have been an important
factor in the decision to maintain the National Retired Teachers Association
as an autonomous group within the NRTA-AARP structure, so the special
situation of the federal government retiree has made possible the survival of
NARFE in the face of newer and more expansive mass-membership
organizations. NARFE was founded in February 1921, around the time of
the passage of the Federal Employees Pension Act, and has served both as a
vehicle for "case work" arising from this act and as a means of pressing for
subsequent enlargement of benefits to federal retirees. The organization had
a hand in the passage of the 1959 Federal Employees Health Benefits Law
and the 1962 amendments to the pension act providing for cost-of-living
annuity increases.

While the existence of federal legislation affecting government retirees
has been fundamental to the survival of NARFE, it has by no means
guaranteed success, even on issues where a narrowly focused group such as

this might be assumed to have an advantage over larger and more amorphous retiree organizations. In recent years, NARFE income, if one discounts the factor of inflation, has grown comparatively little, increasing from $259,000 in 1956 to $329,000 in 1960 and $543,000 in 1971. In 1969 and 1970 the group ran a net operating deficit.[12] During a period of unprecedented membership growth in the other two mass-membership groups, NARFE's rolls have increased only modestly—a 15 percent increase from 1968 to 1971 and a further 17 percent growth—to 182,000—in 1974.

NARFE's lack of substantial growth is at least partially responsible for the organization's tendency to concentrate on bread-and-butter issues of direct substantive concern to members, while relating only marginally to more broadly defined social, economic, and legislative questions. Whereas NCSC and AARP produced a veritable flood of position papers, policy statements, and political propaganda in connection with the 1971 White House Conference on Aging, NARFE leaders did little beyond attend meetings with other senior-citizen groups and, through the organization's house organ, *Retirement Life*, keep members abreast in a general way of the proceedings. (*Retirement Life* accounts of the White House Conference were buried on pages 22, 15, and 20, respectively, in the issues of October and December 1971, and January 1972. Only the last of these editions contained more than six or eight paragraphs on the topic.) The activities and decisions of congressional committees and subcommittees with authority to decide policy for federal retirees, on the other hand, are given frequent and voluminous attention in the publication.

National Council on the Aging

Among the groups treated in this chapter, NCOA, launched in 1950 under its original name of National Committee on the Aging, was the first to be deeply affected by the modern senior movement. The purpose of the organization, as described in an NCOA "Fact Sheet," has been to serve as "a central, national resource for planning, information, consultation and publications devoted to a better life in later years."[13]

Three developments, coming to a focus in the late 1940s, were responsible for the founding of the organization.[14] One factor was the work of the New York Joint Legislative Task Force on Aging—the Desmond Committee. The committee surveyed aging needs, and its reports gave official sanction to an enlarged concern with aging problems in the state. Moreover, the staff director, Albert J. Abrams, in collaboration with Harry Levine of the New York City Welfare Department and Ollie Randall of the Community Service Society of New York, drafted legislation which eventuated in providing state aid for senior centers—an important breakthrough. Second, there was a growing awareness among European scholars and practitioners that the

elderly's needs deserved attention on their own terms, not as a subsidiary of
some larger social issue. One of the NCOA founders, Mrs. Geneva
Mathiasen, was uniquely responsible for bringing this perspective to bear
during the organization's formative years. Finally, there was the senior-center movement, originating in New York City with the founding there in the
40s of the Hodson and Sironich centers. Conferees who assembled at a 1949
meeting at Vassar College drafted a blueprint for encouraging the growth of
such centers, and NCOA later took up this cause.

The immediate occasion for founding NCOA was the Federal Security
Agency's announcement in 1950 of plans to hold a National Conference on
Aging. With the conference impending, Mrs. Mathiasen contacted the head
of the National Social Welfare Assembly to volunteer her services and those
of Ollie Randall to head a new committee of NSWA, the National
Committee on the Aging. Though the Assembly's delegates voted the
committee into existence, they provided only a token budget, and in the
early months the organization led a precarious existence. The crisis of
infancy passed, however, and in a couple of years the committee was in a
position to survive on its own—a change in status formally acknowledged in
1960 with the decision to reconstitute the group as the National Council on
the Aging.

Though NCOA is still not by any means an activist organization (its board
normally forbids adoption of official stands on broadly defined national
policy issues), it does concern itself politically when the issue is one of direct
institutional importance, as in the need to obtain adequate funding for
senior centers under Title 5 of the Older Americans Act. It is quite possible,
moreover, that a recent trend toward increased influence on the part of
senior-citizens spokesmen will have the long-run effect of broadening the
organization's social goals. The NCOA-sponsored National Institute of
Senior Centers (NISC) was founded in 1967, and between 1969 and 1974
the number of NCOA-affiliated centers grew from roughly 2,500 to more
than 5,000. Related to this development has been the fact that the
proportion of dues-paying NCOA members designating ''senior center'' as
their single major interest has grown to the point that fully two-thirds of
national members are in this category. As a result of their ties to senior
centers and NISC, the NCOA policy-makers are apprised of the aspirations
of hundreds of thousands of elderly people.[15] It is not uncommon among
voluntary organizations that an enlargement of political goals should be one
important consequence of a change from caucus-type to quasi-mass-membership structure. Such a shift may be occurring here.

At present, however, it is only an incipient development, and NCOA,
with a dues-paying membership of 1,900, remains essentially a society of
subject-matter specialists. There are basically three tiers in the organization:
(1) a technical, fact-finding and fact-dissemination level composed of policy

analysts; (2) a ''lay tier'' composed of prominent persons interested in aging; old-timers who became interested in aging during the senior movement's ''popular phase'' and (3) an ''affiliated group tier'' consisting of representatives of a host of national organizations, such as the Red Cross, Association of Junior Leagues, National Association of Social Workers, who come regularly together to gain added understanding and a renewed sense of commitment.

Factors in Organizational Strength

The four groups included in this survey, despite differences in resources, goals, and strategies, have in common a cluster of traits which serve to differentiate them from their counterpart organizations of the 1930s and '40s. In large part the difference consists in the fact that the newer groups are steadier and more persistent in their pursuit of substantive goals and less subject to internal and external disruptions. This is related to three factors, two of them having to do with internal arrangements (bureaucratization and revenue supplementation) and a third relating to the external environment (a more benign opinion climate).

Bureaucratization

In the case of the earlier aging organizations, the demise of the founder was typically the occasion for profound organizational trauma, often followed by marked goal redefinition and agonizing reappraisals.[16] In contrast, among the groups under consideration here the death or departure of the founder was accommodated with not such traumatic results. The withdrawl of Aimé Forand in the early 1960s in no way retarded the subsequent growth of his brainchild, the NCSC. The case of the NRTA-AARP is admittedly more complicated, since Dr. Andrus, without intending to do so, placed a severe strain on her organization when , two years before her death, she sought to move its national headquarters from Washington, D.C., to her home in Long Beach, California. The effects of this effort, in terms of stagnating membership and organizational disruption, were not inconsequential. Yet, following her death in July 1967, the organization regrouped itself and went on to new levels of size and significance.

The resignation of National Council on the Aging founder and longtime executive director, Geneva Mathiasen, occurred in 1969. NCOA at the time had become concerned with the need to deal more effectively with the federal government, and the transfer of power to her successor, William C. Fitch, whose reputation had been built in the federal aging bureaucracy, occurred without evident organizational trauma. NARFE, by far the oldest group under study, has, of course, survived numerous changes in its leadership over its fifty years of operation. Such smooth successions of power at the staff level are typical of groups which have evolved meaningful bureaucratic standards and performance criteria.

The attempt to impose bureaucratic standards on an organization composed of the elderly encounters at least one quite significant problem: namely, the rank and file, reversing the usual social bias in favor of youth, may insist that the top executives themselves be persons of advanced age. For example, if a senior-citizen leader were to suggest that a person over age seventy may not be as well-qualified to run a large organization as a person of similar background twenty years younger, he might endanger his own leadership status and risk disruptive internal strife. Yet, the fact remains that advanced age does exact a toll on persons, especially on their ability to labor for long, grueling hours managing a large enterprise. Thus, bureaucratic demands and rank-and-file attitudes are in tension.

In the case of the three organizations with the fastest rate of growth, NCOA, NCSC, and NRTA-AARP, a way of resolving this dilemma has been found. Their formula guarantees that the top honorary posts—in all three cases that of the president—shall be held by a person over sixty-five years of age, while those who carry the main burden of administering the organization may be (and normally are) younger in age. Bernard Nash was only in his mid-forties at the time of his appointment as NRTA-AARP executive director; Nash's immediate subordinates—introduced to the author in the course of recent interviews—also appear comparatively youthful. Prior to his appointment Nash was Deputy Commissioner on Aging and originator of the federal Foster-Grandparents Program. On the other hand, the AARP president, Foster J. Pratt, is in his seventies. A similar pattern has prevailed in the NCSC, where the current president, Nelson Cruikshank, assumed his position at age sixty-six upon retirement as head of the AFL-CIO's Department of Social Security, but where the executive director, William Hutton, was appointed to office ten years ago when he was only forty-six. The NCSC's only full-time field representative, Ken Arvedon, is in his mid-forties. Arvedon and Hutton were obviously chosen on the basis of their vitality and sense of commitment, with age not a determining factor. The pattern has been similar in NCOA.

This is not intended to suggest that aging organizations are predisposed against an individual in the over-sixty-five category for top executive posts, but rather that, in becoming bureaucratized, the groups in question have increasingly insisted on applying performance criteria under which advanced age confers no special advantage. In selecting persons to fill largely honorific posts, where on-the-job performance is a less crucial factor, there is, of course, a continuing preference for over-sixty-five retirees.

Revenue Supplementation

It was one of the chief sources of weakness in the older aging groups that they were almost entirely dependent on member dues as an income source; efforts by leaders to garner revenues elsewhere either came too late or did not occur. In the case of the Townsend movement, for example, the decision to offer for sale a series of goods unrelated to the basic political objectives—for example, Townsend Old Fashioned Horehound Drops, Townsend Club Toilet Soap, Dr. Townsend's Vitamins and Minerals, and so on—came too late to arrest the drastic decline in income that began in the late 1930s.

A markedly different pattern has prevailed in the case of the four groups currently under examination. Although a political objective—the passage of Medicare—was central to the founding of NCSC, the organization has never failed to appreciate the necessity of providing services that would enhance its general revenue picture. The organization offers for a fee to members a wide spectrum of services: travel, drugs, legal aid, and so forth. Moreover, as the semiofficial senior-citizens arm of the American labor movement, the NCSC has relieved the regular labor officials of what might otherwise have been a distraction from their central concern with collective bargaining. In return, the larger industrial unions, particularly the auto workers, machinists, steelworkers, electrical workers, and the AFL-CIO Industrial Union Department, have generously subsidized the NCSC budget. Of a total NCSC budget of $415,000 in 1971, fully 40 percent was contributed by sympathetic unions.[17]

The NRTA-AARP offers an even more striking illustration. Though concerned from the outset with the political matter of state teacher pensions, the organization during its decade of most rapid growth—1958–68—tended to minimize, although without altogether neglecting, the lobbying aspects of its mandate so as to concentrate on elaborating a large range of benefits. This strategy proved markedly successful from a fiscal standpoint, as recent figures make clear. In 1974 the combined assets of NRTA and AARP were $4.4 million and the assets of the NRTA and AARP Administrative Fund—established in 1958 to receive funds which are to be expended for joint administrative expenses—was $6.9 million. There was an additional $1 million of assets in an Appropriated Special Reserve under the Administrative Fund. With regard to current revenues, the two groups had a combined total income in 1974 of $9 million (mostly from membership dues) and the income of the Administrative Fund (mostly derived from the administrative allowance provided for under the group health insurance program) was $8.6 million. It would appear from these figures that member dues account for only about 50 percent of NRTA-AARP assets and revenues—a significant datum.[18]

In the case of NCOA it has been not so much fees for services that have produced substantial nondues income but rather grants, initially derived from private foundations and later from the federal government. In its very first year of operation the organization obtained a grant from the Fred and Alma Schipper Foundation, and, with the exception of one two-year interval, it was not without a grant from this source for the next two decades. But Schipper was a small donor; a far wealthier one was soon to be tapped. In 1956 the Ford Foundation gave NCOA a three-year appropriation of $500,000. Three years later when the agency came back to Ford with a requested renewal, the foundation not only reacted positively but took the step (unprecedented according to one of its vice-presidents) of making a grant 50 percent above that asked for—$750,000 instead of $500,000! An additional Ford grant, this time to cover a five-year period, was made in 1963. The author of a 1969 NCOA staff report evidently was not exaggerating in concluding that "for a period of ten crucial years, the major support of NCOA came from the Ford Foundation."[19] The final payment from the Ford grant came in 1967; after that, while private sources of income remained significant, the organization increasingly looked to the federal government. In 1967 NCOA signed two multiyear federal contracts, one with the Office of Economic Opportunity, another with the Labor Department, totalling $2.5 million—a quite substantial sum considering that the council's 1964 total budget had been only $350,000.[20] In the fall of 1969, in a move evidently related to the shift in its major source of income, NCOA moved its national headquarters from New York, where it always had been, to Washington. A summary of NCOA financial activity for that year showed that, of a total income of $2.1 million, fully $1.9 million was in the category "fees and grants from federal agencies" whereas a mere $27,882 was in the "member dues" category.[21]

In the case of NARFE, selective benefits have consisted in large degree of casework for dues-paying federal retirees and a modest range of economic services, such as a life insurance option.

A More Benign External Environment

A hostile and unreceptive political atmosphere was a basic conditioning factor in the environment of the aging groups of the 1930s and '40s. Francis E. Townsend's plan to pay each person over age sixty a pension of $200 per month, financed out of a national sales tax, was attacked on a wide variety of grounds. While the plan attracted the passionate support of many elderly persons—especially in California, Townsend's home base—it was acceptable to only a small percentage of the electorate: 3.8 percent, according to a 1936

Gallup poll. The plan was vigorously condemned by the Roosevelt administration and met with hostility by the House Ways and Means Committee,
where it died.[22]

Similarly, a pension scheme advocated in California by Robert Noble,
leader of the Ham and Eggs group, proposed that the United States
Congress deal with the Depression by issuing an unspecified amount of
special scrip, the prompt spending of which was to be insured by having the
scrip lose all its value after one year. The plan was roundly denounced by a
host of California interest groups, and after an initial flurry of interest
became a political dead letter. In their efforts to significantly redistribute
public revenue in behalf of relief specifically for the aging, the interest
groups and mass movements of the thirties and forties found public opinion
mostly arrayed against them.

During the past decade, however, the basic issue was not so much the
redistribution of wealth as it was the distribution of a large, predetermined
sum of money available through a variety of government channels. In the
words of Robert Binstock, "adequate amelioration would require direct
transfers of income to the aged poor amounting to at least $6 billion
annually. . . . these are not the kinds of changes actively sought by the aging
organizations."[23] Binstock points out that the efforts of aging groups do not
reflect a vigorous pursuit of goals that could bring about a substantial
"re-equalization" for the disadvantaged aged. Within this scaled-down set
of aspirations, aging groups have labored, with increasing success, to gain
acceptance as "middlemen" between the governmental funding sources
(HEW, OEO, Department of Labor, Administration on Aging) and the
recipients. A particularly lucrative statutory basis for many of these middlemen programs has been the 1965 Older Americans Act, especially Title III,
IV, and V, under which the national government has distributed between
$19 million and $23 million annually since 1969.

Another factor contributing to the more benign setting was the emergence in these years of what Theodore Lowi has termed "interest group
liberalism." Lowi observes that John F. Kennedy, more than any other
previous president, was inclined to encourage and reward group involvement in national policy-making, applying the principle of "participatory
democracy" to the implementation as well as to the formulation of law.[24] The
application of interest-group liberalism principles to the old-age field was the
logical corollary to their acceptance elsewhere at the federal level. Referring to
the 1971 White House Conference on Aging, for example, Binstock remarks
that "the staff officially determined that business, labor, and consumers; the
professions; religious, fraternal, social and service organizations; and community action organizations all deserved representation in formulating national
policy toward the aging in the 1970s."[25] Officials of both the Kennedy-
Johnson and Nixon administrations had come to accept the view that

spokesmen for senior-citizen organizations deserved not only to be heard
when they spoke out but in some cases even to be encouraged to express their
policy preferences.

This change in opinion climate was one which the aging themselves,
through their spokesmen, had a hand in bringing about. In their protracted
struggle with the American Medical Association the advocates of Medicare
succeeded in shifting the general public's view of the AMA. They skillfully
played on the theme that financing health-care benefits through social
security would be the "truly American way" and succeeded in casting AMA
leaders in the hapless role of persons insensitive to older citizens' suffering
and cynical in their use of slogans like "socialized medicine" which were
designed (it was argued) to forestall even modest changes in the status quo.
The AMA's defeat on Medicare, so Max J. Skidmore maintains, was costly to
the organization in more than a financial sense, involving as well a
dislodgement from an accustomed position at the political center and loss of
generalized acceptance as a group interested only in improving national
health-care levels.[26]

An interesting change in the political stance of NCOA also appears
related to the more benign climate of general opinion on aging matters. On
the occasion of the board of directors' 1960 decision to reconstitute NCOA,
a policy was agreed to—essentially a codification of prior practice—which
seemingly barred political activity once and for all. Article 3 of the Articles
of Incorporation stated: "no part of the activity of this corporation shall be
attempted influence of legislation by propaganda or otherwise." This
statement was taken quite seriously among NCOA officials, and for two or
three years it was interpreted as prohibiting stands on any controversial issue
which might be the subject of legislation. But given the changing mood of
the times this prohibition proved unpopular, and in June 1966 the board,
having already broken with tradition by endorsing the Older Americans Act
of 1965, voted to modify its stance. The board now resolved that "as an
educational institution, NCOA may wish to express an opinion on certain
issues and to establish appropriate mechanisms for this purpose." To
implement the revised view, a Public Policy Committee was created.[27] By
the early 1970s this committee had authorized NCOA statements on a
number of rather narrowly circumscribed aging issues.

Given this more friendly atmosphere, aging groups often find themselves
in a position to "shop around" among federal agencies, seeking the best
terms. At the time of the establishment of the Administration on Aging, the
National Council of Senior Citizens first nominated two of its most stalwart
supporters—Charles Odell of the UAW and James O'Brien of the Steelworkers—for the post of commissioner, the agency's top post. Both
nominees were passed over in favor of William D. Bechill, a man with no
strong and active ties with any of the aging organizations. When Bechill

proceeded to allocate funds in ways that did not favor the NCSC, its leaders became highly critical of AOA. At the same time they shifted their pressure to Sargent Shriver, then head of OEO, insisting that he set up a task force on the "special problems of the elderly poor"; Shriver acquiesced. The task force, when established, consisted almost exclusively of the NCSC and its allies, whose own interests were then given the most favored treatment in the subsequent letting of OEO contracts. For roughly the same reasons, the NCSC laid siege to the Department of Labor, with similarly favorable results.[28]

Points of Divergence among Groups

As constituent units in a social movement, the major mass-membership organizations share a fundamental likeness in social outlook. Yet, there is also a range of issues on which they diverge. One difference has to do with how they fall along a partisan-nonpartisan continuum. Easily the most politically activist and partisan group is NCSC, which makes no secret of its close identification with the Democratic party and whose monthly house organ, *Senior Citizens News*, reads at times like a Democratic campaign document. In commenting on preparations for the upcoming 1971 White House Conference on Aging, for example, the publication charged in a news column that "early in the planning for the Conference it became evident that an attempt was being made at the White House to rig the Conference for the political benefit of the Nixon Administration."[29] About the same time NCSC executive director Hutton alluded to "the sad record in dealing with the problems of the elderly in the nearly three years Mr. Nixon has been in office."[30]

AARP and NARFE, on the other hand, have worked to avoid partisan identification. While Binstock is doubtless correct in saying that many Washington politicians look upon the typical member of AARP as "a white collar or professional Republican," the AARP staff contains at least as many persons whose prior employment in government required political clearance from Democrats as it did those who needed clearance from Republicans. Whereas NCSC looked upon the 1971 White House Conference with profound mistrust—fearing a Nixon attempt to co-opt delegates and sneak through unacceptable conference resolutions—AARP took a more detached stance. Executive Director Bernard Nash praised "the favorable climate for change" that the conference created and also Mr. Nixon's address to the delegates, but he coupled this with criticism of the conference's failure to act more progressively on key issues—national health insurance, for example.[31]

NARFE executives similarly work both sides of the political aisle. They seek to ingratiate themselves with Democratic congressmen who control the

powerful civil service committees and at the same time occasionally speak
out in support of policies favored by the Republican White House—for
example, of Mr. Nixon's August 1971 announcement of wage-price con-
trols.

There is also an interesting difference between the two largest mass-membership groups, AARP and NCSC, in terms of their stands on particular
issues. A persistent and basic source of disagreement has been the policy of
denying Social Security benefits to elderly persons who elect to continue
working after age sixty-five. The NCSC, while acknowledging that "a loss of
Social Security benefits for those who earn more than the designated amount
sometimes serves as a barrier to the employment of workers past retirement
age," nevertheless insists that the employment test be preserved in order
"to conserve funds for payment to beneficiaries who are unable to
supplement low retirement incomes with earnings." The number of workers
who desire to continue working past retirement age is comparatively small,
the group maintains, and elimination of the test "would place unfair tax
burdens on younger workers."[32] In marked contrast, the AARP voiced
support for the position taken on the employment test issued by President
Nixon's commissioner on aging, John Martin, and remarked editorially:
"The Social Security Earnings Limitation test is wrong for several reasons: it
penalizes those who need to work to supplement their income, it kills
initiative, it has some grossly inequitable features and it denies some older
Americans the meaningful life that comes through work."[33]

Underlying this policy disagreement are significant differences in the
constituencies of the two bodies: NCSC, with a basically working-class
constituency, finds that its members are concentrated in occupations where
gainful employment after age sixty-five seldom presents itself as a live
option; AARP, having mostly middle-class constituents, many of them
professional people who do have the choice of continuing to work beyond
the usual retirement age, is more inclined to see the issue from their
perspective. When, at the 1971 NCSC convention, an apparently middle-
class clergyman voiced objection to that organization's line on the Social
Security income test, he was sharply rebuked by other delegates, several of
whom identified themselves as union men.

Policy differences between the two largest senior organizations also were
apparent in 1974 in the course of the struggle over national health
insurance. Both groups, admittedly, came out in opposition to the Nixon
administration's proposed Comprehensive Health Care Act of 1974
(CHCA), but they did so for sharply divergent reasons. AARP/NRTA
spokesman Cyril Brickfield maintained that the administration bill was
faulty in terms of scope (for example, failing to provide for voluntary
participation among persons not covered under Social Security). He also had
several other objections and mentioned that AARP had drafted a substitute

bill that Senator Abraham Ribicoff soon would be introducing. But the most striking thing about Brickfield's testimony was that he went on to affirm that the administration bill, despite its faults, contained some sound provisions and that AARP was not unalterably opposed to its general outlines. ''Our organization's bill and the [administration's] address themselves to the same elements,'' he remarked. ''We ask serious consideration of our provisions as a substitute for [one aspect of it]. Such revised provisions could easily be incorporated into whatever national health care plan is ultimately adopted by Congress.''[34]

The view of NCSC, on the other hand, as expressed by its president, Nelson Cruikshank, was that the administration bill was fundamentally and grossly faulty. Cruikshank's remarks amounted to a lengthy indictment of the proposal—''a monstrosity of multiple systems,'' he called it, one which ''fails to protect the working population'' even as it ''violates social insurance principles,'' caves in to the private insurance industry, and ''undermines Medicare.''[35] It was the NCSC view that progress only could be made by casting aside CHCA and, instead, using as a point of departure the labor-endorsed Kennedy-Griffiths National Health Security bill (S.3 and H.R. 22).

The diversity of opinion between AARP and NCSC on national health insurance paralleled to some extent the splits within Congress on the issue, not only between Democrats and Republicans but also among liberal Democrats, Kennedy and Ribicoff and others, who have wavered on the issue and often taken conflicting stands.[36] There does exist a degree of consensus among senior-citizen groups on policy issues, but it exists more at a general level (giving the elderly greater ''national priority,'' ''better health protection,'' and so forth) than at the level of application to concrete cases. Here consensus tends to break down.

Conclusion

In line with what Professors Dawson and Gettys long ago suggested is typical of social movements as they mature, activists identified with the modern senior movement came in the 1960s to the stage of formal organization. At this time viable mass-membership bodies—united on some issues, divided on others—were either formed or else, having been formed at an earlier point, now reoriented themselves so as to give voice to a wider social impulse. The foundation for this emergent strength came in part from an increasingly benign climate of national opinion regarding aging needs and from the groups' increased lobbying and internal managerial skills. By supplementing their modest member-derived resources with subsidies from outside sources and by focusing their energies through efficient bureaucracies, they were already having an impact on the national political scene.

I should like to reiterate, in order to avoid possible misunderstanding, that the four groups treated in this chapter are not the only aging interest-groups which are politically active in Washington. The other six groups mentioned at the outset, though small in membership and more limited in scope, also appear to be influential on certain issues.

In a larger sense the findings in this and the immediately preceding chapters offer a striking example of "issue expansion." The contemporary old-age organizations have proved adept in the art of propaganda and symbol manipulation, as illustrated in their rhetorical triumph over the AMA in the Medicare struggle. They have successfully expanded their audience, moving beyond what Cobb-Elder define as "identification groups," namely, the elderly as such and a small number of others with an immediate, perceived stake in the senior-citizen cause, and have framed slogans and issues with an obvious appeal to "attention groups" and to "mass publics" that in varying degrees became aware of the struggle and, by becoming involved, helped tip the balance.[37] Senior-citizen organizations have gained legitimacy for themselves as major spokesmen for the elderly and have provided policy-makers with needed technical information. In so doing they have been significantly involved in gaining a high-priority place for aging issues on the national agenda.

It is interesting, moreover, that one of the groups treated above, NARFE, has not in recent years experienced any substantial enlargement in social goals nor, as will become apparent later, has it been a prominent participant in recent public-policy struggles on broadly defined issues. NARFE's rather anomalous position seems related to the fact that it, alone among the mass-membership groups, did not originate in a prior social movement and remains largely aloof from the one presently in existence. NARFE is essentially an "interest" group, concerned with the narrowly defined needs of its dues-paying, retired-civil-servant constituency. Its leaders do not conceive of themselves as part of a social reform vanguard, and their policy views reflect this fact.

3

The Movement in Action

8 Senior Citizens and the Older Americans Act

The year 1965 was a major turning point for federal policy toward the aging. The enactment of Medicare, climaxing a long struggle between two enormously influential political giants, the American Medical Association and the AFL-CIO, plus their allies in and out of Congress, was by far the best-known action affecting the elderly in that session of Congress. As befits a controversy of such intensity and fiscal magnitude (the initial price tag was $6 billion), Medicare has been the subject of several booklength studies as well as of shorter treatments in works dealing generally with the Kennedy-Johnson years. But in the same year Congress passed another statute affecting the elderly, the Older Americans Act, and this has received far less attention. Though the measure's initial dimensions were quite modest both as to range of programs and spending levels (the initial authorization was for $5 million—more than a thousand times smaller than Medicare's), the act did provide a framework which has facilitated a substantial program enlargement in the years subsequent. Furthermore, the Administration on Aging (AOA) created by the statute has become a highly visible and significant agency in the executive branch.

Scholarly treatments of the Older Americans Act have been sparse. Robert Binstock, in collaboration with others at Brandeis University, has offered penetrating treatments of the statute as it pertains to state-level leadership planning, while Robert B. Hudson of the same university has considered the act in light of the larger issue of federal-state relations and has given attention to the area agencies on aging as mandated by the 1973 amendments.[1] There also have been brief but pertinent comments on the act by other analysts.[2] Yet, up to now no one has provided a general treatment of the legislative process leading up to the act or of the years immediately following, when the task was one of administrative implementation. Such a treatment will be important for the present work both because of the act's obvious substantive importance and also because the environment in which it matured differed considerably from that affecting Social Security legislation and other programs relating to the elderly.

While focusing its attention largely on trends in the Older Americans statute and in related AOA administrative behavior, the present chapter will also consider how statutory developments have affected the national old-age organizations, especially AARP, NCSC, NCOA, and the National Association of State Units on Aging (NASUA).

The Gestation Period of the Older Americans Act, 1958–64

At the time the bills which were later to find expression in the Older Americans Act were first given serious congressional attention, the attitude of the White House was decidedly unfriendly. During the years of his presidency, from 1953 to 1961, Dwight Eisenhower was committed as a matter of principle to fostering state initiatives in the social policy field, and as a consequence his administration endeavored wherever feasible to "devolve" federal programs on the states. While inclined to look favorably on programs to aid the elderly, the White House was not responsive to appeals for a new federal agency in this field or to the establishment of new grants to states financed out of general revenues. For different reasons, there was an equal lack of enthusiasm on the part of the then-existing interest groups concerned with senior-citizen matters. The groups were either insufficiently "political" in their general approach to national policymaking (the case with AARP/NRTA and NCOA) or else were involved in a quite different field of federal policy (the case with the National Association of Retired Civil Employees). Given these circumstances, congressional activists found their range of legislative options rather limited and were obliged to focus attention more on the need to build grass-roots support for their ideas than on the technical details of proposed statutes.

In the second session of the Eighty-fifth Congress, beginning in January 1958, several bills concerned with aging matters were introduced in the House. (Similar bills had been offered before, but now, with the gradually increasing interest in the elderly occasioned by the Forand Medicare bill, introduced in the previous session, chances seemed improved for actually scheduling committee hearings and getting favorable floor action.) An idea embodied in several of the bills was that of creating a "Bureau of Older Persons" in the Department of Health, Education, and Welfare. Essentially this would amount to giving a firm statutory base and enlarged staff to the Special Staff on Aging established in the HEW secretary's office two years earlier by executive order.

A rather unique idea was embodied in a bill introduced by Congressman John E. Fogarty, a Democrat from Rhode Island. In its initial form, Fogarty's bill (H.R. 9822) called for the convening of a White House Conference on Aging not later than December 21, 1958. (He was shortly to modify the conference year to 1961 so as to allow time for preliminary state conferences on aging.) Though not himself a member of the Committee on Education and Labor, the body having House jurisdiction in such matters, Fogarty had long since established himself as a man to be reckoned with on legislation broadly defined as social welfare. As the long-standing chairman of the Subcommittee on Labor, Health, and Education of the House Appropriations Committee, he had used his position as a leader of the majority party in Congress to prod the Republican administration into acting more decisively in a number of areas. In 1955 he had procured a $750,000 appropriation for mental retardation at a time when there was almost no federal activity in this field.(Within a decade, during which time the Democrats regained control of the White House, this authorization had been enlarged to more than $4 billion.) For years during the Eisenhower period Fogarty was able to carry the House with him in winning health-research appropriations exceeding administration requests by as much as 40 percent—a feat of legislative leadership that won him the label of "Mr. Public Health." Soft-spoken and considerate of his colleagues, Fogarty was immensely popular in the House, and his fellow members of both parties weighed carefully his views on matters within his field of competence. Fogarty's particular concern with national activity in the aging field went back as far as the Truman administration, when he had criticized Oscar Ewing, the Federal Security administrator, for "not doing anything in this field" and for allegedly assigning only one man, Clark Tibbitts, to handle problems in this area. For years Fogarty had been convinced that the executive branch was "way behind the people," whereas to his mind Congress was in step with popular sentiment.[3]

It was thus Fogarty's immense prestige in the House as much or more than the inherent logic of his arguments which accounts for the attention given his views when his bill and the related ones came up for hearings before Congressman Roy W. Wier's safety and compensation subcommittee in March 1958. The fact that hearings were even scheduled was itself partially attributable to Fogarty's stature.

Fogarty was the lead-off witness. After a polite bow to the "distinguished chairman, Mr. Wier," who also had introduced "a very excellent bill," he launched into a justification for his view that the establishment of a Bureau of Older Persons should give way for the moment to the more urgent need to hold a White House Conference on Aging. The congressman from Rhode Island, who regarded the elderly as a population category whose needs could be addressed in roughly the same way as was already the case with younger age-groups, remarked that:

> One of the motivating factors behind my thinking in calling this a White House Conference is that, in the years that I have been serving on the Appropriations Committee we have had a White House Conference or we have been providing funds for a White House Conference on Children and Youth. The last one was in 1950 and the next one is in 1960 . . . .

Then as you well know, you on the Committee on Education and Labor, when it was authorized by your Committee and by Congress to hold a White House Conference on Education, which was held a couple of years ago, we had reason then to go into the benefits of the White House Conference on Education. . . .[4]

Further elaborating on his bill, the Congressman stressed that he was much concerned about the rapidly increasing population of older persons, already 15 million in 1958 and likely to almost double by the 1970s.

There followed questioning of Fogarty by members of the committee. Representative Herbert Zalenko, a Democrat from New York, posed the question that lay at the heart of the choice involved:

> *Mr. Zalenko:* May I ask the gentleman just one question. You agree that all of the other legislation has great merit. But, as I understand it, you feel that, by H. R. 9822, *we should first have these conferences* [on aging] *at all levels* [state, local and national] *in order to first get the awareness or conditioning on the part of everyone for the problem and, secondarily, to get the benefit of the collective thought of the most people before going into specific legislation;* is that correct?

> *Mr. Fogarty:* Yes, sir. . . . I have been told by some of the experts working in the field that this is a good solid basic approach to the overall program in a way that will come up with a good solid recommendation.

> *Mr. Zalenko:* Is it your feeling that by proceeding this way *we would, in the initial stages, overcome, let us say, any uninformed or other opposition to this vital legislation* by proceeding in your way [i.e. the White House Conference approach] rather than going into specific legislation which might be blocked and thereby set us back in the program?[5] [Emphasis added.]

Fogarty did not directly answer this second question, but the tenor of his remarks was that he had been correctly interpreted.

The importance of prior conferences at the state and local levels was a point to which Fogarty returned more than once in his remarks. Commenting on the testimony of an administration witness, he affirmed that "you can call a national conference on anything. The President or Secretary can if he wants to. But I do not think that these conferences are going to be effective unless we have some real work done at the State levels and come right up through the line that way."[6] At such state-level conferences delegates to the national meeting could familiarize themselves with the issues, and the fact of the conferences being held in each state would stimulate grass-roots interest in the national conference to follow. Quite probably, Fogarty was reflecting on Oscar Ewing's 1950 conference on aging problems, which had had no such preparatory meetings and whose subsequent results had been meagre.

Conceivably, the House subcommittee could have endorsed both Fogarty's White House Conference idea and the Bureau of Older Persons
concept, there being no logical inconsistency between them; but after the
hearings concluded it chose to endorse Fogarty's idea and to shelve others for
the moment. Legislative strategy, more than the merits of the case, lay
behind the decision; the Eisenhower administration strongly opposed the
Bureau of Older Persons proposal, and this posed the threat of a veto if
Congress pursued this course of action. Speaking for the administration,
Louis H. Ravin, secretary of the Federal Council on the Aging (an
interdepartmental coordinating committee created by executive order in
1955), had voiced several objections at the hearings to creating a new agency
to deal with aging problems:

> You cover in aging all aspects of life—employment, health, retirement,
> recreation, income maintenance, everything that you can think of for the
> young or an old person. Those things are being carried on fairly effectively
> already within the Federal Government. If you are going to set up a
> bureau the first question you have in mind aside from organization, is
> who are the people, what are the competencies you will need? You will
> need people who are conversant with the processes of aging, with health
> of the aging, with employment service functions, with housing. Those
> specialists are now available in the agencies with government and can be
> drawn upon by a coordinating group like the Federal Council. If you set
> up a bureau you would have to recruit these people. Are they going to be
> able to attract physicians away from public health who are any more
> competent than the ones we have in public health now?[7]

Ravin had gone on to reject the idea put forward by members of the
subcommittee, that a bureau of older persons was needed to coordinate
federal policies toward the aging, insisting instead that coordinating
machinery already in existence was fully adequate.

On the other hand, the administration's initial reaction to the proposal to
hold a White House Conference on Aging had been one of apparent
indecision. Louis Ravin, without denying that such a conference might be
helpful and constructive, remarked that legislation on the matter was not
necessary and "perhaps would not be appropriate in this area at this time.
Conceivably in the future it might be helpful."[8] Nowhere in his testimony
had Ravin voiced opposition to the basic concept, and a later administration
witness had affirmed that the White House was itself giving consideration to
calling such a conference, though not on the basis of an act of Congress.[9]
When the full Education and Labor Committee endorsed Fogarty's bill, the
administration did not oppose its passage by Congress.

One can see in retrospect that the decision to lay aside temporarily the
suggestion for an older-persons bureau and to shift the focus of attention to
the White House Conference was tactically shrewd. As the congressman
from Rhode Island correctly anticipated, the conference was instrumental in

enlarging substantially the base of popular support for federal initiatives in the aging field. Coming as it did in January 1961, after John F. Kennedy's November election victory but before Dwight Eisenhower left office, the conference's call for the federal government to both consider "the establishment and increase of grants-in-aid to States to promote and expand services to the aged" and to create a coordinating agency to deal with problems of the elderly helped to build pressure on Mr. Kennedy for substantial aging initiatives.[10] It has been generally appreciated that the 1961 White House Conference made a major contribution to the enactment of Medicare four years later and that it also served to crystallize sentiment for the establishment of a major nongovernmental group, the National Council of Senior Citizens.[11] Less well known is the fact that the conference had a good deal to do with stimulating President Kennedy's February 1963 appeal for a program of categorial grants in the aging field—an important precursor to the Older Americans Act—and with the decision to found the National Association of State Units on Aging (NASUA), an influential lobby composed of the executive directors of the various state units.[12] (NASUA's members consisted of the heads of state agencies, many of which were initially created just prior to the White House Conference and with the help of federal funds allotted to the states for the purpose of organizing pre-White House Conference assemblies.) In roughly the same way that the vote endorsing Medicare through Social Security (a vote by the conference's Section on Income Maintenance) had amounted to a setback for the Eisenhower administration on the health-care front, so too the appeal for new federal categorical grants in the aging field (an appeal by the Section on State Organization) constituted a rebuff to the same administration, which also had objected to most new federal grant proposals.

In both cases the loss of control by the White House related to an inability to constrain its nominal HEW subordinates. As Richard Harris has revealed, the cooperation between Arthur Flemming, the HEW secretary in the later Eisenhower years, and his longtime friend Nelson Cruikshank had a major bearing on both the appointment of a liberal Republican as conference chairman (Representative R.W. Kean of New Jersey), and on the unexpected sending of the Medicare proposal to the liberally inclined Section on Income Maintenance where AMA delegates, hostile to Medicare, were not in control.[13] Similarly, the support, albeit cautious, given by the conference to the idea of categorical federal grants in the aging field was related to the fact that the head of the HEW Special Staff on Aging, William C. Fitch, and Congressman John Fogarty had developed an unusually close working relationship. Though the tie involved obvious risks for Fitch, a political appointee of the Eisenhower administration, he managed to become one of Fogarty's closest associates, an "alter ego," as Fitch was later to characterize himself.[14]

In the months subsequent advocates for the elderly in both houses of Congress stepped up pressure for creation of a new agency. The Senate Special Committee on Aging was constituted in 1961, and its chairman, Patrick V. McNamara of Michigan, introduced a bill in that year calling for a United States Office on Aging within HEW, headed by an Assistant Secretary for Aging. In the House, Congressman Fogarty and other influential members continued their quest for an agency constituted similarly. Capitol Hill hearings on these various proposals were scheduled in 1962 and 1963, and the sentiment among those appearing to testify was strongly supportive.

President John F. Kennedy, in a major departure from the views of his predecessor, recommended in "Elderly Citizens of our Nation," a February 1963 message to Congress, that there be established "a five-year program of assistance to State and local agencies and voluntary organizations for planning and developing services; for research, demonstration, and training projects leading to new or improved programs to aid older people." As to the idea of creating a bureau of older persons with clear legislative mandate, however, the president's proposal was conspiciously silent. Bills embodying the president's recommendation were introduced in that congressional session. A second approach, vigorously endorsed by Congressman Fogarty and embodied in H.R. 7957, largely paralleled the adiminstration's plan, but went beyond the president's thinking by proposing an Administration on Aging to be located in the office of the HEW secretary. Hearings on both ideas were held in September of that year before the Select Subcommittee on Education of the House Education and Labor Committee. Since the White House and Congress were now both securely in Democratic hands, one might have expected these hearings to proceed smoothly toward a compromise agreement. Instead, the administration found itself decidedly on the defensive, with Fogarty and his allies in a mood of outrage. For the first time, moreover, the national old-age organizations entered significantly into the picture. Since the arguments presented on both sides of the issue were to be repeated in more recent years with only minor variations, it is worthwhile to consider this confrontation at some length.

What lay beneath the dispute was an order the previous January by the HEW secretary, Anthony Celebrezze, downgrading the Special Staff on Aging from its accustomed place in the secretary's office and redesignating it as the Office on Aging under the jurisdiction of a newly-created commissioner on welfare. The action was doubly offensive to old-age activists, both as threatening to remove aging from the center of focus in HEW and as linking aging with the unfortunate connotations of the term "welfare." In his testimony before the education subcommittee, Congressman Fogarty stormed that "this is contrary to everything that has been researched and recommended to change the image of aging from a sickly, indigent

individual to a dignified, responsible person. The welfare setting has wiped
out most of the social progress that was made over the last fifteen years in the
field of the aging."[15] In a similar vein William C. Fitch, having recently
become the executive director of AARP, remarked that "at a time like this
when we are trying to have 18 million old persons stand up and accept
responsibility, when you tell them you actually are standing in line for
public assistance or welfare, I think we have reversed our goal."[16] He
observed that editorials in AARP publications had taken exception to the
relocation of the aging staff and noted that no articles in recent months had
elicited such articulate response from readers. The coordinator of the UAW
Older and Retired Workers Program, Charles E. Odell, spoke out in a
similar vein: "[This decision] was taken without consultation. . . . I know of
no expert in the field, no state administrator or state commission person, in
fact I know of no person on the immediate staff of the Office on Aging who
were [sic] consulted in the decision to make this shift. . . . I submit, in large
measure, it was a decision taken expediently in order to round out a
sufficient cluster of responsibilities under the Welfare Administration to
justify the grade and title and scope of the position."[17] The views of the
acting president of the National Council of Senior Citizens and of the
chairman of the retired workers committee of the United Steelworkers were
equally emphatic.

The solid front presented by the old-age clientele groups made an
impression on the subcommittee members, one of whom, Congressman
Carey, summed up his views at the hearings' conclusion: "This is how
strongly [the various aging groups] feel and when people feel that strongly, I
am going to be guided by what [one witness] referred to as the growing
political muscle among aging Americans. I do not want that muscle to come
down on me in the next election and say, 'You put me where I did not want
to go.' "[18]

Aware that his January reorganization decision was a controversial one,
Secretary Celebrezze appeared before the subcommittee to present the
administration's case against the Fogarty bill, which he charged amounted
to a threat to his own ability to manage the department effectively and to
efforts to give the aging issue its deserved emphasis. He maintained that, far
from minimizing the importance of the aging issue, his action actually
constituted a way of dealing with it more effectively; the aging staff, in his
words, now would be located under a welfare administrator "who is known
both nationally and internationally as an outstanding leader and program
expert in the fields of social welfare and aging. I think this committee must
appreciate," he continued, "that I have 138 separate programs going and
everyone wants to be in the Office of the Secretary. Likewise every agency
which has any program at all wants a commissioner, a commissioner on
water pollution, and so on. Every agency wants status. I think our

reorganization program did much to lift the Office of Aging from the stagnation it was in when I became Secretary.'' He argued the need for "administrative flexibility" in handling the internal affairs of his department (threatened by the Fogarty bill), and strongly urged the deletion of that portion of the bill fixing the position of the proposed office within the HEW hierarchy.[19]

Nevertheless, faced with overwhelming sentiment among those in its own ranks best informed on the matter, and with a parallel sense of outrage among clientele groups, the subcommittee decided to disregard the secretary's preferences and to adopt a proposal to create a new unit within HEW, the Administration on Aging, and it was this that two years later would be enacted into law. Yet this was not a complete victory for the congressional viewpoint on the issue, considering that Congressman Fogarty, the House sponsor of the bill, had really preferred and advocated the creation of an independent commission on aging which would report directly to the president. The congressman spoke candidly on this point during the course of his subcommittee testimony:

Mr. Martin [Republican, Nebraska]: What is the advantage of setting up a separate department in HEW over another agency?

Mr. Fogarty: There is not any. I am just giving in. The Department opposed the independent agency last year and due to their opposition, nothing has been done for a year now, so I am just giving in on that for the time being. I just think an independent commission is the best thing but to get some action I am willing to cooperate with the Department and hope they will support this kind of legislation. I thought the independent commission concept was a good idea then, I still think it is a good idea, but we have to get some action, and to do something in this area this is our solution.[20]

Though Secretary Celebrezze's unpopular decision nine months previous was the immediate focus of attention, it became evident in the course of the hearings that the effort to upgrade the aging matter bureaucratically and give it greater status arose as well out of more long-standing concerns among advocates for the aging. William C. Fitch of AARP remarked, for example, that "the impression yesterday might well have been there had always been 48 members on the staff on aging. Congressman Fogarty knows only too well for many years there had been three. At the time I was there in 1956 and 1957 [as Director of the Special Staff on Aging] we struggled along with 10 and 12 hoping we might get more. So ... there has been some activity but it has not been as practical or as far-reaching as many of us working in the field would like it to be."[21] Though the committee members evidently did what they felt was the minimum necessary, legislatively, to upgrade HEW's old-age agency, there remained doubt that very much would change so long as the secretary continued to regard aging as a relatively low-priority matter; in the course of the hearings several of them remarked that a mere reshuffling of the bureaucratic cards would not guarantee the desired "action program for the aged" in the absence of a genuine commitment from those in higher executive offices. Yet it was a step.

When the House Education and Labor Committee's Older Americans Act bill (H.R. 3704) came up for House floor discussion early in 1965, Congressman Fogarty was asked to present it and to lead off debate. Given that congressional committees typically guard their prerogatives jealously, the fact that the congressman from Rhode Island was singled out for this role, even though not himself a member of the committee, was regarded by observers as a remarkable testimony to his House influence in this particular field. The final House vote was near-unanimous, 394-1, with Congressman David Martin of Nebraska casting the sole dissenting vote.

The pattern was much the same on the floor of the Senate, where the companion legislation had come up after hearings skilfully led by Senator Patrick McNamara of Michigan. McNamara's interest in this legislation was equally as long-standing as Congressman Fogarty's. As far back as January 1959 his Subcommittee on Aging of the Senate committee on Labor and Public Welfare, in a report titled "Problems of the Aged and Aging," had called for the salient points covered in the 1965 act and his Special Committee on Aging (created in 1961) had been a major force in helping to generate national interest in the proposed legislation.[22] In the Senate the measure passed unanimously, and it was signed into law by the president on July 14, 1965.

To see how the Older Americans Act has affected the pattern of power and influence on old-age matters, one needs to recall, again, that these same years were witnessing a much more highly publicized struggle over the Medicare issue. In the House, Medicare, defined as a tax measure, fell under the jurisdiction of the tax-writing Ways and Means Committee, and in the Senate it was under the aegis of the Committee on Finance. According to informants, there was a sense of frustration among certain members of the Education and Labor Committee and among members of the Senate Committee on Labor and Public Welfare that the glow of publicity over Medicare was leaving them essentially in the shadow, and that in part their enthusiasm for the Older Americans Act represented an effort to gain some of this popular attention.

The struggles for Medicare and the Older Americans Act made important indirect contributions to legitimizing senior-citizen group involvement in the legislative process. Yet it would appear that of the two bills, the latter was more significant in this regard. In the first place, only the Older Americans Act provided for the establishment of a new agency, the executives of which, as is typical of all newly created bureaus in government, would presumably seek an accommodation with the political environment, in which old-age organizations were becoming more and more important. Medicare, on the other hand, was to be administered by the long-existing Social Security Administration, whose environmental accommodations had been worked out before national old-age groups became significant. Second, the fact that Medicare was financed out of a permanent tax on workers and employers, one not requiring renewal at periodic intervals, would reduce the frequency of congressional hearings on it and thus the visibility of interest-group testimony and comment; the Older Americans Act, on the other hand, would come up annually for renewal of its appropriations and, additionally, once every two or three years before the appropriate substantive committees for a renewal of its spending authorizations. Such hearings would provide repeated opportunity for interest-group responses.

Third, there was a difference in the relative importance of senior-citizen organizations in the enactment of the two measures. In the Medicare case such groups by and large took a back seat, notwithstanding the fact that the National Council of Senior Citizens was vocal on the matter and appears to have been modestly influential in the final outcome. The largest aging organization, AARP, was not actively involved, even though it did offer committee testimony at one point; similarly, the National Council on the Aging (NCOA) was reluctant to become embroiled in the controversy. In the case of the struggle over the Older Americans Act, on the other hand, the AMA, AFL-CIO, and other political giants on Capitol Hill took no direct role, whereas the aging organizations were actively interested. As recently as 1958, when the Weir subcommittee had held its hearings, no organization composed of or primarily concerned with the aging had appeared to testify. Yet by 1963, partly as a result of the stimulus provided by the White House Conference, partly because of Secretary Celebrezze's action, the old-age groups were present in force, and they would remain active in the matter until the act was signed into law two years later.

Infancy of the Older Americans Act, 1965–70

The major focus of leadership in the passage of the Older Americans Act was decidedly in Congress. The administrations in the White House—first Eisenhower's, then Kennedy's, then Johnson's—responded to initiatives emanating directly or indirectly from congressional leaders without ever managing to gain a sense of leadership on the issue. Firmness and a sense of resolve on the part of legislative aging activists stood in contrast to executive branch indecisiveness and, occasionally, outright confusion.

Once President Johnson's signature on the act was dry, however, marking as it did the act's progression from a stage of gestation into infancy, there occurred an important shift in the focus of initiative. In the period from 1965 to 1970 a marked administrative and managerial perspective came to prevail, displacing the previous legislative dominance. Decision-makers in the Department of Health, Education, and Welfare and their allies in the state units on aging, united in the newly organized National Association of State Units on Aging, were now at the focus of action.

While the change in emphasis can be attributed in part to the normal shift of attention toward administrative matters that follows the enactment of new programs, there was a good deal more to it in this case. So marked did the managerial emphasis become that, by the close of the decade, persons who were interested in aging matters but who were not situated in the executive branch were expressing concern. In 1969 the chairman of the Select Subcommittee on Education of the House Education and Labor Committee, Congressman John Brademas of Indiana, was demanding to know whether, as he suspected to be the case, congressional intent with respect to the Administration on Aging had been reversed administratively. In 1971 an investigative committee was appointed by the Senate Special Committee on Aging. The committee's report, "The Administration on Aging: or a Successor?" seriously questioned the effectiveness of the existing agency and recommended a new aging unit at a higher administrative level in the executive branch—the inference being that the Administration on Aging had somehow lost sight of congressional expectations. Throughout the five-year period mentioned, the major aging organizations, especially NCSC, NCOA, and AARP, chafed under their lack of apparent influence over old-age agencies in the government, their leaders in many cases being convinced that group views were neither being solicited nor heeded. The important 1969 amendments to the Older Americans Act, though necessarily passed by Congress, were essentially the product of deliberations among White House and HEW executives—an "inhouse product," in the words of the then-commissioner on aging, William D. Bechill.[23]

If one is to properly interpret the early years under the Older Americans Act, then, a convenient point of departure is to ask why this managerial perspective came to predominate and what were its long-term implications.

The most apparent explanation for the decline in congressional influence under the act was personnel turnover and a consequent absence of legislative leadership. In April 1966, less than a year after the measure went into effect, death deprived the Senate of its foremost spokesman in the aging field, the chairman of its Special Committee on Aging, Patrick V. McNamara of Michigan. Though McNamara was replaced in office by his energetic colleague Harrison Williams of New Jersey, the loss was not easily remedied. Similarly, the death in January 1967 of Congressman John E. Fogarty eliminated McNamara's counterpart in the House. There were also problems stemming from leadership turnover in the key House subcommittee responsible for the Older Americans Act, the Select Subcommittee on Education. For several years prior to the act's passage this subcommittee had been chaired by Congressman John Dent (Democrat, Pennsylvania), but this relative stability did not last. The subcommittee was briefly (1966) chaired by Roman Pucinski (Democrat, Illinois), who in turn yielded it to Dominick Daniels (Democrat, New Jersey), who held it for two years (1967–69). Only after 1969, when the chairmanship went to John Brademas (Democrat, Indiana), did the subcommittee leadership stabilize and a high degree of congressional expertise begin to emerge.

It is not without significance, furthermore, that the same five-year period was one of rapidly rising executive-branch influence on the part of Wilbur J. Cohen, one of the most seasoned and articulate experts on aging matters. Having served since the beginning of the Kennedy administration as assistant secretary of HEW, Cohen was promoted in May 1965, to the post of undersecretary in the department, and early in 1968 to the secretaryship itself. Cohen was widely respected both in the bureaucracy and in Congress, and congressmen frequently deferred to his judgment on old-age matters.

Another factor in the relative freedom from political constraints affecting administration under the act was the inability of old-age groups to mobilize in behalf of their public policy demands. As was the case with Congress, part of the explanation was personnel turnover. John Edelman, who had succeeded to the presidency of NCSC upon the resignation of Congressman Aimé Forand, died in the late 1960s. AARP's founder and longtime president, Ethel Percy Andrus, died in 1967 at the age of eighty-three. At various times three men held the post of executive director of AARP: William Fitch up to the death of Dr. Andrus, Cyril Brickfield from 1967 to 1969, and Bernard Nash from 1969 on. There were unsettling changes, too, at the top level of the National Council on the Aging. The Association relocated its headquarters twice during the period, in 1966 from one site to another in New York City and again in 1969 from New York to Washington. And in 1969 Mrs. Geneva Mathiasen, active in the organization since its founding in 1950, retired as executive director, yielding the post to William C. Fitch, who was himself to leave the organization only a year or so later.

The Bechill Era

The lack of group political effectiveness in the 1965–1970 period may also be attributed to antagonisms arising out of an effort to influence the selection of the first commissioner on aging, an administratively and symbolically important post. In mid-1965 a coalition was formed consisting of the executives of the National Council of Senior Citizens, the National Association of Retired Civil Employees, the National Farmers Union, and the National Council on the Aging, to urge upon President Johnson and other concerned officials the credentials of Charles Odell, a prominent and seasoned individual in the aging field with good connections in the labor movement and in the Democrat party. Senator Patrick McNamara also threw his considerable influence behind the Odell nomination effort; AARP/ NRTA remained neutral. Odell was then director of the United Auto Workers' Older and Retired Workers Department, the country's largest labor union retiree group, and previously had been special assistant to the undersecretary of labor for older worker programs. As one of the participants in the coalition later remarked to an interviewer, the effort in behalf of Odell signified a commitment to the philosophy that the Administration on Aging ought to opt for an expansive role, so that it would become not merely the mechanism for implementing the categorical grants to states mandated under the act but a point for rallying the entire federal establishment as well as nongovernmental groups in behalf of a coordinated attack on aging problems. As the informant put it, what the coalition sought was a "bold, dynamic, forceful program for the elderly" that would give positive meaning to the sweeping ten-point declaration of objectives spelled out in the preamble to the act.

In furtherance of their goal the coalition participants pursued the Odell candidacy vigorously in meetings with officials and lawmakers. Nevertheless, President Johnson, disregarding their entreaties, on October 1 nominated William D. Bechill for the post. This action obliged the coalition to prevail upon Senator McNamara to hold up confirmation in the Senate in hopes of forcing the president to withdraw Bechill's name. The deadlock continued for a time, and it was not until October 22 that McNamara backed down and the Senate voted confirmation; Bechill was sworn into office on November 2, 1965.[24]

Quite evidently, then, other factors than pressure from lobbying organizations were controlling in this decision; it would appear that administrative and managerial considerations, related to the terms on which Congress had approved the Older Americans Act, were the real key to it. The two officials under whose jurisdiction the Administration on Aging fell initially were the secretary of HEW, John Gardner, and his subordinate, the undersecretary of HEW, Wilbur Cohen. (In July 1965, when the act was signed into law, both men were newly appointed to office, Gardner having moved from the presidency of the Carnegie Corporation and Cohen having been promoted from his former post as an HEW assistant secretary.) The decision to recommend Bechill's name to the president was one in which both men were directly involved, Gardner handling the direct negotiations with Bechill, and Cohen closely advising Gardner on the matter.

Cohen had become acquainted with Bechill when the two of them were on the faculty of the University of Michigan School of Social Work in the years 1955 to 1960. Later, when Bechill left Ann Arbor to take up the post of chief of medical care of the California Department of Social Welfare, and, in 1964, to become executive secretary of the California Advisory Committee on Aging, Cohen remained aware of his activities, especially in the 1964–65 period when Bechill's job entailed his taking frequent trips to Washington. The fact that Bechill's administrative experience was at the state level was also to his decided advantage, since in debate on the floor of Congress the bill's supporters had referred to it as a "states' rights" measure, with the categorical grants under the act intended to stimulate state activity.

The fact that Cohen elected to push vigorously in support of Bechill, a virtual unknown among activists in the senior-citizen movement, was evidently related to Cohen's own uneasiness over the decision to create the agency in the first place. As early as May 1962, when he had testified for the Kennedy administration before the General Subcommittee on Education of the House Education and Labor Committee, Cohen had voiced reservations about the need for such an agency, being convinced that the Special Staff on Aging in the HEW secretary's office and the President's Council on Aging were together adequate to coordinate federal efforts in the field. A year later, at the time that Secretary Celebrezze had appeared before the same subcommittee to object strenuously to the creation by act of Congress of the Administration on Aging, his deputy, Wilbur Cohen, was at his side. It was not that Cohen was indifferent or insensitive to the need for federal initiatives in behalf of older persons; indeed, since his service on the Committee on Economic Security under Edwin Witte thirty years previous, he had been a leading advocate of such initiatives. Rather, his concern focused around the need to maintain effective discipline in his agency. Bechill, a man with strong roots in state government and with no significant ties to any of the aging groups active on the issue, would help to reduce to a minimum the danger or an AOA "capture" by outside forces, while guaranteeing the new agency's effective subordination to Secretary Gardner and to Cohen himself.[25]

Once installed in office, Bechill was able to move with a fair measure of effectiveness to implement the intent of Congress as he understood it. By the time he left office in January 1969, there were permanent agencies on the aging in all fifty states. The funds appropriated for various purposes under the act went from $7.5 million in fiscal 1966 to $23 million in fiscal 1969. With very limited funds available, a beginning was made in many localities where there had been nothing before. Yet the performance under the act seemed meagre indeed to many whose hopes has been inspired by the 1961 White House Conference. In the words of one outside observer, Robert B. Hudson, "While being the core of the Act, Title III grants were inadequately funded, had no service priorities attached to them, and were so numerous and small that it was generally agreed the basic needs of most older persons were not being met through them. For the most part the state units on aging (SUAs) did little more than get themselves established and disburse funds as best they could.''[26] A presidential task force reporting in 1968 concluded that, among the numerous federal and state agencies operating programs for older Americans, there had not developed a sustained and comprehensive approach.[27]

Without suggesting that it was the only, or even the most important factor, in the Administration on Aging's inability to combat adequately these early problems, one should take account of the atmosphere of distrust on the part of several interest-group leaders toward William D. Bechill, an attitude which had marked their stance prior to nomination and which continued to be displayed throughout his term in office. Having been selected in the first place partly because of his relative lack of group associational ties, Bechill found it difficult if not impossible to gain the confidence of old-age group spokesmen, and this was to remain a serious problem for him.

From the time he was first called into Secretary Gardner's office and informed that he was being considered for the commissionership, Bechill had been conscious of the campaign to block his appointment. "Once Gardner made it clear that he wanted me for the job," he later told an interviewer, "I made it a point to go up to the Hill and see whether I would have the support there necessary for me to fulfill my mandate. I talked to John Fogarty, and he alluded to the opposition, and asked whether I could perform adequately. I recall telling him that of course no one can predict how things may transpire, but that I felt I had the background, and was dedicated to doing the very best I could. That seemed to satisfy him, and he did not oppose my appointment." As the intensity of opposition mounted, Bechill discussed seriously with Gardner the possibility of asking the president to withdraw his name from nomination, to which Gardner responded in strong terms that as a new appointee himself he could not, and would not, back down in such a test of strength with congressional leaders. Bechill was thus under no illusions that his task in office would be an easy one, but it was nevertheless a source of frustration to him that his subsequent relationship with leaders in the senior-citizen movement a-mounted, in his words, to "almost an adversary relationship.''[28]

During his almost four years in office Bechill encountered recurrent barrages of criticism from old-age organizations. The Farmers Union and the National Council of Senior Citizens accused him of being seriously deficient in the area of coordination of federal agency approaches to aging needs; the National Council on the Aging viewed his agency in some degree as a competitor for the right to coordinate state units on aging, a task which NCOA executives Ollie Randall and Geneva Mathiasen believed could be better handled by a seasoned and knowledgeable private agency like NCOA; NCOA, after all, predated AOA by fifteen years. As might be expected of an executive in a newly created agency with uncertain support in the general public, Bechill endeavored to allay these antagonisms, for example, traveling to New York on several occasions to meet with NCOA officials in their headquarters and meeting with the heads of other groups. But basic differences, both philosophical and interpersonal, persisted.

The breakdown in communications between Bechill and the major aging organizations was nowhere more vividly apparent than in the 1967 decision, formally promulgated by Secretary Gardner and Wilbur Cohen but acquiesced in by Bechill, to transfer the AOA out of the office of the HEW secretary and to place it into a newly created Division on Social and Rehabilitation Services. (This move resembled the previously discussed January 1963 decision to relocate the Special Staff on Aging under the commissioner on welfare; the responses of the leading old-age organizations were in both cases equally vigorous.) Though the members of the Advisory Committee on the Aging had been given, or at least thought they had been given, a solemn pledge from Gardner and Cohen that no organizational changes affecting AOA would be made without first consulting them, the move of the agency was presented as a fait accompli. Just as aging activists in the earlier instance had objected to the linking of the elderly with "welfare," so they now took exception to the association with "rehabilitation." In the words of one of their number, William Fitch, "to place the aging agency under the aegis of Social and Rehabilitation Services created the undesirable impression that the aging need help in order to be lifted up, that they are not already upstanding citizens."[29] The post of commissioner of Social and Rehabilitation Services was given to Mary Switzer, a dynamic and very shrewd executive, and Secretary Gardner argued before congressional committees and elsewhere that, given her expertise, the AOA would now gain a new stature, one denied the agency as long as it had to confront many other, wholly unrelated, agencies competing directly for the secretary's attention. This argument did not appeal to the leading senior-citizen groups, although some of them were prepared to argue that, if the AOA were to be relocated anywhere in the HEW complex, it should be in the Social Security Administration, which at least had a long record of concern with aging problems.

Had Bechill elected to make an issue of the demotion of his agency bureaucratically, the result could have been seriously embarrassing for the Johnson administration. The old-age groups, even when divided on other issues, invariably were at one on an issue involving prestige and, to use a favorite term, "visibility" for "their" agency in the government. In the words of William Fitch, then executive director of AARP, "Had Bechill just given us the word, those of us in the old age groups could have rallied a tremendous outpouring of support for keeping AOA where it was." Fitch personally phoned Bechill on this point, offering to protest the alleged indignity in the best interests of older people. In a subsequent interview with the author, Bechill pointed out that, no matter where the AOA was positioned, he had "a hell of a lot of access" to the White House (where he attended a minimum of fifty top-level meetings) as well as to both Cohen and Gardner.[30]

This is not the place to attempt to resolve the complex issue of whether older Americans are better served by an agency positioned high in the executive branch (as the aging activists insist) or one which is grouped with other, related agencies under the supervision of a subject-matter expert (as administrative management principles would seem to dictate.) The key point for the present argument is that these two rival schools of thought were brought to a sharp focus early in the history of the Administration on Aging and that there was consequently little opportunity during the Johnson years for an aging "subgovernment" to emerge.

Perhaps the most interesting question which arises in the course of examining the Bechill years is why the commissioner adhered to what amounted to an antigroup strategy. Part of the answer is of course implicit in what already had been said—officials of the leading national organizations, by opposing the Bechill nomination initially and by continuing to harrass him after he was installed, helped engender an atmosphere that would have made an accommodation difficult in any case. But it is also true that the commissioner's strategy was something that he deliberately chose. In seeking an answer, one may begin by noting that the bulk of federal money appropriated under the Older Americans Act was in the form of Title III grants-in-aid to states over which the commissioner in Washington essentially had no control. His discretionary funds, a far more limited amount, consisted of money for research and development and for training grants, under Titles IV and V. When it became clear that the state aging agencies, in allocating Title III funds to organizations in their jurisdictions, were responding almost entirely to state-level political constraints and that nationally based groups like NCSC and NCOA were almost completely shut out, Bechill took this as a cue as to how the fiscal resources at his disposal could be most prudently allocated. Robert Binstock, who was on the HEW staff at the time and in a position to observe Bechill closely, has since written that: "If he [Bechill] had any doubts that state politics rather than the politics of the existing aging organizations would dominate Title III, they were quickly dispelled. In their year of operation, the state executives formed their own trade association—NASUA—which quickly began to serve as an instrument of solidarity against even minor threats of interference or nuisance from NCSC and NCOA." Moreover, Binstock continues, Bechill "was not especially impressed by the capacity of the two organizations to wield influence in Congress."[31] In light of this general assessment, Bechill elected to bypass the national aging organizations and to use his discretionary money in an effort to improve his direct bargaining position vis-à-vis specific congressmen or, more generally, to improve the HEW and White House position vis-à-vis Congress. In his own mind, he had the funds earmarked, and he would say to his aides, "This is where such and such money is going eventually."[32] Thus, for example, an AOA grant to a Peoria long-term-care institution was made at a time when President Johnson was desperately seeking support from Minority Leader (and Illinois senator) Everett Dirksen on major tax legislation.

In the case of the Title V training-grant funds decision-making power was essentially delegated to Clark Tibbitts. Bechill relied on Tibbitts, an authority on aging matters with decades of experience in the federal bureaucracy, as a source of advise and counsel, and in exchange gave him a relatively free hand in the Title V area. Tibbitts, like Bechill, had no prior attachments to NCSC or NCOA, and he too chose to bypass them, in this case in favor of grants to NASUA and practice-oriented programs in universities. And he did so for essentially the same reasons that animated Bechill in the Title IV area.[33]

In addition to these political calculations, Commissioner Bechill's attitude also was influenced by a conviction he had arrived at concerning how government ought properly to function. As he later told an interviewer, he had "a very strong feeling about the importance of public responsibility and accountability," and he interpreted this as meaning that only a public official, responsible through the president to a national electorate, could adequately meet this criterion. In such a conception, the role of clientele groups in helping to shape policy was necessarily minimal.[34]

The Martin Years

Richard Nixon's victory in the 1968 presidential election, entailing a broad shift of national policy away from the principles embodied in the Great Society-New Frontier of the Kennedy-Johnson years, clearly had important implications for the aging field. Whereas a liberal Democratic administration quite probably would have introduced further significant enlargements and refinements of health care programs for the elderly (Medicare), the Nixon administration was inclined to go slowly on this front. The 1969-70 budget requests approved by the Nixon White House actually involved a reduction in funding under the Older Americans Act, where a Democratic administration almost certainly would have continued the existing pattern of steadily increasing expenditures. Yet, notwithstanding the importance of these and other substantive changes, it is interesting to note that the broad cleavage between the officials of the Administration on Aging and old-age interest groups and their congressional allies tended to persist into the first year or so of the Nixon administration.

Though the man selected by President Nixon to replace William Bechill as commissioner on aging, John B. Martin, was necessarily a Republican rather than a Democrat, he did not differ greatly from his predecessor in administration style. Like Bechill, Martin had a background in state adminstration; at the time of his appointment he was the chairman of the Michigan Commission on Aging and had a long-standing interest in the aging field. He had once been auditor general of Michigan. Martin also resembled Bechill in his lack of any marked linkages with the larger old-age groups. Moreover, while prominent politically in his home state, Martin, like Bechill, was not well known in Washington, even though Congressman Gerald Ford was an old friend and Martin at the time of his appointment was a Republican national committeeman from Michigan. It is true that in some ways Bechill's and Martin's backgrounds differed: Bechill had an academic background which Martin lacked, and Martin was more prominently identified with his political party, having served in the Michigan legislature and having been elected to statewide office as a Republican. Martin thus reflected a degree of partisanship not present in Bechill's case, but this was a minor matter, as it turned out.

Martin's assumption of office early in 1969 marked no sharp break in the administrative style of the Administration on Aging. Beginning slowly during the closing months of the Bechill era and now with increasing speed under Martin, plans were developed for the convening of the 1971 White House Conference on Aging, a conference provided for under an act of Congress passed in 1968. The early planning for the conference was, typically, of an "in house" character. As Martin himself was later to describe the process to an interviewer:

> I got Wilma Donahue [of the University of Michigan's Institute of Gerontology] and Clark Tibbitts together and we drew up a plan which contemplated a three-year program. We would encourage older people to get together at pre-Conference forums in each of the states. The older people were saying that they were tired of always being lectured to by "experts" and they wanted to gather just among themselves. We had in mind 200 to 300 such forums around the country, but the thing mushroomed beyond all expectations, and as it turned out there were over 6,000. Congressmen suddenly became aware of old people as a political force. We just didn't anticipate the intense interest in these things and the fact that they wanted to be heard.

While desirous of involving the nation's elderly in the planning process, both individually and collectively, Martin and his advisors held at arm's length the larger mass-membership organizations: "We tried to keep the old-age groups advised; we were open to their suggestions. But I would say their input was limited."[35] Among the ninety-nine members of the conference planning board appointed in 1969, only ten were in the category

"National Organizations of Older People" ("Youth Representatives," in contrast, had fourteen planning board members).[36]

Martin was functioning in a larger administrative and political setting, and it should be noted that his administrative style during the White House Conference planning phase was in part an accommodation to the concerns and anxieties emanating from the Nixon White House. In his capacity as director of the conference, Martin was charged with proposing members for the planning board. Since the White House was concerned over the danger that the conference on aging might be "captured" by outside forces and adopt resolutions embarrassing to the administration (this had happened at the first White House aging conference in 1961 and later at the White House conferences on children and youth and on nutrition), the Nixon staff insisted on clearing each board member proposed by Martin. Delays and a marked tendency toward caution were the result. The danger that the conference might involve a "disproportionate" number of Democrats was equally a matter of distress. Martin's initial idea had been to allow the governors to appoint their state delegations. The White House worried that this would mean that Democratic governors would appoint only Democrats, and consequently the Nixon staff announced a plan whereby each governor would appoint 50 percent more "delegates" than would actually be invited to attend, thereby enabling Washington to filter out the most activist and potentially embarrassing among them. The suggestion was eventually abandoned in the face of charges that the White House was attempting to impose a political test on the delegates. But the fact that the plan was put foward, without Martin's prior involvement or assent, suggests the degree to which his range of administrative discretion was constricted by criteria imposed on him externally.[37]

By the opening weeks of 1971, then, there was a growing sense of exclusion from the decision process among the leading senior-citizen activists in Washington, both in Congress and among leaders of the larger national groups. The resulting anger, which in some cases was reaching truly explosive proportions, was to have significant consequences, especially since the Washington leaders of the senior movement were now less troubled than they had been earlier by the problem of top-level personnel turnover. Now in a position to mobilize their considerable resources to influence public opinion, the senior-movement leaders turned their guns on the process by which the White House Conference planning was being conducted. The results of this effort were to be far-reaching indeed, affecting not only the White House Conference itself, but more fundamentally the very basis on which old-age policy henceforth would be discussed and decided. Since these developments marked the end of what we have characterized as the "managerial phase" of decision-making under the Older Americans Act, it merits separate treatment, and will be the focus of the chapter to follow.

Summing up the period covered in the present chapter, one is struck by the difficulty experienced by senior-citizen activists in demanding and achieving an acknowledged place for themselves in the inner circles of the Administration on Aging during its infant years. As has been seen, the explanation for this is essentially twofold. In the first place, senior citizen organizations had been neither strong enough nor sufficiently politically adept in the late 1950s and early 60s to make the Older Americans Act an expression of their will. Their access to the AOA, created by the statute, was therefore less than it otherwise might have been. Second, despite the growth in their memberships and leadership skills in the later part of the 1960s, these organizations were unable for a variety of reasons, some of them internal to the groups and some having to do with the temperament and backgrounds of those in key HEW positions, to crack into the inner administrative circles of HEW. All of this would change in time, but the change did not occur quickly or without a struggle.

Since the image of aging groups emerging from this chapter has been one of thwarted ambitions, it is well to recall earlier chapters suggestive of more successful efforts by the groups. NCSC, it will be remembered, is generally viewed as having been significantly involved in the Medicare struggle. In addition, this group along with others was successful in negotiating lucrative contracts with various federal agencies—OEO, Labor Department, and so on—in which they served in a "middle man" role between the agency and old-age clienteles. Through their own house organs and contacts with the press they apparently had a continuing influence on public opinion. While it remains true that the groups in question were generally unsuccessful in piercing the protective bureaucratic armor of AOA and higher-level HEW officialdom, their spokesmen in the sixties do seem to have helped sustain a general "atmospheric pressure" and helped to insure that aging concerns would remain a high-priority national agenda item.

9 The 1971 White House Conference on Aging

As has become evident, federal old-age policy evolved initially without benefit of sustained, informed inputs from national voluntary association. It is true that old-age associations were on the scene in the early 1960s but they did not generally define their mandate as entailing a pronounced "intercessor" function.[1] When they intervened politically at all, the intervention was limited in scope and low in intensity. In the early 1970s, however, there occurred a significant alteration in this pattern, and the 1971 White House Conference on Aging was to be a major catalyst in the reaction. In order to assess this development, one may begin with the White House Conference's 1968 authorizing resolution enacted by Congress and then turn to the planning and eventual execution of the conference (1969–71). My consideration of the consequence of these developments for subsequent policy in the aging field will be reserved for the chapter to follow.

Legislative Origins of the White House Conference

As has been shown to be true of most federal old-age action of the period, the 1968 authorizing resolution (PL-90-526) which provided for the convening, roughly a decade after the comparable 1961 assembly, of a White House Conference on Aging was enacted almost entirely as a result of initiative from within Congress. In the Senate, the bill (S. J. Res. 117) was introduced by the chairman of the Senate Committee on Aging, Senator Harrison Williams. The hearings on the bill, held on March 5 and 6 of that year before the Special Subcommittee on Aging of the Committee on Labor and Public Welfare, were chaired by another vocal and influential senator, Edward M. Kennedy of Massachusetts. In the committee report published subsequently, the members alluded favorably to the testimony presented by various academic experts, especially that of "sociologists, economists and others" concerning the anticipated "far-reaching changes in the composition and expectations of the aged." Moreover, in justifying the need for a White House conference the report quoted at length anthropologist Margaret Mead and Duke University economist Juanita Krebs, as well as various heads of state units on aging. Yet the report made but passing reference to the testimony of spokesmen who had appeared to represent the NCSC, the

National Catholic Conference of Services for the Aging, the National Farmers Union, and other nongovernmental groups. It was not that such groups were unhappy over the proposals but simply that their views did not seem to weigh heavily.[2]

In the House, hearings on the companion bill (H. J. Res. 1371) were held June 18 before the Select Subcommittee on Education of the House Education and Labor Committee. Of the four witnesses called to testify, only one, William C. Fitch of the Naitonal Council on the Aging, was associated with a private voluntary organization. Judging by the way he was quoted in the subsequent committee report, even Fitch was asked to testify because of his long association with the late Congressman Fogarty and not because of his current associational involvement. The other witnesses called before the committee were all public officials.[3]

But as the national aging associations in the late 1960s began to overcome their internal managerial problems, they became increasingly conscious of the need to influence public policy. Haltingly at first, and then with increasing vigor, they began to coalesce, even though pronounced differences of outlook and policy remained. In so doing they overcame a long-standing reluctance to engage in joint legislative effort. Several years previously, in the middle 1960s, there had been a series of informal meetings among group leaders sharing a concern with old-age matters. The members had met to discuss their common concerns, legislative issues among them, but they adhered to a rule against taking stands on pending legislation or otherwise engaging in joint political activity. Though these meetings had important long-range effects insofar as they helped to get the various leaders acquainted, they lacked a central focus; for a period of months in late 1969 and early 1970 they were suspended altogether. With the approach of the White House Conference on Aging, however, legislative issues literally thrust themselves on old-age group attention. A reconstituted body of senior-citizen leaders, more compact in size than the earlier one and less wary of taking political risks, though still quite fragile as to its sense of common purpose, came into existence. Whereas the earlier grouping had included some members representing groups only secondarily interested in the aging, this one consisted of the leaders of only six organizations, all of them with aging as their primary concern. The six included NARFE, NCSC, NRTA/AARP, NCOA, the Gerontological Society, and the National Caucus on the Black Aged.

Given the participants' mutual jealousies, diversity of internal structures, and varying constituencies, their initial collaboration might not have endured had there not been an outside person, respected by all the participants, who was able and willing to serve in the role of mediator. Such a person was found in Arthur S. Flemming, the man named by the President in April 1971 to serve as the White House Conference chairman. Many of the group leaders' meetings were held in Flemming's Executive Office Building suite close to the White House, and when the conference actually convened in late November of that year, Flemming labored strenuously to maximize the areas of consensus among the group representatives.

Since the conference chairman's willingness to foster actively group involvement constituted a sharp break from previous practice and was to have far-reaching implications, Flemming's behavior at this juncture merits close attention. Important clues to his motivation are to be found in his own prior career and in the political environment he entered at the time of his appointment, and it will be helpful to take up these two points in order.

Most successful federal officials are obliged to deal with the leaders of lobbying organizations as a condition of their effectiveness in office, and in so doing they presumably gain at least a rudimentary understanding of the lobbyist's own problems with his constituency. Yet few of them can match Arthur Flemming's personal knowledge of the world of private associations, a knowledge derived from a lifetime of direct involvement. After a period of service in the 1930s as head of the School of Public Service at American University, a Methodist-related institution, Flemming from 1948 to 1953 and again in 1957–58 served as president of Ohio Wesleyan University and from 1968 to 1971 as president of Macalaster College in St. Paul, Minnesota, both private liberal arts institutions. His service in voluntary organizations has been equally extensive. After many years as a lay leader of the Methodist church, Flemming was elected in 1963 a vice president, and three years later the president, of the National Council of Churches of Christ, a federation of which the Methodist is one of the larger participating churches. At other times he held the presidencies of the World Council of Churches and the National Conference on Social Welfare. In all of these groups Flemming was generally identified with those who wanted the organization to become more conscious of the moral and ethical dimensions of public policy decisions and to attempt to wield policy influence. During his years in the NCCC, for example, he was instrumental in getting the federation to face up more squarely to the moral implications of the federal school aid and civil rights controversies.[4] With this background, Flemming was presumably favorably disposed toward the view that old-age associations, like voluntary associations generally, should be encouraged to adopt stands on public issues and to assert them strongly before decision-makers.

Reinforcing this inclination was the prevailing political atmosphere at the time of Flemming's White House Conference appointment, one which found the old-age organizations in a mood of rebellion and seriously considering protest actions which could have seriously endangered the conference's success. As noted above, the initial planning for the White House Conference had been carried on under the direction of John B. Martin, the commissioner on aging and, until April 1971, the conference's

acting chairman. Under Martin's leadership six thousand community meetings—called Older Americans White House Forums—were held across the
country beginning in the fall of 1970. Organized without direct national
senior-group involvement, these conferences presented themselves as a
convenient target for antagonism by the leaders of old-age groups. Nelson
Cruikshank, the president of NCSC and in the opinion of many the "elder
statesman" of the senior movement nationally, attacked the forums and the
contents of a questionnaire drafted by the conference staff to determine the
problems of greatest concern to the elderly. Cruikshank charged that the
questionnaire was "superficial" and that the forums could be reached only
by those affluent elderly who had the means and mobility to get to the
meetings. By the winter of 1971 Cruikshank's sense of foreboding had
deepened. "Things were coming apart at the seams," he later told a
reporter for the *National Journal*, and at that point the best he was hoping
for was that "the conference would not be a disaster."[5] NCSC was close to
backing out.

Another source of resentment was the lack of consultation with national
senior groups and the apparent effort to impose a "political test" on
conference delegates. Initially, each senior-citizen organization was allotted
two delegates with one vote apiece, whether the organization had a
membership of 300 or 3 million, a plan which drew criticism from the larger
mass-membership groups—a "horse and rabbit sandwich" method of
assigning delegate slots, as one of their leaders characterized it. The
committees which collected preconference information and drafted recommendations were appointed by Martin and his staff without consulting the
participants; William Fitch, executive director of the National Conference
on the Aging, said the appointment of an insurance man as chairman of the
section on spiritual well-being was the last straw as far as he was concerned.
No cluster of groups felt more alienated than the National Welfare Rights
Organization, the National Caucus on the Black Aged, and other more
militant groups interested in the problems of the aging. They were initially
given no role at the planning stage and were not assured of being able to
send delegates to the conference itself. Hobart Jackson, the chairman of the
black caucus group, told a Senate committee in March that "all of this
contributes to a feeling among participants of being used." Jackson began
laying well-publicized plans for a *"Black* House Conference on Aging."[6]
Even the organized state units on the aging, normally to be found among
the commissioner on aging's warmest supporters, found cause for alarm.
They were angry because the apportionment of conference delegates gave a
majority voice to rural states rather than to the urban states where most of
the aged resided, and because HEW secretary Elliot Richardson asked the
governors to propose half again as many delegates as their states could send,
leaving final selection to the federal government, not the states.

This rebellious mood was given pronounced focus and visibility in the course of the March 25–31 joint hearings in Washington before the Senate Special Committee on Aging and the Subcommittee on Aging of the Senate Committee on Labor and Public Welfare. The hearings were intended to investigate criticisms of the AOA, to evaluate AOA performance, and to inquire into preparations for the White House Conference. Of the fifteen witnesses who appeared (exclusive of those who participated in panel discussions), the overwhelming number, twelve, came representing nationally based senior-citizen groups, whereas only one, Garson Meyer, head of the President's Council on Aging, spoke as an administration witness. The domination of the hearings by the national senior-citizen groups was itself remarkable, considering that the congressional hearings leading up to the 1961 White House Conference had heard from almost every kind of association and expert in the field except groups of this type, and considering also that as recently as the 1968 hearings mentioned above, such groups had been regarded as only secondary in importance.[7]

In their initial statements and again under the sympathetic questioning of liberal Democratic senators, who predominated among the joint committee members, the witnesses spelled out their sense of frustration with the conference planning process. While the most vocal critics predictably spoke for senior groups generally identified with a pro-Democratic of left-of-center viewpoint—NCSC, the National Farmers Union, and the National Caucus on the Black Aged—the spokesmen for groups with no particular ideological or partisan coloration were only slightly less vehement. Bernard Nash of AARP spoke of "roadblocks that have been thrown in the way of the planning process"; William Fitch of NCOA introduced a resolution adopted the previous weekend by a meeting of more than two hundred senior-center directors which deplored "the failure to involve the elderly directly, especially the elderly poor" and the "rejection of minority groups"; the chairman of the Public Policy Committee of the Gerontological Society, Elias Cohen, charged that "the issues to be presented have been designed to produce a platitudinous type of report. Those running the conference are staying away from controversy and criticism. There is no proper input for national organizations like our own"; even the spokesman for the American Association of Homes for the Aged, by no means an activist organization, spoke out against the lack of any substantial input from his group. Only one old-age-group witness, Thomas G. Walters of the National Association of Retired Federal Employees, had nothing but praise for the way the Conference was being organized.[8]

As evidenced in their questioning of witnesses and in the contents of their subsequent report based in part on the hearings, a solid majority of the joint committee members agreed essentially with the changes leveled by the complaining witnesses. The report, released in October 1971, and rather ominously titled *The Administration on Aging: or a Successor?* sharply criticized the level of AOA administrative performance and took up a variety of bureaucratic alternatives aimed at giving older Americans higher executive-branch status and visibility. The report also drew upon the findings of an advisory council appointed by the committee leadership and charged with inquiring into AOA operations. National aging organizations and officials of state aging agencies largely made up the body's membership, whereas White House Conference planning officials and others identified with the Nixon administration were not invited to participate. An item-by-item comparison of the various alternatives discussed in the report and the prior proposals offered by AARP, NCSC, NCOA, and NASUA reveals a striking parallel between them. After sifting the various alternatives, the authors of the report finally favored a recommendation which blended the thinking of interest-group leaders, though it was not identical with what any of them had proposed. The proposal, which suggested creation of an independent agency on aging in the executive office of the President and encouragement for creating parallel units in state government, has received little support to date, but coming as it did in 1971 the report indicates the trend of Senate joint committee thinking at the time, in particular the increased responsiveness of the committee to old-age associations.[9]

Faced with the prospect of having the White House Conference end up as so much wreckage, the president's staff moved urgently to get the proceedings back on track. There appears to have been no significant opposition to the appointment of Arthur Flemming either inside or outside the executive branch. John Martin, until then the acting chairman of the conference and the person whom one might have thought would have the most to lose by Flemming's arrival, was not unhappy about the appointment and in fact endorsed Flemming's name in conversation with the president.[10] In all likelihood Mr. Nixon needed little urging in the matter, considering that he and Flemming had a personal relationship going back to the days when Nixon had been vice-president and Flemming the HEW secretary. Moreover, Flemming's credentials for the office were impressive. His active involvement in the aging field went back many years; in 1939 he had been appointed to the old Social Security Board, and he served as director of the 1961 White House Conference on Aging, chairman of the 1969 Social Security Advisory Board, and as a member of the 1971 White House Conference Planning Board. In addition, he was generally well acquainted with old-age group leaders; Flemming's friendship with Nelson Cruikshank, for example, went back to the days when the two were fellow undergraduates at Ohio Wesleyan.

On assuming office in April 1971, then, Flemming took as his first priority conciliation of old-age-group leaders and reactivation of the stalled conference planning process. Though the fact of his being selected chairman

was itself a major concession to old-age-group restiveness, positive steps
seemed necessary to involve the leaders. As mentioned above, the top
executives of the six most active and concerned groups were called together
for a series of consultations; in addition, Flemming and HEW secretary
Elliot Richardson established a task force to inquire into the effectiveness of
the Administration on Aging as an advocate for aging interests and to
explore how the AOA, if not functioning adequately, might be appropri-
ately restructured. (It was significant that Flemming should be called upon
for this task, since he was not at the time the administrative head of AOA.)
As was typical of his approach to problems, Flemming established a task
force to look into the matter, with two of its four members having been
closely identified with old-age groups—Garson Meyer being a former
president of NCOA and Hobart Jackson heading the National Caucus on the
Black Aged. In discussing the information-gathering duties of the task force
Flemming was later to list "taking testimony from organizations of elderly
persons" first in order. In the same vein Flemming arranged to enlarge
substantially the official representation of old-age organizations among the
conference delegates and within a month of his appointment had arranged
for a meeting in the White House between President Nixon and the
representatives of national aging organizations.[11] In addition, he scheduled
an open forum for the evening of the first day of the conference—selecting
former U.S. Supreme Court chief justice Earl Warren to chair the meeting—
and in so doing promised that all issues could be raised at the conference,
while assuring dissidents that the conference would not be manipulated.
Flemming also instituted a special-concerns session for the morning of
Wednesday, November 30, where attention would be focused on particular
problems of the aging that delegates might feel had not been properly
treated on the formal agenda. Finally, and not least important, Flemming
used his influence with President Nixon to set up a final session of the
conference where cabinet officers could come and respond publicly to the
recommendations previously adopted.

These various initiatives achieved their intended result. Group leaders,
even the most critical ones, now begin voicing words of optimism, and the
conference planning went forward without further interruption. Indicative
of the changed mood was the remark of Hobart Jackson that "Mr. Flemming
has brought a new posture which at least holds out some hope." Jackson at
the same time quietly dropped his thought for a "Black House Conference
on Aging." Another former critic, William R. Hutton of NCSC, now
contrasted Flemming's "vigorous and effective action on behalf of the
aging" with earlier rebuffs which Hutton had received from Commissioner
Martin and the secretary of labor. "As a matter of fact," he remarked to a
House committee, "after more than two years of foot-dragging and
inaction, the spreading reaction of low-income elderly finally did raise some

concern at the White House.''[12] Other group leaders spoke in similar approving terms.

As the November White House Conference approached, several aging-group leaders were concerned that it might end up like the earlier Conference on Children and Youth, whose delegates had dissipated much of their energies attacking what had been done and not done, while devoting only minimal energy to identifying viable options and pressing for action. With this concern in mind, the leaders of the six senior-citizen groups met with Arthur Flemming just before the opening session and drafted a joint statement affirming their common hope that the discussions and recommendations of the conference would contribute to ''just one objective: the enlistment of widespread support . . . in behalf of action programs that will make available to older persons increased resources, services and opportunities.'' The joint statement went on to warn that ''Our most serious problem is a lack of commitment to action in the field of aging'' and noted the danger that ill-considered actions might ''drive persons within these groups apart as they confront issues in the field of aging.'' The joint statement was quoted in full by Arthur Flemming in the course of his November 28 opening remarks to the conference. (For the full text of the resolution, see the Appendix.)

As the three thousand delegates settled into their work, it became evident that the national old-age organizations were the key to the whole conference. Although it had not necessarily been planned that way, fully one-third of the delegates were members of one or more of the larger aging associations. The remainder, though numerically larger, formed an amorphous body lacking in a sense of shared purpose distinct from that of the others. At least three of the larger associations—AARP, NCSC, and NCOA—maintained hospitality suites, and these proved important in channeling information to delegates, monitoring events, and generally maximizing group influence. As a practical matter, agreement among the leaders of the six organizations upon any goal, such as the need for higher executive-branch status for the AOA, was tantamount to the adoption of that goal by the delegates. There was usually little difficulty in passing even those resolutions which did not engender total concurrence among the groups; the other associations were prepared to go along on an issue in which one group had strong convictions. Thus AARP's strong feelings about the need for national legislation in the private pension field as well as its advocacy of a ''community resources emphasis'' in dealing with old-age needs were both acquiesced to without serious opposition. Similarly, NCSC was instrumental in getting the delegates to approve a series of far-reaching commitments in the income maintenance area. This involved resolutions favoring a guaranteed income floor for those over age sixty-five, an immediate 25 percent across-the-board increase in Social Security benefits, expansion of Medicare to include prescription drugs, and comprehensive health care for the aged. Even without this organized group pressure, the conference delegates would likely have taken some significant actions, but they probably would not have been so explicit or so far-reaching.

Yet despite the efforts to sustain an atmosphere of mutual tolerance, there were fundamental areas of disagreement between the aging organizations, and it was only with considerable effort on Flemming's part that these were channeled so as not to threaten the conference's progress. On the one hand there were those groups, particularly NCSC, the Black caucus, and NCOA, which were concerned with getting a more active and vigorous federal role in finding solutions to old-age needs. To their way of thinking only marginal advances could be achieved through strictly private channels. On the other hand, AARP and NARFE believed that the conference should stress what could be accomplished through the private sector—voluntary associations, community groups, churches, and so forth—with the government being looked upon as a last resort. Out of this diversity in basic philosophy there arose sharply differing policy views, and these opinions generated some sharp conflicts.

It was almost inevitable that some of this controversy would reach the various sections of the conference and, ultimately, the convention floor. In the Employment Section and again in the Section on Mandatory Retirement, AARP tried to get its position adopted that a mandatory age for retirement is unconstitutional. But NCSC fought this bitterly. The issue finally went to the conference floor where a bruising debate ensued. Many of the delegates were genuinely confused by the complexity of the points raised and, unable to arrive at an independent judgment on such short notice, tended to cast their votes along "party lines." In the final outcome it was NCSC's view which prevailed.

Flemming took the diversity of opinion seriously, devoting fully half his time during the convention to chairing closed-door sessions with group leaders. An important result of these meetings was a six-hundred-word joint statement, a kind of negotiated settlement, which committed the six signatory groups to working collaboratively during the upcoming "Post-Conference Year of Action." On the one hand they pledged to do "everything possible to develop strong political backing at all levels of government for [Conference] recommendations" (a position resembling that previously taken by NCSC, NCOA, and the Black caucus); on the other hand, they agreed to take "seriously the recommendations addressed to the private sector" (reflecting AARP and NARFE thinking especially). Lest there be any doubt about chairman Flemming's own convictions in this area, the statement affirmed that "the chairman advises us that he recognizes the importance of commitments for action from the public sector to parallel those he is seeking from the private sector." Mr. Flemming read the text of the agreement to the assembled delegates at the closing December 2 plenary session. (For the full text of the agreement, see the Appendix.)

As a number of commentators have pointed out, the 1971 White House Conference had an important effect on the nation's chief executive, at least in the short run. Whereas the Nixon administration had started off in 1969 by reducing the budget of AOA and by depriving the agency of significant administrative jurisdiction (sending RSVP and other volunteer programs to another agency), the White House mood now changed. In the words of one analyst Robert B. Hudson, ''Many speeches [by conference delegates] were prefaced with comments about the lack of long-term effect which conferences such as this had, and the speakers stated their determination that this one would be different. The conference leadership also sought to impress upon higher officials, including the President, that it would be wise to go beyond restating earlier achievements and making a series of vague promises.''[13] Appearing before the final session of the conference, Mr. Nixon pledged to support a five-fold increase in the AOA budget over his original 1972 budget request, a $100 million nutrition bill for the aging, the upgrading of nursing homes, and private pension reform. Within two years' time all the above-mentioned presidential commitments had found their way into federal legislation. As will be shown in the next chapter, other policy recommendations, adopted by the conference but not endorsed specifically by Mr. Nixon in his speech, in many cases have either failed of enactment or though enacted in form have had little practical effect for lack of funding. But that the mood of the conference had a positive influence on the president, at least within a limited sphere, there can be little doubt. John B. Martin, the commissioner on aging, later put the matter succinctly in the course of an interview with the author: ''the old-age organizations had a good deal to do with the White House Conference. They were only a fraction of the delegates, but they had the advantage of being organized and that gave them tremendous leverage.''[14]

An increase in the level of visibility for old-age groups has been identified as associated with the White House Conference, and it will be the task of the next chapter to determine the extent to which this momentum was sustained in the period immediately following. But before that is done, it is important to consider some theoretical implications implicit in the material that has been covered.

A number of analysts, beginning with E. Pendleton Herring in his pioneering work on interest groups in the legislative process, have commented on the importance of group coalitions as a tactic in gaining needed legislative leverage.[15] There is a persistent tendency in these writings to assume that such cooperative efforts are directed, primarily if not exclusively, toward influencing the *legislative* branch of government and furthermore that the goals jointly sought are initially worked out in private before any approaches are made to government officials. (This emphasis on the legislative branch, one should note, is consistent with the usual legislative connotations of the term "lobbying.")

A recent work devoted entirely to the topic at hand, *Cooperative Lobbying*, by Donald R. Hall, illustrates the problem strikingly. Hall's discussion is weighted heavily on the side of efforts to lobby among Capitol Hill lawmakers and makes only the most incidental reference to pressure directed at the executive branch. Moreover, Hall's leading cases of successful cooperative lobbying involve groups getting together privately in advance of their approaches to policymakers. Aside from one or two minor exceptions, federal officials or lawmakers are not pictured as direct participants in these joint efforts—instead, they are almost invariably the objects, not the agents, of pressure. Hall devotes a section to the matter of how groups manage to reach consensus, but his data contain no instances of an appointive official assuming a mediating or arbitrating role.[16]

In contrast, the present findings call attention to the possibility that collaborative effort may have as its primary object the need to influence the executive branch. Even though statutory change may occur from this effort as a by-product, the achieving of basic changes in administrative policy itself can fully justify the participants' time and energy. It is evident, moreover, that a federal official (or officials) may actively involve himself in bringing about the collaboration.

To a limited degree earlier authors have considered the phenomena described in this chapter but under a different rubric than cooperative lobbying. David B. Truman, for example, some years ago traced the path by which major "peak associations" are brought into existence—such an association being defined as a structured, enduring alliance between interest groups functioning in the same policy area. It seems that the United States Chamber of Commerce and the American Farm Bureau Federation, both "peak associations," were founded in part through a direct intervention by a top-level government official with leaders of existing groups.[17] But the creation of a peak association is a rare event in national government, whereas presumably the more ad-hoc coalitions such as this chapter has treated are rather common. The closest thing in the political science literature to what I have been considering is a phenomenon analyzed by Lester Milbrath in his book, *The Washington Lobbyists*. Milbrath remarked that: "Groups commonly bring their quarrels to Congress or an executive agency and ask the government officials to arbitrate or choose between conflicting policies. A decision that helps one may hurt another. In a sense, the members of Congress sit as judges deciding contending interests."[18] There seems to have been some of this arbitrating element in what Flemming did with the aging-group leaders in 1970–71, but his role was more energetic, prolonged, and change-directed than that which Milbrath seems to have in mind.

10 The Bid for
Sustained Senior-Group
Policy Influence

As we have seen, the 1971 White House Conference on Aging involved a break from the decision-making patterns of earlier years. Under the aegis of Arthur Flemming the notion was advanced, novel in the aging field, that senior citizen mass-membership groups have the right both to express themselves on major issues and to expect a warmly sympathetic listening from policymakers. Yet the change in outlook had occurred in the context of a particular conference, one conceived, planned, and executed on the premise that old people are entitled to a national forum. Given such a setting, it was not surprising that their organizations and spokesmen should have played a prominent, even a decisive, role. There was no necessary reason to believe, once the White House Conference was over, that those federal officials and lawmakers who would be obliged to make pro or con judgments on conference recommendations would be similarly receptive to senior-group inputs. On the contrary, considering that officials had been deciding policy in the aging field a long time prior to the appearance of mass-membership groups and believed themselves fully apprised of "old folks'" needs, one might assume that things would return to the pre-conference pattern; continuity in official Washington is more the norm than change, and the old-age lobby (such as it was) had been only a marginal participant in the established order of things in Congress and in the executive branch.

The question then arises: has the long-term trend toward increasing senior-group political influence continued into the post–White House Conference period or, on the contrary, has there been a return to the practice of deciding policy 'essentially through negotiations between executive agencies and congressional committees? In confronting the question one must not confine one's attention to events observable in the public record but must also probe beneath the surface. Only in this way can the causes of behavior be analyzed: if senior groups have been successful, how have they achieved this success? If not, why? An analysis of the 1972–74 period should shed light on these issues, although considering the recentness of events to the present writing, the answers will have to be phrased tentatively.

The working hypothesis, subject to testing and possible refutation in this chapter, will be that the 1971 White House Conference did indeed mark an important change in the level of access accorded to senior groups by policymakers—a genuine shift in direction, not a mere momentary deflection. One should not imagine that this is a matter on which consensus already exists. Contrary to my premise, there has been a tendency among some observers to "write off" the White House Conference as noble in intent but without significant consequences. An executive of the National Council of Senior Citizens, for example, remarked to the author that participating in meetings of the Post–White House Conference Planning Board was like "attending a wake," so little of substance was accomplished, and Nelson Cruikshank of the same organization stated in an address to the New York Golden Ring Council, almost exactly a year after the conference closed, that, "Now that the [White House] Conference has failed we shall have to initiate more forceful and positive action."[1] There is of course no inherent contradiction between the views of NCSC leaders regarding policymakers' alleged failure to follow up on conference recommendations and the rather different tone of the hypothesis offered above, since the former is concerned with manifest public-policy results and the latter with significant indirect consequences. Yet, clearly, in suggesting that the 1971 gathering amounted to an important watershed I am by no means merely repeating the conventional wisdom, and it is this that makes the hypothesis a challenging one.

White House Conference Effect on Federal Policy

By examining the manifest changes during the 1972–74 period one can gain an impression regarding the general political atmosphere and assess the readiness of officials to accept initiatives in behalf of the aged. To examine such changes, an evaluation of the carry-through on conference recommendations seems appropriate as a point of departure.

The White House conferees made recommendations on a broad front, including proposals directed at the private sector, at local communities, at state national governments. For present purposes it is appropriate to set aside much of this and deal exclusively with proposals relating to federal policy. Listed below are the nine federal policy areas considered by the conference and the more important recommendations under each heading.[2]

Summary of Major White House Conference Recommendations

1. **Income Maintenance**
   a. Increase widow's benefit to 100 percent of covered worker's benefit
   b. Tie Social Security benefits to the cost-of-living index

    c. Change the retirement test to allow up to $3,000 of earned income without reduction in Social Security benefits

    d. Increase benefits across-the-board 25 percent

    e. Raise the minimum monthly benefit to $150

2. Pension Reform

Enact federal legislation to enforce national minimum standards for private pensions

3. Health Care

    a. Finance a certain percentage of Medicare expenses out of general revenues

    b. Enact national standards to regulate state Medicaid plans

    c. Eliminate all Medicaid deductibles

    d. Include prescription drug costs in Medicare coverage

    e. Enact a national health plan providing medical care for persons of all ages

4. Employment of Older Workers

    a. Establish a federally funded training and job-assistance program for older workers

    b. Improve effectiveness of the act barring age discrimination in employment

5. Housing

    a. Create an office for housing the elderly in HUD

    b. Establish a housing program designed specifically for the elderly

    c. Require that all federally assisted public housing include a fixed percentage of old-age tenants.

6. Nutrition

    a. Establish the equivalent of a national school lunch program for the elderly

    b. Increase utilization of the food stamp program by liberalizing standards and designing a distribution system that does not inconvenience the physically handicapped

7. Transportation

    a. Subsidize mass transit services from federal gas tax revenues

    b. Appropriate funds to establish special transportation subsystems for the aged in mass transit

    c. Reduce transit fares for aged users of trains, planes, and buses

8. Gerontological Research

    a. Establish a National Institute of Gerontology within the National Institutes of Health

    b. Increase funding for research in gerontology

9. Reorganizing and Strengthening Old-Age Agencies

    a. Establish a committee on aging in the House of Representatives

    b. Create a special department on aging in the Office of Management
       and Budget
    c. Reenact and expand the Older Americans Act of 1965
    d. Elevate the Administration on Aging into the office of the HEW se-
       cretary
    e. Establish a National Information and Resource Center for the Aging

Of the nine major areas listed in this summary, none is more important than the first, income maintenance. Indeed, some have argued that raising income levels is the key to the whole problem of the aged in this country. In view of this it is of great significance that in the course of its 1972 amendments to the Social Security Act, Congress enacted, and the President rather reluctantly went along with, changes fully embodying White House Conference demands. (Indeed, the combined 1972–73 boost in Social Security benefits of 27 percent actually overfulfilled the conference's mandate in this area.) In another area, the enactment of the Older Americans Comprehensive Services Amendments of 1973 amounted to a major change in focus and a substantial enlargement in the authorization level informally agreed upon, a level estimated by Senator Thomas Eagleton at $1 billion.[3] While it is true that in the area of health care the policy response has fallen short of White House Conference demands, there nevertheless was significant motion represented by the enactment of H.R. 1, including (*a*) expansion of Medicare coverage to include the permanently disabled, (*b*) federal payments to prepaid group health plans (HMOs), (*c*) home health insurance, and (*d*) coverage of persons in need of kidney dialysis and kidney transplants. A major campaign for national health insurance involving significant benefits for the aged as one facet, was launched in 1974. A major nutrition program, directly in line with conference demands though thus far poorly funded, was signed into law in 1972 and in the following year incorporated as Title 7 of the Older Americans Act amendments. With reference to section 9 in the table, the House has established a Committee on Aging, an expanded Older Americans Act has been passed (1973), and Congress has acted to remove the Administration on Aging from its lowly status as a subunit of Social and Rehabilitation Services in HEW and to place it under the secretary's overall jurisdiction. And there has been a major pension-reform act passed. Indeed, of the nine areas identified in table 10.1 only housing, gerontological research, and transportation have seen little or no statutory change, and even in those areas there have been important congressional initiatives which have failed to be adopted only through White House opposition or inaction.

As viewed by the more aggressive champions of the aged, such as the leadership of the National Council of Senior Citizens, the actions of a fiscally conservative President Nixon in vetoing major legislation affecting the aged and in failing to provide adequate budgeting for certain key programs amounted to slamming the door in the face of the White House Conference recommendations. But considering the legislative accomplishments in the aging field during the 1972–74 period, this assessment appears unduly somber. There would seem to be a more compelling argument for the view embodied in a 1973 Senate report which reviewed accomplishments during the first sixteen months following the close of the conference. The report concluded that "bipartisan interest and support in the Congress—together with some initiatives by the Administration—have resulted in far-reaching accomplishments [since the White House Conference]."[4] In his introduction, committee chairman Senator Frank Church (Democrat, Idaho) characterized the year 1972 as one which older Americans could look upon "as ranking only behind 1935, when Social Security was enacted, and 1965, when Medicare became law."[5] Church's introduction and the text of the report both underscore the numerous areas where policy accomplishment has fallen short of conference recommendations, but the overall tone of the commentary is emphatic regarding the conference's generally positive outcome. Quite possibly, even those who initially were displeased with conference results may have occasion to revise their judgment on the basis of a larger, three-year assessment such as the one presented above.

By comparison with previous White House conferences in other fields, several of which gained a reputation for failing to achieve much in concrete policy terms, the 1971 Conference on Aging can be judged relatively influential. Though it alone was not responsible, there would seem to be a causal connection between the conference and the initiatives alluded to above. The gathering's "success" was admittedly a qualified one, considering that in certain areas there has been little or no progress and in at least one case, the issue of Medicare hospital insurance deductibles, the trend of policy has been the reverse of that demanded by the conferees. Additionally, the success was by no means of such magnitude as to substantially alter the circumstances of most elderly Americans; even if the White House Conference recommendations were miraculously to be adopted *in toto*, a very considerable number of elderly persons would still remain poor and inadequately protected against ill-health, malnutrition, inadequate housing, and so forth.

Considering that the gathering seems to have positively influenced the course of events, it is highly plausible that old-age associations, which played a key role at the conference, may have gained in stature and political influence as a by-product. But rather than leave it as a mere supposition, I shall now address this issue directly.

Changes in Old-Age-Group Political Access

It is a noteworthy fact, though scarcely a surprising one, that senior-citizen orgainzations were an important factor in the "Post–White House Conference Year of Action," namely 1972 and early 1973. The one-hundred-member Post-White House Conference Board, chaired by Arthur Flemming, was composed predominantly of nongovernmental groups of various kinds, old-age mass-membership groups constituting one important segment. The conference board was assigned the task of screening the work of a still larger number of groups and associations, all of them former participants at conference sessions, and of determining which of the conference recommendations they supported and with what intensity. As Flemming explained to a House subcommittee, "We will put before the [conference board] a synthesis of the reports of the 340 national organizations, and we will likewise put before them whatever information we receive from the governors, and then ask them for their recommendations as to further strategies for action."[6] In saying this, of course, Flemming yielded none of his independence of judgment or action, but from the context it is apparent that he and the old-age association leaders continued to see important payoffs from continued collaboration. When, early in 1973, Flemming closed out his duties as conference board chairman, the president named him to succeed John Martin as commissioner on aging, and presumably his responsiveness to group initiatives will continue to characterize his administrative style.

Yet a trend toward increased old-age-group involvement in policy probably would be apparent even if Flemming were not in the picture. A person of his administrative sagacity responds to, as much or more so than he creates, fundamental changes in the political atmosphere. As a way of identifying possible trends in associational involvement in old-age policy, it is worthwhile to consider how the major groups have been behaving and with what responses from officials and lawmakers. The largest and wealthiest of such bodies, the American Association of Retired Persons-National Retired Teachers Association (AARP) can usefully serve as the primary focus in this assessment, with other senior-citizen associations brought in incidentally to round out the picture. My approach will be to examine AARP's role from various angles, beginning with how it is viewed in the Administration on Aging, continuing with a congressional perspective, and finally as it appears through interviews with the association's own staff.

The 1969 decision to name Bernard Nash to the post of AARP executive director implied a shift in the association's role vis-à-vis the Administration on Aging. Nash had served for a time in the old Office on Aging in HEW and after that as assistant to the commissioner on aging during the Johnson administration. During the five years that Nash has served as the association's top-salaried officer, relationships have shifted from the earlier pattern of relative noninvolvement with AOA to fairly active collaboration. In 1970, during the early stages of planning for the White House Conference, AARP donated $50,000 to the effort—$1,000 to each of the fifty states—in order to assist in the convening of the "senior forums" projected by conference director Martin. (Congress had appropriated some federal funds for this purpose, but the amount was found to be quite inadequate.) The $50,000 of AARP money had symbolic as well as obvious practical importance, since it was granted "selflessly" and entailed no tangible, immediate benefits for the donating organization—a fact whose significance presumably was not lost on budget-conscious AOA officials. Around the same time, the administration came up with a "senior companions" proposal designed to assist elderly persons who had become feeble or were otherwise unable to meet their daily needs. Though the proposal was objectionable to the National Council of Senior Citizens, which saw it as interfering with the Labor Department's already-existing "senior aides" program that NCSC was helping to administer on a contractual basis, AARP lobbied in its favor. After several setbacks the program was eventually created—though it was located in ACTION, not in AOA. Speaking of these and related actions, a long-tenured AOA bureaucrat remarked to the author, "The AARP has really gone to bat for us at times, sometimes when no other group would do so."[7]

There is also evidence of increasing AARP policy involvement in Congress. In the course of an interview, the counsel to the Select Subcommittee on Education of the House Education and Labor Committee (the Brademas Committee) identified four noncongressional inputs that are typically important as key subcommittee members and the staff deliberate about legislative proposals in aging: (1) individuals like Bernice Neugarten, of the University of Chicago, and William Bechill, the former commissioner on aging, both of whom combine expertise in the technical aspects of gerontology and a grasp of political realities; (2) articles in the press and in leading journals bearing on aging matters; (3) career executives in the Administration on Aging; and (4) AARP and NCOA, two groups which the informant stressed "are in touch with us on a very regular basis." An informant in the Finance Committee of the Senate presented a similar picture of linkages between legislative committees and aging groups.[8]

The National Council of Senior Citizens, although rivaling AARP in size and scope of legislative interests, is not among the groups identified as closely in touch with the staffs of the Administration on Aging or the House education subcommittee. This is not to suggest that NCSC is lacking in influence in either place—it has made known its views through appearances at committees and in letters to administrators and lawmakers. But, as will be shown in a later chapter, the organization's more intimate and informal involvements with policymakers have been confined largely to other areas, especially that of income maintenance.

Though Capitol Hill and AOA interviews provide ample evidence of increased AARP policy involvement, one must turn to that organization directly for an adequately rounded picture of its activities. In early 1972 and

again in 1973 the author conducted a series of interviews among top-echelon
AARP executives, including Bernard Nash. The information gained in this
manner reveals the existence of both formal and informal channels between
the association and official Washington, especially (though not exclusively)
in the area of service programs for the elderly.

Formal Channels

AARP has become an increasing source of information for lawmakers and
agency officials. Reports prepared by the association's staff serve as a basis for
formal appearances by AARP spokesmen before House and Senate committees. One not atypical report, a 148-page document concerned with "The
Present Income Situation of the Elderly and Prospects for the Future," was
reprinted in its entirety by the Senate Special Committee on Aging as an
appendix to its 1973 hearings on future trends in Social Security.[9] While not
generally regarded as an "activist" organization, AARP does express itself
on major issues, and its views are difficult for lawmakers to ignore
considering the association's six-million strong, generally middle-class constituency.

Informal Channels

Informal linkages help to give substance and thrust to the formal ones. By
their very nature such ties are difficult to identify, since their manifestations
may consist in nothing more accessible to the analyst than a private phone
call, a conversation in a lobby, or even a significant nod of the head.
Without suggesting that they are in any sense exhaustive, the following
quotations, drawn from interviews with staff informants, are suggestive of
the scope and intensity of such ties. "Senator Thomas Eagleton relied
primarily on our staff to size up his position on the bill to exempt income
from Social Security in determining a person's eligibility for welfare
benefits." "Senator Hiram Fong has sent his staff people to our offices
several times to get our views on pending bills, and, on one occasion, he
actually reversed his thinking on a given bill after hearing what we had to say
on it." "Before his recent defeat for reelection, Congressman David Pryor
was one of our best friends in the House. As is well known, Pryor was one of
the leading advocates for the aging on the Hill and campaigned for creation
of a Committee on Aging in the House of Representatives. What isn't so
well known is that it was Bernard Nash of this association that first
mentioned the aging committee idea to him and pointed out the benefits."
"During President Nixon's first term in office [1969-73] the White House
had a staff man, Evans was his name, assigned to dealing with old-age
problems. He kept us informally apprised of White House thinking, and

they wouldn't make a move on a major old-age issue without first consulting
AARP.'' ''During the 1972 campaign the Republican National Committee
had a senior-citizens committee and the head of that worked with us a good
deal. We would have worked willingly with the Democrats, too, but they
failed to create a senior-citizens committee in the '72 election.'' These
comments are intended as illustrative, not as exhaustive. Implicit in them is
the notion that AARP legislative representatives cultivate their congressional
contacts and that these contacts are responsive to what the association has on
its mind.

The staff has cultivated ongoing relationships with several members of
Congress who are influential on aging matters. In the Senate these members
include especially Frank Church and Harrison Williams (the chairman and
past chairman, respectively, of the Special Committee on Aging), Thomas
Eagleton, Walter Mondale, and Hiram Fong. In the House some of the key
contacts are John Brademas, Albert Quie, John Heinz III, and Joe Waggonner. With any of the persons mentioned, Nash and his subordinates usually
can arrange an appointment on short notice simply be identifying themselves to the legislative aide or staff assistant. As Nash put it, ''They know who
I am and that if I request an appointment with the Senator or Congressman,
it is something important and I won't waste his time with trivialities.''
Moreover, John P. Martin, in the course of an interview with the author, was
questioned regarding the effects of such interest-group interventions during
the years (1969–73) that he held the office of commissioner on aging.
Without hesitation Martin enumerated six major pieces of legislation in
which AARP and its sister groups were significantly involved in both the
formal and informal process of enactment—measures ranging from the
automatic cost-of-living escalator in Social Security to the Title 9 community
services program in the Older Americans Act. The former commissioner
conveyed the impression that he could have extended the list of group-
affected legislation if he had thought about it longer.[10]

While the very existence of informal contacts between AARP and
policymakers has obvious importance on its face, one usually cannot show
direct causal connections between what the association does and subsequent
policy outcomes; in most cases such connections can only be inferred from
indirect evidence, and often even that is impossible to do. Occasionally,
however, there is a case in which such a linkage can be demonstrated, one of
them being President Nixon's decision to sign into law, rather than veto, the
Older Americans Comprehensive Services Amendments when they came
before him a second time in 1973. Considering its importance, Bernard
Nash's account of what transpired is worth quoting at length:

> We were concerned, of course, about the President's veto late in '72 of
> the amendments in their initial form. Early in '73, when Congress passed

them a second time, now somewhat modified, there was still no guarantee that Mr. Nixon would not veto them again. We drew up a three-page memo based on our research into the matter and including the results of an informal poll we had conducted through our contacts among both Republicans and Democrats on the Hill. The memo suggested a compromise package that we knew would win majority support in both Houses and at the same time would not offend Republican sensibilities.

We were very anxious to get it into the president's hands, by-passing the White House staff which normally screens out such things, and we picked Congressman Joe D. Waggonner of Louisiana, hoping he could get it through. (While Waggonner is a Democrat, his voting record is such as to make him very acceptable to the White House.) Waggonner was in a reception line waiting to greet the president one day, and when his turn came he thrust a copy of our memo into Mr. Nixon's hand and said something like, "Here, this will allow you to sign the Older Americans Amendments." As he reported it to us later, Nixon took it, read it over quickly while he stood there, and expressed satisfaction with what it contained; he said it was the kind of document he had been looking for. Within a couple of hours a White House Staff man had called Congressman Quie, the ranking Republican on the Education and Labor Committee, to check it out, and one of Quie's people called us.

One always hesitates to say that any one move was decisive, but in this case we feel that what we did had a very obvious impact on the president's decision to agree to the compromise and place his signature on the act.[11]

This case is not intended to suggest that AARP or, for that matter, any interest group, is influential to the point of routinely gaining access to the president; indeed, in the instance cited it is unclear whether Mr. Nixon was aware that the document he read was an AARP product or that, if he was aware of it, the fact made any difference to him. Rather, this case demonstrates the high level of political sophistication present in the AARP staff, involving both an ability to anticipate the responses of officials and to propose viable options—a datum of considerable interest in gauging AARP's probable influence on issues elsewhere in the federal establishment.

Conference Impact on Internal Life of Groups

In May 1969, AARP named its first full-time staff executive in the legislative relations area, Peter Hughes. The combined dues-paying membership of AARP and NRTA at the time was around 1 million. Few, if any, linkages based on extended personal contact existed between the Association and AOA or, for that matter, between it and any other executive agency. The brief space of five years, however, saw a fundamental change in this picture. On November 1, 1973, the combined memberships of AARP and NRTA stood at the very substantial figure of 6,020,000, and in the state of

California alone there were 600,000 members. The national legislative staff was enlarged to four full-time personnel—Hughes and three other. The association also employs several special consultants—Cy Brickfield and former aging commissioner John Martin on a regular basis and others, for example, former Congressman David Pryor and former commissioner of Social Security William Mitchell, on an ad hoc basis for special projects such as reading testimony before congressional committees. (Mitchell, it should be noted, is also an AARP national board member.) Outside the legislative staff, particularly, there are specialists in other departments who are in fairly regular contact with federal agencies; Harriet Miller is the AARP housing specialist and Robert McAlpine of the national affairs division deals with a number of federal agencies. Beyond this there is a state legislative department employing an additonal four full-time professional staff persons. And, not least in importance, the AARP executive director, Bernard Nash, and his deputy, James Sullivan, both have backgrounds in federal service and keep closely in touch with federal agencies. Thus, not counting those who are employed on a purely ad hoc basis, there are fourteen executives whose work involves fairly continuous contact with state and national government—an immense change for so short a period.

While it is true thus relatively easy to show a relationship in time between the 1971 White House Conference and important developments internal to AARP, proving a causal connection is by no means so simple. Conceivably, both sets of events were a response to some still more basic factor, a groundswell of public interest in the aging, for example, and bore no essential connection to one another; and indeed there is evidence which lends a certain plausibility to such a contention. Bernard Nash came into office at a time (December 1969) when AARP membership was growing, its financial structure was strong, and the prospects for the future were bright. Nash who had a mandate to streamline the organization, found that a large proportion of the staff of 160 was performing routine clerical duties, mainly mail handling. He shortly persuaded the board to employ a management consulting firm to study the situation, and the consultants came up with a recommendation that automated equipment be installed, thereby making it possible to achieve a substantial reduction in the mail-handling staff (from 120 to 45 persons). Having implemented the consulting firm's suggestions, Nash had funds available for other purposes, and he made the decision to employ a larger number of highly qualified professionals.[12] These decisions had an inherent logic to them and appear to have been essentially unrelated to any changes occurring in the larger social and political environment.

Where this contention breaks down, however, is that the professional staff added at this juncture were not evenly distributed throughout the organization but were concentrated primarily in the field of state and national legislation, just as one would expect if one assumed that the White House

Conference was having a major effect on the external environment and was helping to generate greater political self-awareness among AARP constituents. The AARP staff personnel interviewed by the author were cognizant of the difficulty in sorting out the relative importance of any single factor in organizational change, but (in line with my own contention) they nevertheless alluded repeatedly to the White House Conference in the course of their remarks. One staff man's comments were typical:

> It's hard to say for certain how this enormous increase in staff in such a short time came about. You've got to keep Nash's able leadership in mind. But I would stress the White House Conference primarily. The conference helped us to expand our membership by stimulating the interest of many aging persons in old-age issues, and this in turn made it possible for us to afford more staffing. Also, the conference increased congressional willingness to listen to what we had to say. When you go, for example, into Senator [John] Tunney's office [Democrat, California] and you say you have 600,000 members in his district alone, that makes an impression. Our membership is big enough now that a word of thanks in our newsletter often makes a big difference to a politician. We can't go in with money, like the dairy lobby with a half-million bucks, but we do have publicity to offer. A kind word from us is remembered.[13]

To phrase the informant's point slightly differently, the White House Conference could be said to have affected AARP both in overt, direct ways and also subtly and indirectly. In the former sense it fostered a major growth in membership and income and did so without entailing any apparent increases in internal factionalism, as has been known to accompany such explosive growth elsewhere. In the more indirect sense, it produced changes in AARP by changing the political atmosphere in which federal and state lawmakers function, sensitizing them more to old-age needs and fostering in them a greater receptivity to what the organized aging were saying. AARP thus enlarged its legislative-relations staff with reasonable assurance that the new personnel would find an attentive audience among influential members of Congress.

The evidence above squares with views expressed by former commissioner on aging Martin, who was in office when the changes described were occurring. To an interviewer Martin remarked, "the White House Conference was really the turning point for old-age organizations and the senior-citizens movement generally. The aging have come more into their own in the last four years [1970–73] than in the previous fifty years."[14]

During the three-year period of planning, execution, and follow-up of the White House Conference, the internal life of the second largest mass-membership organization, NCSC, also underwent significant changes. Whereas prior to the conference a large number of the Council's 3,000 constituent local clubs—at least a third—existed mainly to foster conviviality and provide diversion, by 1973 this "borscht and bingo circuit" had pretty much disappeared. Existing clubs in many cases were recast along more socially activist lines, whereas newer ones just coming into existence were mostly founded with social reform as one of their primary goals. The change was essentially qualitative and is not fully reflected in quantitative indices of growth. It is interesting, nevertheless, that between the beginning of 1971 and the end of 1973, the number of NCSC national dues-paying members ("Gold Card Members") increased from 100,000 to 250,000—a dramatic change for so short a period and one indicative of growing support for the national headquarters' politically activist approach.[15] NCSC officials are reluctant to attribute this development to the White House Conference—it will be recalled that their general attitude has been to minimize the consequences flowing from the conference—but nevertheless the change was probably a function of conference-generated momentum, at least indirectly.

Turning from intraorganizational changes to relationships among the various old-age groups, one finds additional evidence of White-House-Conference-generated momentum. It will be recalled that intergroup cooperation was an important underlying dimension to the conference, both beforehand and while it was actually in session. In the months following, this growing interrelationship did not come to an end. What had been a precarious ad hoc coalition called into being in the hothouse atmosphere of a national assemblage, now began to take on permanent organizational form; as a direct outgrowth of the Post–White House Conference Board, there emerged a new body, the Conference of Interested Agencies in Aging (CIAA). Launched in mid-1972, CIAA members now gather on a regular basis, and Harry Walker, the president of the National Association of State Units on Aging and the head of the Maryland stage agency on aging, serves as chairman. Six associations currently make up CIAA, and in all but one case they are the same ones previously active in connection with the White House Conference, the single change being the replacement of the Gerontological Society by representatives of the National Conference of Homemakers and Home Health Aides.

In conclusion, there is strong presumptive evidence that the 1971 White House Conference on Aging has had a major effect on the trend of events during the subsequent two and one-half years. The impact is measurable partly in the significant legislative developments of the period and, not less importantly, in developments internal to the larger senior-citizen organizations. Admittedly, even in the absence of the conference, old-age associations probably would have addressed themselves more forcefully than before to public policy questions, having already begun such a shift in the late 1960s before the conference became a factor. But the weight of evidence is that the change would neither have been so swift nor so fundamental without the conference. The data also have considerable interest from a theoretical standpoint. It is striking that AARP, at a critical point in its development, elected to make use of "organizational surpluses" typified by those arising out of the administrative reorganization carried out by Bernard Nash in order to become more directly concerned with influencing state and national policy. One is dealing here, it would appear, with an instance of a fairly general phenomenon among American interest groups, one which Robert Salisbury has shown to typify the way that associations generally move from an initially apolitical to a rather overtly political stance. With an association's internal maintenance needs fully provided for, Salisbury has noted, whatever organizational surpluses as may be present are available for various noncritical functions, and addressing the political sphere more directly is one function that many associations view as a shrewd long-term investment.[16]

11   Old Age Groups
and Enactment of
the 1972 Social
Security Amendments

In the summer and fall of 1972 Congress enacted legislation which forced dramatic and fundamental changes in the Social Security system. On June 30 it passed H.R. 15390 (the Mills-Church Amendments), which raised the Social Security tax rate and wage base, authorized an automatic cost-of-living adjustment, and most important, provided an across-the-board 20 percent benefit increase. On October 30 President Nixon signed H.R. 1, which provided, among other things, an increase in recipients' earnings limitations, an elimination of the dollar-for-dollar benefit reduction, and an increase in benefits for widows and widowers. The bills represented a continuation of a legislative trend that many had believed unlikely under a fiscally conservative administration; between 1969 and 1973 Social Security benefits increased 51.8 percent and the cost of benefit payments lost more than $25 billion. As a result of the legislation embodied in H.R. 1 and H.R. 15390, Social Security now accounts for more than 20 percent of all federal spending.

The enactment of the 1972 Social Security Amendments raises two major questions: Why did the passage of this seemingly costly and inflationary legislation occur at a time when politicians of both parties were attempting to reduce government spending? Which individuals or groups were responsible for the dramatic increase of the legislation's provisions? Heretofore, analysts have provided facile answers to these questions, concluding that the amendments passed because it was an election year and because they were sponsored by Wilbur Mills, Frank Church, and other leading congressmen and senators. Both of these answers are valid in part, but they reflect a superficial analysis of the political processes involved. Although the passage of these amendments was partially due to the upcoming election and the sponsorship of powerful legislators, their substance and success were also attributable to less publicized but critically important factors.

The purpose of this chapter is to demonstrate the correlation between the passage of these amendments and the activities of old-age interest groups. To illustrate the subtle but substantive influence of group pressure, the

This chapter was written with Nancy Gina Bermeo.

analysis will center on the role of the National Council of Senior Citizens in
the legislative history of H.R. 15390. NCSC was not the only old-age interest
group which advocated substantive Social Security changes, but it was
certainly the most active. Its leaders took adamant and highly visible
positions on the issue of Social Security reform, whereas the more middle-
class AARP, which was willing to accept arguments that major changes
would prove inflationary, consequently stayed more in the background.

Before attempting to illustrate the nature and magnitude of the NCSC's
"group influence" we must first clarify the meaning of the term itself. For
the purposes of this discussion group influence is defined as the ability to
affect the outcome of events in a manner which appears to serve or partially
serve a group's expressed needs. The following chronological analysis will
illustrate that the National Council of Senior Citizens affected the outcome
of events at several crucial stages in the legislative history of the Mills-Church
Amendments.

The Advisory Council on Social Security (1971)

The nomination and convening of the Advisory Council on Social Security
marked the first phase in the legislative history of the Mills-Church
Amendments. Analysis of the council's activities reveals that the group
functioned as a vital though informed link between NCSC and key
decision-makers in Congress.

The complexity of the advisory council's political role is best understood
in the context of its officially sanctioned purpose. According to federal
legislation, the council meets every four years to review the status of the
Social Security program and to examine the scope and adequacy of the
program's benefits. The 1971 advisory council first convened in June 1969,
and in accordance with federal law comprised thirteen individuals, each
chosen by the secretary of HEW and representing employers' associations,
unions, and a variety of other groups. The council met on seventeen
occasions and submitted its advisory report to Congress in April 1971.

The report contained recommendations for fundamental changes in the
nature of the Social Security system, suggesting specifically an alteration of
the program's accounting methods to allow expansion and liberalization of
the system's benefit payments. Since the program's initiation, Social
Security Administration actuaries had assumed static wages when projecting
Social Security revenues and expenditures. Due to the influence of continuous inflation, the tax rate deemed necessary to finance a given level of
benefits invariably produced a surplus of revenues. This surplus was kept in
a trust fund which was periodically tapped when legislators sought to expand
benefits and coverage. The advisory council advocated changes which would
permanently reduce the growth potential of this surplus and proposed that

the official actuaries discard the "assumption that earnings and benefits will remain level over the valuation period." It recommended that: "the actuarial cost estimates for the cash benefits program be based ... on the assumption that earnings levels will rise, that the contributions and benefit base will increase ... and that benefit payments will be increased as prices rise."[1] In addition to suggesting that the program be financed on a current cost basis and that the trust fund not exceed more than one year's benefits, the council made more than thirty other recommendations which, if embodied in legislation would serve to increase the magnitude and cost of the benefit system.

Why did a council which was hand-picked by representatives of a fiscally conservative administration recommend such a dramatic and far-reaching overhaul of the Social Security system? And why were these actuarial changes not made previously, during Democratic administrations, if the system had always produced surpluses?

Analysis of the council's composition and its connections with senior-citizen interest groups provides a partial answer to these questions. The council was more liberal than observers had expected, largely because its composition was determined by Arthur S. Flemming and merely rubber-stamped by the HEW secretary. As was mentioned in previous chapters, Flemming was a liberal Republican, had been involved in various social welfare programs, and had close ties with a spectrum of liberal interest-group leaders. The council's membership[2] included four representatives from employer and professional organizations and four representatives from labor unions.[3] The five additional members ostensibly represented the council's neutral interests but almost invariably supported liberal proposals.

The council was, according to one of its staff members, "definitely weighted in favor of the elderly," and its leaders managed to steer clear of White House dictation. The council's statement regarding the relationship between the federal budget and the Social Security system illustrates the point:

> Even though the operations of the Social Security trust funds and other federal trust programs are combined with the general operations of the federal government in the unified federal budget, policy decisions affecting the Social Security program should be based on the objectives of the program rather than on any effect that such decisions might have on the federal budget.[4]

As is generally true when advisory councils are created in the federal government, the effect, if not the manifest intent, in this case was to guarantee privileged access for the interests represented.[5] According to interviews with council staff members and NCSC leaders, privileged access did indeed occur in this case; one informant maintained that there existed, "an almost incestuous political relationship between Nelson Cruikshank and the council membership." Cruikshank had known the council's chairman (Flemming) since college. One of the union representatives on the council occupied Cruikshank's former post as director of the AFL-CIO Department of Social Security and had worked with him for a number of years. Bertha Adkins, Arthur Flemming, and Nelson Cruikshank held positions on the National Planning Board of the 1971 White House Conference on Aging. (Adkins and Flemming were actually chairpersons of the board itself.)

We conclude that on the basis of personal relationships alone the Advisory Council on Social Security was at least moderately accessible to NCSC. While it is apparent on the face of it that the council's final recommendations were in line with NCSC demands, it is more difficult to show that the group's efforts had a direct impact on how the council acted. It might be argued that what the council recommended arose purely out of an incontrovertible actuarial analysis, one showing large surpluses in the trust fund and a lowering of benefit-payment purchasing power resulting from high inflation rates. While such an analysis would be valid in part, it cannot adequately account for what transpired. There existed a good deal of internal dissension among council members, and it was by no means obvious at the outset how the available actuarial data would be interpreted. Illustrative of this was J. Douglas Brown's opposition to special minimum benefits. As a Princeton economist and a founding father of the original Social Security system, Brown was one of the council's more knowledgeable and influential members. In the spring of 1972 he wrote a letter to the *New York Times* expressing adamant opposition to the concept that individuals who had contributed to Social Security for several decades should be guaranteed a minimum benefit regardless of their contribution rate. Brown argued to the contrary that "contributory insurance and public assistance cannot be mixed" and that congressional support of the concept would constitute "a most serious threat to the soundness" of Social Security as a whole.[6] Brown was not alone in his opposition. A number of nationally prominent actuaries spoke out against the council's recommendations and the legislation which followed them. Robert J. Meyers, president of the Society of Actuaries and former chief actuary of the Social Security system criticized the proposed actuarial changes as highly imprudent. In a *The Wall Street Journal* article Meyers suggested that the changes might "create a difficult, perhaps even intolerable financial situation for future generations that have no way of avoiding it once it has occurred." He cautioned that the council's assumption that national production would increase at a constant rate of from 2 to 2.25 percent was extremely unwise and asserted that the

Advisory Council's recommendations did not properly assess the impact of
Zero Population Growth:

> in the 1990s and increasingly in the immediately following decades, the
> immediate ZPG conditions will produce fewer individuals at the working
> ages to support the same number of aged beneficiaries. Eventually, the
> total aged population will rise from about 29 million in the 1990–2010
> period to about 45 million in 2025, an increase of about 55% as against a
> rise of only about 15% for the productive population.[7]

The criticisms leveled by Brown and Meyers indicate that the actuarial
reasoning behind the 1972 amendments was not as cut-and-dried as its
advocates implied. The council's final report thus implied political as well as
logical reasoning. First, the concept of an "overfinanced" trust fund is
essentially relative and derives its meaning from a political rather than a
mathematical context. Second, its assertion concerning the trust funds'
independence of the federal budget was fraught with obvious political
implications. Aaron Wildavsky's statements on budget reform are relevant
to understanding the intrinsically political nature of the council's operations: "the budget is inextricably linked to the political system. Enabling
some political forces to gain at the expense of others requires the explicit
introduction and defense of value premises."[8] Interviews with council
staff members revealed that council members had frequent conversations
with NCSC leadership throughout their deliberation period. We can safely
infer that NCSC affected both the introduction and subsequent defense of
the value premises which were embodied in council recommendations and
that this constituted a subtle but very crucial form of group influence.

The White House Conference on Aging

The 1971 White House Conference provided an official forum from which
senior citizens and old-age interest groups could express their legislative
demands. According to its director, John Martin, the conference functioned
to provide "an integrated set of guidelines for further action on behalf of
older Americans."[9] The guidelines which emerged were largely those set
forth by major old-age organizations; and in the income-maintenance area,
especially, conference recommendations were adopted mainly at the behest
of NCSC. Nelson Cruikshank would later remark to an interviewer that his
group's advocacy of Social Security changes at the 1971 White House
Conference was analogous to the advocacy of Medicare at the 1961
conference. Though demands for policy changes in both areas had been
expressed previously, each White House Conference provided a means by
which Cruikshank and his allies could energize the impetus for legislative
change. Through the conference, organized advocates could gain access to

communications media, solicit the attention of a wide spectrum of decision-makers, and derive support from delegates who were not affiliated with the organization itself. Each conference served, in essence, to publicize the nature of the advocates' demands and to reinforce the importance of their proposals by broadening their base of support. Regarding the 1971 conference in particular, informed staff personnel in the House Ways and Means Committee and in the Finance and Special Committee on Aging of the Senate are unanimous in believing that the national assemblage was an important source of political leverage.[10] Moreover, the frequent mention of the conference and its proposals in subsequent congressional debate on the Mills-Church Amendments is further testimony to its legislative impact.

NCSC, having thus succeeded in its initial task of influencing both the Social Security Advisory Council and the White House Conference, early in 1972 turned its attention to Congress directly and to the task of soliciting support for specific proposals embodying its Social Security recommendations.

The Process of Formulation

On February 23, 1972, Congressman Wilbur Mills of Arkansas submitted the first piece of legislation embodying the provisions which were eventually to be included in H.R. 15390. Mills proposed an amendment to H.R. 1 which provided a 20 percent Social Security increase instead of the 5 percent increase originally provided for in the bill. Since subsequent congressional debate on the measure involved repeated references to the recommendations of the Advisory Council and only occasional allusions to NCSC and other old-age groups, one might infer from the record that Mills's amendment was a direct outgrowth of the advisory group's work, while NCSC was influential mainly to the degree that it managed to affect that body's report. But as we shall see in some detail below, the evidence is to the contrary. It appears that the legislation's substance and its movement through the legislative labyrinth was in large degree a function of activity by NCSC and other aging groups.

To some extent the influence of aging groups is apparent on the face of events, since key provisions of the bill find no precise parallel in Advisory Council recommendations but are decidedly in line with prior recommendations of NCSC. (Judging by their remarks from the floor, many congressmen and senators appear to have been under the impression that the Advisory Council had itself recommended the 20 percent increase in Social Security benefits. The report of the Advisory Council had recommended that benefits be increased but failed to recommend a specific amount.)[11] In one sense the Mills amendment actually ran contrary to Advisory Council recommendations, since that body had suggested the trust fund retain financing for approximately one year's benefits at all times, whereas the Mills proposal called for a minimum-benefit reserve of only nine months. On the other hand, the amendment paralleled NCSC thinking not only with regard to its absolute amount but also in respect to the potentially controversial issue of whether benefits should be across-the-board, with all beneficiaries, rich and poor alike, receiving the same percentage increase, or graduated, with poorer recipients receiving a greater proportional increase. Though Mills was known to be aware that a graduated benefit scale might marginally improve the economic status of the poorest senior citizens, he and NCSC were both of the view that tactical considerations involved in securing the necessary votes outweighed this consideration.[12]

Interviews with informed congressional staff personnel lend added weight to the view that senior-citizen groups were decidedly influential in this case. According to a staff member of the House Ways and Means Committee, the concept of an across-the-board 20 percent increase was formulated during discussions involving old-age interest group leaders, bureaucrats, legislators, and actuaries. He explained that, "The trust fund allowed a large increase and there's no doubt about that. . . . But the increase which was finally proposed would not have been as high if the NCSC and other senior-citizen groups hadn't pushed for it on the Hill and at the [White House] Conference." To state that NCSC had a critical effect on the substance of Mills's amendment is not to state that Mills was controlled by old-age interest groups but merely that his actions were influenced by publicly and privately articulated group preferences.

Senate Phase of the Struggle

But the NCSC's role did not end with the process of legislative formulation. Shortly after Mills submitted his amendment he met with Nelson Cruikshank and William Hutton of NCSC. The congressman suggested that NCSC concentrate on lobbying among senators since the amendment was then under consideration by the Senate Finance Committee. Accordingly, NCSC leaders met with Finance Committee chairman Russell Long and suggested that he cosponsor Mills's amendment in the Senate. When Long declined to commit himself, NCSC leaders sought the sponsorship of Senator Frank Church who, as chairman of the Special Committee on Aging, was also a likely sponsor. Church was initially unwilling to sponsor the amendment because, as an informant put it, he was wary of "offending Long." His reluctance also may have stemmed from an unwillingness to jeopardize his own already-introduced Social Security amendment.[13] Nevertheless, after conferring further with staff members and NCSC leaders, Church changed his position and on March 7, only two weeks after Mills submitted his proposal, presented the amendment on the floor of the Senate.

With the official backing of Congressman Mills and Senator Church, NCSC began to publicize the merits of the new amendment among potential legislative supporters. In this endeavor they were aided by the Special Committee on Aging. NCSC had worked with this committee since both came into existence in the early 1960s. A member of the committee staff told an interviewer that NCSC employers "were very friendly" with committee staff members and that "a lot of respect existed" between the two groups. A senior staff member discussed NCSC's activities and committee alliance in an interview: "NCSC played a very important role in the amendment's passage. Other groups made some contributions but NCSC was definitely the leading force. It served ... to energize senators' support and, working in close cooperation with our committee, made out very well."

NCSC energized support through a variety of means. Rather than try to influence every congressman directly, the organization made extensive use of grass-roots solicitations of support for Mills-Church. In retrospect it appears that these mailing campaigns varied in effectiveness. In the case of a midwestern Republican who eventually voted in favor of the increase, the avalanche of mail supporting the amendment had little or no significance: according to one of his staff members, the senator "paid no attention to what was going on in terms of mail and just looked at what the bill promised and who was backing it." In other cases, the mail campaigns appear to have been decidedly influential. Senator Hubert Humphrey was said to be responding to a barrage of mail requests when he submitted a proposal to make payment of the 20-percent increase immediate.

The NCSC monthly house organ, *Senior Citizens News*, with an estimated readership of 4 million, appears to have been an effective means of mobilizing rank-and-file support. In addition to containing articles and commentary on all national legislation concerning the elderly, *Senior Citizens News* often prints lists of proponents and opponents to major age-related proposals. According to NCSC leaders, expressions of support for the Mills-Church Amendments increased markedly just before the *Senior Citizens News* went to press, a not-untypical development when a major floor vote impends on which the organization has taken a strong stand. In William Hutton's words:

> When we have one of these issues we notify [legislators] that we intend
> to list the names of the co-sponsors in the next issue of the *Senior Citizens
> News*. You'd be surprised at the influence this has—when it comes down
> close to our editorial deadline we have [legislators] calling us frantically
> sometimes way past working hours. They don't want to be left off [the list]
> because the old folks back home pay attention.

Reinforcing the impact of mailing campaigns and other efforts to arouse supporters, NCSC leaders made direct personal contact with many senators and congressmen. Nelson Cruikshank described one crucially important lobbying effort:

> There was a time when we were trying to get Russell Long of Louisiana to fall behind our position. He had refused to co-sign the [Mills-Church Amendments], and this was evident from the listing in *Senior Citizens News*. NCSC doesn't have a large number of supporters in Louisiana, but it happened that about this time an old gentleman, a long-time liberal, was in Washington to attend our annual convention. This man was from one of the first families of New Orleans and he agreed to accompany a group of us up to Long's office. Long greeted the man warmly, and for several minutes the two of them engaged in one of those classic southern conversations about relatives and kinfolk. . . . Then the old man turned to Long and said, "Russell, here's a list of the supporters of the latest social security increase. Every liberal in the Senate is on this list but I don't see your name. Russell, your name ought to be here!" Long stammered something about having to weigh pros and cons, but the old man was adamant. Finally, Long relented and pledged that he would support the bill when it came up on the floor.

By focusing on Russell Long, NCSC leaders recognized that they were dealing not just with an undecided member of the upper house but with a decidedly influential one. In addition to Long, proponents made a concerted effort to solicit the support of other influential senators and congressmen during the first stage of their lobbying efforts. As a Senate informant remarked, "Once NCSC and its allies gained the sponsorship of certain key senators, a lot of others just fell right in line. . . . After they got Mansfield to cosponsor, a large group of Northern Democrats followed the lead. . . . The situation repeated itself several times." This snowballing of support would later occur in the House as well. An informant in the House Ways and Means Committee stated, "As soon as the senior citizens got the support of Mills and some of the other House bigwigs, the rest came comparatively easily."

Despite the successful lobbying efforts, it appeared at one point that NCSC and its allies would be unable to gain Senate passage of the Mills-Church Amendments. Though the amendment had gained a large number of cosponsors in less than four months, the bill to which it was attached was not meeting with comparable success and was unlikely to be reported out of committee until the following session of Congress. Senator Church decided that such a lengthy delay would be intolerable, and with the concurrence of NCSC moved to have the amendment detached from H.R. 1 and attached instead to the National Debt Ceiling Bill (H.R. 15390). Though this tactic insured that the measure would reach the Senate floor before the end of the fiscal year and would, if passed, almost certainly be signed into law by the president (Church was aware that debt ceiling bills are traditionally deemed veto-proof), it nevertheless involved the obvious risk that some senators, otherwise favorably disposed, might refuse to vote for the amendment on the grounds of its being "nongermane" to the bill at hand.

Moreover, there was significant political opposition developing. President Nixon and many of his close advisors voiced adamant disapproval of the amendment. At a news conference Mr. Nixon described the 20 percent increase as "dangerous" and "highly inflationary," while in an April 1972 interview with the *National Journal*, presidential advisor John Erlichman evaluated the Mills-Church Amendments in the following terms: "We think twenty percent is a political ploy and cannot be considered seriously.... We can't take twenty percent.... We've got a budget crunch."[14]

White House opposition was supplemented by that coming from the United States Chamber of Commerce, whose spokesmen argued that expansion of the Social Security system would have deleterious effects on private pension plans. William R. Brown, associate director of the Council of State Chambers of Commerce, described this effect during a congressional hearing: "[The Chamber] envision[s] the day when employers will not be able to maintain and absorb the costs of both Social Security and private pension plans. The Social Security program inexorably will force industrial retirement plans out of existence if present trends continue to accelerate."[15]

The tactical wisdom of NCSC and its allies was put to the test on June 29 when the Mills-Church Amendment reached the Senate floor. The measure by now had forty-three cosponsors (only eight short of an absolute majority), but it is not unheard of for measures with broad sponsorship to nevertheless fail to pass. Republican Senator Carl Curtis of Nebraska led the opposition during floor debate, arguing that the 20 percent increase was inflationary and would impose unnecessary tax burdens on non-aged Americans. When Senator Church countered with the assertion that his amendment would actually decrease taxes, Curtis asked, "Can the Senator point out a single social security taxpayer who will pay fewer dollars in 1973 than in 1972 on the same earnings?"[16] Church was forced to reply that he could not, and Curtis appeared to gain the ascendancy.

Yet this sort of rhetorical triumph was the only form of success the amendment's opponents experienced. The opposition proved so weak that even its administration-backed offer of compromise was badly defeated. Wallace Bennet, ranking Republican on the Senate Finance Committee, submitted a compromise amendment which provided a social security increase of 10 percent. Bennet's amendment received only twenty votes, and sixteen of the senators who supported it voted for the Mills-Church Amendments as well. The Senate finally passed H.R. 15390 by an overwhelming 84 to 3 majority the morning of June 30.

House Phase of the Struggle

Despite this success in the Senate, NCSC leaders were far from complacent concerning the ultimate passage of their proposal. Cruikshank and Hutton were suspicious of the Senate's overwhelming responsiveness and suspected that many fiscally conservative senators had voted in favor of the increase under the assumption that the measure would be killed in the House on a procedural point. NCSC's suspicions regarding conservative motivation cannot be confirmed, but the group was certainly correct in predicting procedural hurdles in the House. According to House rules, committee reports must be held over for three days before they are put to a vote on the floor, and conservatives in the House and Senate allegedly were planning to postpone or prohibit passage of the amendments by invoking this rule. NCSC leaders predicted this hurdle and confronted Mills in his office on the morning of June 30. According to an informant, Mills was sympathetic to the group's concerns and suggested that NCSC contact the conferees as soon as possible. Several hours later Mills arranged a meeting of the conferees but did not convene them formally as the conference committee. The group voted on the Senate version of the amendments and agreed by majority vote that the legislation should remain unchanged. Mills thus laid the basis for thwarting procedural objections when he brought the amendment to the floor of the House. He introduced the Senate-passed version not as a conference report, but as "an amendment in disagreement." This move prevented any insistence that the measure be held over for three days because the "holdover rule" is only applicable to conference reports.

Mills's actions created a heated debate. Representative James Byrnes, the ranking Republican on Ways and Means, leapt up and demanded that Mills present the conference report. Mills responded that House rules prevented him from doing so. The Mills-Church Amendments were considered "nongermane" because they did not relate to the National Debt Ceiling bill to which they were attached. According to House rules, every nongermane amendment must be presented as "an amendment in disagreement," whether the conferees disagree or not.

Despite the procedural dispute which resulted from the actions of Wilbur Mills, the House debate shared important similarities with that in the Senate. In both cases members made direct references to aged interest-group influence; in the House Congressman Ray Madden quoted Nelson Cruikshank in his debate speech, while in the Senate George McGovern earlier had argued that "all the national organizations of the elderly are calling for at least a 20 percent social security increase."[17] The disarray of the opposition forces was also as apparent in the House as it had been in the upper chamber. Congressman Byrnes offered a compromise amendment involving a 10 percent increase which was defeated 83 to 253. As had been the case in the Senate, supporters of the 10 percent increase were even less unified than the votes initially reflected. This is exemplified by the fact that Congressmen Collier, Rangel, and Halpern changed their votes from Yes to No after they realized that the Byrnes amendment would lose by such a landslide.

When the 20 percent amendment finally came to a vote, the true strength of the bill's proponents was made manifest by an overwhelming victory of 302 to 35. The president signed H.R. 15390 into law on July 1.

Analysis of the Outcome

The success of NCSC in engineering passage of H.R. 15390 can best be accounted for on two grounds: tactical miscalculations on the part of the opposition and NCSC's own marked skill at capitalizing on its initial legislative advantage. In what follows we shall consider these two points in some detail.

While the available data on the opposition's behavior is more limited than in the case of those who advocated the Mills-Church Amendments, it is reasonably clear that the opposition erred in several significant respects. First, they appear to have assumed that, as a cautious and fiscally conservative congressman, Wilbur Mills would be responsive to their thinking. As things actually developed, of course, Mills not only agreed to lend his name to the measure but also worked actively for its enactment. In so doing he radically altered the legislative calculus. In their comments during the course of House floor debate several congressmen justified support of the amendment with the affirmation that, as one put it, "Mills' reputation for [fiscal] responsibility is beyond question."[18] Additionally, many congressmen and senators perceived Mills as the foremost authority on Social Security legislation; Congressman Hale Boggs, for example, remarked that Mills "probably knows more about [Social Security] than any other member of Congress."[19] Opposed by such a widely respected and knowledgeable fiscal conservative, the president's arguments seemed ill-founded to all but a few Republican legislators.

The second factor which debilitated the opposition's impact was a perceived fragmentation of administration opinion. Congressmen and senators believed that the amendments had the support of the Advisory Council on Social Security and several other administrative bodies. This belief gave proponents of the amendments increased leverage. A Republican senator's staff member explained the effect of this leverage in an interview.

All the people backing the 20 percent increase used the Advisory Council's report to their advantage. NCSC, for instance, is full of liberals and [usually] has most influence with liberal Democrats. With this amendment things were different. They had less trouble getting the support of

Republicans because their proposal was backed by an administration-picked committee.

As was discussed previously, the Advisory Council did not endorse the Mills-Church Amendments per se, but the widespread belief that it did served to neutralize the president's opposition anyway. It is likely that many legislators believed that the amendment was opposed, not by the Republican party, or by the executive branch, but only by the president and his closest advisors.

Opposition from the United States Chamber of Commerce was adversely affected by the nature of the Chamber's lobbying practices. Though the organization has a membership base of more than 5 million, it is not commonly regarded as a consistently powerful interest group. Patricia A. Goldman, a former employee, believes that "Despite a gigantic membership base, the Chamber is written off by some close Capitol Hill observers as [often] ineffective."[20] In an interview, Representative Frank Thompson of New Jersey echoed this view. Though he described the Chamber as "very effective" in terms of publicizing its views, he believes that it is normally "unsuccessful" in fulfilling its substantive objectives. The Chamber's lobbying techniques were different from those of NCSC and apparently less effective. Chief lobbyist Dixie Davis explained that the Chamber places least reliance on personal contact between lobbyists and legislative representatives. This accounts for the fact that the group's only steadfast allies on Mills-Church were individuals such as Senators Fannin and Curtis and Bennett who had been long characterized as friends of business and staunch Republicans. Chamber executive John J. Meehan stated that "the chain of influence seldom runs directly from the Chamber to the Hill. It runs from the Chamber to its members and then to the Hill." While NCSC, as noted, likewise made use of indirect lobbying as an important tactic, it did not use this to the virtual exclusion of direct contacts with key lawmakers, as seems to have been the case with USCC.

On the other hand, it is likely that proponents of the Mills-Church Amendments would have been successful even if the opposition had been stronger. NCSC and its allies were greatly helped by the intrinsic appeals of the legislation itself. As one Senate informant put it, "old-age groups like NCSC had a good case. They needed the increase; it wouldn't cost much and there were a lot of aged voters who would get furious if we didn't support it. The question wasn't whether we should support it but whether we could afford not to." The preceding statement documents the humanitarian, fiscal, and political appeal of the legislation. Each of these appeal factors can be linked to the activities of old-age interest groups. By analyzing these factors, we can demonstrate that, in addition to influencing critical stages of the amendment's history, group pressure affected the very essence of the legislation's attractiveness.

The Mills-Church Amendments were given substantive humanitarian appeal by the portrayal of the aged as an outcast and impoverished minority. Proponents were able to establish the need for the benefit increase by presenting impressive statistical information concerning poverty among aged Americans. These statistics were compiled and publicized by NCSC and other old-age interest groups or were compiled and analyzed by decision-makers who wished to evaluate the validity of the demands which the interest groups presented. Even in the latter case, the existence of the interest group was the motivating factor, because without group demands no evaluation would have been necessary. Largely due to the efforts of senior-citizen organizations at the White House Conference on Aging, the humanitarian justification for the increase was well documented and publicized long before Mills and Church submitted their amendments. The information supplied by old-age organizations served to stimulate interest in the sponsorship of the amendment and, concomitantly, to justify the validity of the measure to other legislators.

The amendments' fiscal appeal derived from the recommendations of the Advisory Council on Social Security, influenced, as we have seen, by NCSC leaders and the individuals who sympathized with their demands. The council's report made it possible for legislators to argue that the increase would be financed from surplus trust funds and thus would have little effect on taxes. In the absence of NCSC influence the report would have been different, and this appealing "something for nothing" argument would have been a good deal less persuasive.

The amendments' political appeal was substantial, especially in the light of the upcoming election. The importance of this political appeal is exemplified by the sponsorship decision of Wilbur Mills, who was a publicly announced aspirant for the presidency at the time he agreed to lend his name to the amendment. It is significant that he submitted his amendment less than two weeks before the New Hampshire primary and three weeks before the Florida primary (21.1 percent of the electorate in Florida is over sixty-five). The fact that Mills chose to submit the legislation just before the presidential primaries implies that he viewed the aged and their potential partisans as a possible voting bloc. That he subscribed to such a view was at least partly attributable to the activities of old-age interest groups and the concomitant growth of political self-consciousness among group members and affiliates. Ordinarily, a set of individuals with certain shared characteristics will not be perceived as a political group unless they demonstrate through some form of organizational behavior that their shared characteristics constitute the basis for a specialized set of political interests. Aged Americans are perceived as an electoral grouping because they have banded together in organizations like NCSC which have, in turn, manifested an ability to deliver votes. As one of his staff members remarked, "Mills knew the increase was a good thing for the aged and, accordingly, a good thing for him at the polls. . . . there are a lot of organized senior citizens in this country and their voting turnout is relatively high.'' The rationale behind Mills's sponsorship was undoubtedly similar to that of many other supporters.

Conclusion

The present analysis demonstrates that NCSC played a complex and important role in the legislative history of H.R. 15390. Although its most highly visible activity on the measure was in the first half of 1972 when the bill was under consideration in the House and Senate, the organization actually became active on the issue much sooner, in the course of deliberations by both the Advisory Council on Social Security and the 1971 White House Conference. Taken in its entirety, the study of the Mills-Church Amendments illustrates the substantive and often disregarded manner in which interest groups influence congressional decisions. Obviously, NCSC could not have wielded the kind of influence it did in the absence of favorable conditions in the political environment—the upcoming presidential election in which Wilbur Mills was an aspiring candidate, the prestige of the amendment's sponsors, the apparent ''surplus'' in the Social Security Trust Fund, and so forth. But had NCSC, or some like-minded group with similar resources, not intervened, the legislative result would almost certainly have been different.

As a case study our findings are necessarily limited to what one can validly generalize from them to other issues of concern to NCSC. Clearly, the organization is not equally successful on all policy questions, even ones on which its dues-paying constituents are as aroused and vocal as they were on this one. Nevertheless, while bearing in mind the limited nature of our findings, it seems reasonable to conclude that in the income-maintenance field Nelson Cruikshank and others identified with NCSC have managed to establish a clear claim on the time and attention of federal policymakers, both in the executive branch and in Congress. Considering the substantial sums of federal expenditures involved, this is a not inconsiderable achievement.

12 Constraints in the Political Environment

In the preceding two chapters it has been shown that senior-citizen organizations in the early 1970s achieved a level of access and influence unparalleled in the forty years of federal government involvement in the aging field. While it is yet too soon to say whether this level of influence can be sustained, there seems to be no apparent reason for it to diminish. Senior-citizen groups from time to time may elect to shift their focus of political energies, occasionally leaving certain issues to be decided by an exercise of administrative discretion. But one should not expect any decline in their determination to maintain recent gains and even to enlarge their overall level of political access.

Implicit in these developments is the obvious question of whether the enlargement of old-age group political importance may soon reach the point of threatening, or seeming to threaten, the balance of forces necessary to an ordered society. This is an anxiety that has not seemed at all farfetched or unwarranted by some observers, past and present. The political resources latent in the country's old-age population—time, money, political skill, and commitment—thus far have been tapped only to a limited degree by senior organizations at various levels. With the American birthrate now at an all-time low—at or even slightly below the 2.1 children per family needed to achieve "zero population growth"—the proportion of elderly persons in the population inevitably will increase, with obvious consequences for their relative strength in the electorate.

Even though most observers continue to regard the elderly as one grouping among a number in American society, and scarcely among the politically most potent, a few see their strength in truly apocalyptic terms. F. G. Dickinson warned some years ago of the imminent risk of a "class war between young and old" and voiced a fear that the voting power of older people might be used "to exploit youth." As one approach to overcoming this danger, Dickinson went so far as to suggest that the law might have to be amended so as to provide a maximum voting age.[1] In a similar vein, an essay published under the auspices of a major-oil company raised the following specter: "If a sizeable portion of this over sixty-five group were to band together . . . the weight of their combined support would be the most

169

powerful force the country has ever known''—and the clear implication of the essay was that such a development would be ominous for American society.[2] And political scientist Harvey Wheeler, senior fellow at the Center for the Study of Democratic Institutions in Santa Barbara, recently voiced the following view: "What I'm trying to portray is a situation in which we may well see an active political group forming around age spans, and the aged becoming a more insistent force politically. *One gets the vision of the most powerful political grouping in society* of necessity becoming the group of the elderly because that's the one group that we can all identify with'' (emphasis added).[3] Though these are minority opinions, they are voiced by responsible observers and are not to be taken lightly, particularly since ones like them are frequently found elsewhere. A legitimate question to ask is whether the aging are in the process of becoming a dominant political force in American life. Are there any genuine limits to their organized strength and, if so, in what do the limits consist?

Earlier chapters have offered a partial answer to this question. I have pointed out that the aged have a highly ambiguous status in American life and are by no means always esteemed by a youth-oriented culture; that the aged are riven internally by cleavages along sectional, partisan, class, and racial lines; and that they are frequently isolated both from one another and from easy access to the levers of social power. It also has been noted that the very diversity of national senior-citizen organizations, arising in part from these cleavages, is a limiting factor on the ability of the elderly to coalesce. Implicit in what has been said is the reality that factors internal to the senior movement are likely to remain a major constraint affecting old-age political activism.

Yet I have observed, too, that despite these endemic problems, the various segments of the movement are (within limits) beginning to coalesce. And it consequently would be unwise to lay aside prematurely the anxieties alluded to above. The question arises: what, if any, are the *external* limitations on further substantial increases in senior influence in national affairs? Whatever external constraints exist are presumably not embodied in overt hostility among lawmakers and officials, since any such expressions could prove extremely costly for them politically. It seems more plausible that the constraints emerge out of the very structure of the political system which limits national government responsiveness not only to the elderly but to all socially disadvantaged groups. The present chapter will consider such structural limitations, focusing particularly on the structure of Congress, of the presidency, and of the federal bureaucracy.

Congressional Constraints

While Congress is sometimes thought of as a branch of government with a collective will, united in purpose, it is more aptly conceived as a kind of

feudal kingdom with many autonomous fiefdoms; the 435 House members
and 100 senators have grouped themselves into committees and subcommittees having varying and often inconsistent viewpoints and goals. In such
a setting, the spokesmen for any large and vocal grouping in the population
normally can identify certain members of each house who sympathize with
them and are willing to champion their cause. But building from this to
achieve the needed majorities in both houses often proves to be an
exhausting and frustrating task.

The Senate Special Committee on Aging constitutes the most enthusiastic
nucleus of supporters in either house for old-age group demands. The
committee originated prior to the time that national old-age associations
became a significant legislative factor and is by no means dependent on
them for continued survival and sense of direction. Yet the committee staff
and the personal staffs of the senators on the committee are in close working
contact with senior-citizen groups, and there is typically a commonality of
purpose. A second committee in the Senate, the Subcommittee on Aging of
the Committee on Labor and Public Welfare, has close structural links with
the Special Committee, since fully 40 percent of the members of the latter
body also sit on the former one, and its leaders are also in close touch with
old-age groups.

Until late in 1974 the House of Representatives lacked a general oversight
committee on aging similar to that in the Senate, and the view was widely
held that this militated against a comprehensive or systematic approach in
the House to aging problems. The path leading up to the House decision
finally to create such a body was tortuous and long for the members but is
highly instructive for the analyst, and it will be useful to describe what
happened. I shall test the hypothesis that the decision was not essentially a
response to direct political intervention by the organized elderly (though
aging groups may have been marginally involved) but was the outgrowth of
a felt need emanating from within the House membership itself.

As compared to the Senate, the House has been decidedly more reluctant
to establish special committees of any kind, the reluctance being largely a
result of the greater relative power of House standing committees and the
jealousy with which committees have come to regard their legislative
domains.[4] In the House committee-endorsed bills are normally reported to
the floor under a rule that bars nongermane amendments; the Senate
adheres to an open-rule tradition. The House is more hierarchically
structured, and what goes on in standing committees there has a more
decisive effect on subsequent floor action. Committee chairmen and ranking
minority members in the lower house do not willingly brook interference in
their legislative fiefdoms, and they generally look on proposed special or
select committees as threatening such a result.

Yet, despite these adverse prospects, in the early 1970s there began to be
increasing talk among House members of making an exception in the aging

case. The resolution adopted by the 1971 White House Conference, for creating a joint Senate-House aging committee (similar to the Joint Economic Committee and Joint Committee on Atomic Energy) helped crystalize sentiment that some action was called for. Responding to the conference's resolution, Congressman Albert Quie (Republican, Minnesota), introduced a bill to establish such a joint body. But it died without reaching the House floor. Around the same time Congressman David Pryor (Democrat, Arkansas), circulated a resolution proposing creation of a House standing committee on aging. Pryor had the advantage of being identified with the majority party, and he managed to get the resolution signed by a clear majority of House members—230. It also had the active support of the largest mass-membership organization, AARP. Bernard Nash of that organization had early urged this idea on Pryor, and indeed Nash may have been the original source of it. But after thinking the matter over, the House Democratic leadership informed Pryor that a lack of sufficient office space made his proposal impractical. This was the ostensible reason; the real reason, according to an informant, was that the chairman of the House Rules Committee, Congressman William Colmer (Democrat, Mississippi), was angered when he learned of Pryor's plan to challenge incumbent Senator John McClellan in the 1972 Arkansas Democrat primary, McClellan and Colmer being longtime friends. Also, Colmer was upset by Pryor's identification with the insurgent Mississippi delegation which challenged the right of the Mississippi regulars to be seated at the 1968 Democratic National Convention, a challenge that provoked a bitter floor fight. It was clear as well that Congressman John Brademas (Democrat, Indiana) and chairman of the Select Subcommittee on Education of the Committee on Education and Labor, regarded such a committee as infringing on his subcommittee's domain. In late 1972 Pryor yielded up his House seat to run against McClellan for the Senate (a race he lost), and this foreclosed the possibility of his later resuming the aging-committee struggle.

Following the collapse of Pryor's effort, the initiative in the movement to create an aging committee increasingly came into the hands of Republican members. Shortly after the White House Conference ended, a group of fifteen congressmen, identifying themselves as the House Republican Task Force on Aging, began to meet under the chairmanship of Robert H. Steele of Connecticut for the purpose of informing themselves on aging problems and discussing alternatives. Though not a highly visible group, the task force managed to exert influence in several areas, for example, nursing home reform. Steele and his colleagues were strongly supported in these endeavors by the national old-age associations; he was later to speak glowingly of the "working relationship" that had developed between his task force and "all the elderly advocacy groups."[5] Among the more active participants in the task force were H. John Heinz III of Pennsylvania and C. W. Young of

Florida. Their special contribution to the campaign will become apparent
shortly.

Since the proposal to create a committee on aging involved consequences
for the regular age-related standing committees, their chairmen inevitably
would scrutinize the idea for possible threats to their domains. In addition,
the aging-committee movement could not be separated from the effort
being waged around the same time by Congressman Richard Bolling
(Democrat, Missouri), to legislate basic reforms in House committee
structure and jurisdiction; the committee chairmen inevitably would view
his efforts anxiously and with misgivings. Despite the concern that Bolling
aroused in certain quarters, the support he generated led the House
democratic leadership to agree to his chairing a newly created Select
Committee on Committees, the committee's mandate being to look into
committee jurisdiction and bring recommendations to the House floor for
action.

In the fall of 1973 the Bolling Committee held hearings, and one of those
appearing to offer testimony was Congressman Heinz, who read a statement
that embodied an idea he already had introduced as a bill in the Ninety-
second and Ninety-third Congresses. Heinz argued in favor of a *select*
committee—one having fact-finding and general oversight responsibility
but with no legislative role or authority to act on bills. Such power would
remain with the standing committees. Heinz's strategy for avoiding a
jurisdictional squabble made tactical sense, though judging by their subsequent behavior it did not greatly diminish the anxiety felt by affected
committee and subcommittee chairmen. Bolling's initial response to Heinz's
proposal seemed quite positive: "I want you [Heinz] to know that you
happen to have struck a chord that I respond to in your suggestions for this
kind of committee," he remarked, "I understand what you are saying and I
tend to agree with it."[6] But subsequently he and his committee decided not
to go along with what Heinz demanded.

When the Bolling Committee report was released early in 1974, there was
no mention in it of a select committee on aging. Instead, it proposed to
meet the need for increased legislative focus on old-age problems by
splitting the existing Committee on Education and Labor into two committees, one on labor and one education, and granting the newly created
Education Committee general oversight responsibilities in the aging area. In
support of his view that a new House body modeled on the Senate Special
Committee on Aging was not desirable, Bolling was later to maintain before
his House colleagues that he was opposed on principle to "the proliferation
of select committees."[7] Quite possibly there was a more basic consideration
than this involved. By proposing to split the Education and Labor Committee and to make other far-reaching changes, the Bolling reform package
already was assured of staunch floor opposition. He may well have feared

that endorsement of an aging select committee, whatever the merits of the case, would needlessly intensify the opposition. This interpretation is consistent with the fact that in July 1974, when the House Democratic caucus got together and drafted a set of reforms far milder than Bolling's and essentially intended to counter his suggestions on the House floor, their reforms similarly contained no mention of an aging select committee. Obviously, leading Democrats regarded the proposal as potentially divisive and preferred to avoid the matter if possible.

Debate on the Bolling proposals was conducted under a rule permitting the introduction of amendments from the floor. It quickly became apparent that the Bolling forces lacked the strength necessary to carry the day. But rather than have the issue of committee reform removed entirely from the agenda, Democratic floor leaders decided to substitute the Democratic caucus recommendation introduced on the floor by Congresswoman Julia Hanson of Washington. It was, therefore, as an amendment to the Hanson substitute that old-age committee proponents hoped at last to get their scheme to the House floor for a vote. In the course of discussion on the floor Congressmen Heinz and Young jointly introduced an amendment for the now-familiar idea of a select committee on aging. In the course of a half hour's debate on the matter both opposition and support for the amendment were voiced. Bolling was one of those speaking in opposition, and, interestingly, both of the other two members who did so (Brademas of Indiana and Dent of Pennsylvania) chaired key subcommittees having old-age jurisdiction. When the members got around to a preliminary vote, there were 84 voting against, and among these a disproportionate number were committee chairmen who likewise had jurisdiction on elderly matters. In addition to Brademas and Dent, those voting no included Al Ullman of Ways and Means and Carl D. Perkins of Education and Labor; the Democratic majority leader, Thomas O'Neil of Massachusetts, also voted no. But this was not the sentiment prevailing among rank-and-file Democrats, who voted overwhelmingly, along with most Republicans, in favor. In the preliminary test occurring that day the vote was 322–84 in favor, and on the final vote several days later (October 8) it was 299–44 in favor.

Within weeks of the vote establishing the new select committee, the House granted it a generous initial appropriation, $600,000. Chosen for the chairmanship of the new body was William J. Randall (Democrat, Missouri), a member with long tenure in the House (he was first elected in 1959) and at least a modicum of understanding of aging matters gained as chairman of the Special Studies Subcommittee of the Government Operations Committee, the subcommittee in the Ninety-second Congress that investigated certain aspects of the aging issue.

In terms of its manifest jurisdiction and powers, the new body closely resembled its Senate counterpart, but it is by no means a certainty that it will have the same functional significance. In the Senate, the Special Committee on Aging was launched from within the dominant political party by a member (McNamara) was was closely linked to the party's presidential wing. The committee gained great initial impetus by virtue of its identification with the crusade for Medicare. As one analyst has noted, the committee even before being granted permanent status by the Senate in 1961 had already become a vital clearing house for pro-Medicare information.[8] In the House, on the other hand, there was no such national political movement with which the committee sponsors could identify, and on the whole those who led the effort were members with low national visibility. Whereas Mc-Namara stood out among his Senate colleagues as a recognized authority on aging matters, Congressman Randall will have a difficult time simply coming abreast of the esteem already enjoyed in this respect by Congressman Brademas and others. The Senate special committee has gone beyond mere fact-finding to fulfill an initiating and problem-solving role; in the House the select committee is not likely to be given any such expansive mandate, at least not in the short run.

And there have been other ways in which the House has manifested a reluctance to respond enthusiastically when old-age demands have been advanced. An analysis was undertaken of twenty-nine major old-age bills submitted in the 1972 session of Congress, their subject matter spanning the nine areas identified by the 1971 White House Conference as crucially important. Seventeen of these bills, or 59 percent of the total, were favorably acted upon in the Senate, whereas only thirteen, 41 percent, got through the House—a difference of 18 percent. One gains a similar impression in the course of interviews with informants from the committee staffs of the two houses. One House staff member complained of the way that the Senate often loads up "like a Christmas tree" legislation primarily concerned with other matters and thereby makes it difficult for the House to exercise its traditional restraining role. He mentioned the 1972 nutrition bill as a case in point:

This was a proposal to provide at government expense one good meal a day to every needy elderly person. It involved a tremendously expensive budget, and after we held hearings on the matter we decided that there should be other options considered. It wasn't that we opposed good nutrition for the elderly, of course; it was just that we weren't sure this was a particularly good investment. So in effect we put the idea on the shelf—quietly. Then Senator Teddy Kennedy grabbed hold of the idea, made a big thing of it and tacked it onto a Senate bill. It passed the Senate in a landslide. Then the Nixon administration began to feel the political heat and the White House withdrew its initial objection. So when the Senate bill came over to us it had overwhelming support and it eventually got through the House too.

Although in this particular case the House eventually capitulated, it frequently holds out against the Senate's alleged fiscal extravagance, and in so
doing becomes an important roadblock to bills sponsored by old-age groups.

Further reinforcing one's impression that the House has been something
of a roadblock in the path of far-reaching old-age legislation are data showing that the lower house is more conservative on domestic issues generally.
On the basis of an investigation of congressional behavior during the
Kennedy era, one analyst Louis A. Froman, determined that the House is
consistently less willing than the Senate to accept an enlarged federal role as
a means of dealing with social problems. The Senate's greater liberalism was
attributed in the study to the fact that committee chairmen, who in both
houses tend to be more conservative than rank-and-file members, are
more able in the House to stamp their policy views on legislation, and also to
the fact that Senate districts are more heterogeneous—they contain more
nonwhites, urban residents, and low social-status persons on the average,
and this condition results in a greater willingness among Senators to view
issues from a non-social-elite standpoint.[10] Since the findings of the study
were based on only a single session of Congress and also are somewhat dated,
the present author tabulated the findings of the *Congressional Quarterly's*
"conservative coalition index" (an index generally considered valid) over a
ten-year period beginning in 1964 (see table 12.1).

Table 12.1 Conservative Coalition Victories, 1964–73

	Senate	House		Senate	House
1964	47%	67%	1969	67%	71%
1965	39	25	1970	64	70
1966	51	32	1971	86	79
1967	54	73	1972	63	72
1968	80	83	1973	54	67

Source: *Congressional Quarterly Weekly Report,*
2 February 1974, p. 199.

In seven out of the ten years the House is seen to be the more conservative
body, and in the most recent five-year period this was true in four out of five
cases. These data help one better to understand the political world in which
senior-citizen groups must function. In the House they often encounter an
environment which regards their liberal proposals suspiciously, while in the
Senate, which is overtly more responsive, senior-citizen leaders may not in
all cases be sure whether a given member's "favorable" vote is cast out of
genuine conviction or is somewhat cynically cast in the belief that Senate
"extravagance" will normally be checked by House fiscal conservatism.

The relative conservatism of the House is also quite likely related to the
tendency for congressmen not to become program specialists to the degree

that is typical of many senators. As a number of analysts have noted, senators find it useful to their careers to develop significant expertise in a given area and to become identified as the spokesman for a particular clientele group. Senator Henry Jackson's initiatives in the area of federal energy policy, Edward Kennedy's efforts in behalf of health care, Harrison Williams's leadership in the urban mass-transit area, all come readily to mind. In the aging field, specifically, no member of the House has ever managed to equal the level of visibility achieved by a senator, the late Patrick V. McNamara; and a strong argument could be made that the current chairman of the Special Committee on Aging, Senator Frank Church (Democrat, Idaho), similarly has high status not enjoyed by his House counterparts in the aging field.

Presidential Constraints

While they are not always successful in their dealings with Congress, old-age organizations do at least enjoy a significant access in both houses, their opinions finding their way into committee reports, bills introduced into the legislative mill, and speeches on the floor. And, as has been noted, this level of access appears to be increasing steadily. One might reasonably deduce that the behavior of presidents would similarly reflect this growing trend. The national chief magistrate is answerable to a national electorate and the elderly, a grouping widely dispersed in the population, would seem to have a special claim on occupants of that office (assuming that Froman is correct in thinking that heterogeneity contributes to liberal responses). Moreover, presidents, no matter what their party, have been shown to be more liberal, on the average, than their fellow party members in Congress, a fact partly attributable to the president's need to appeal to the large industrial states in elections. Since aging organizations typically favor liberal spending measures, the relative liberalism of the presidency should insure these groups a favorable White House reception. Still further enhancing one's expectation of presidential responsiveness is the fact that both major parties now include a major section in their quadrennial platforms calling attention to aging problems and promising action. Presidential candidates at least nominally run for office on these platforms, even though from time to time they may choose to modify or ignore specific planks.

Yet the level of manifest presidential support for demands supported by national old-age leaders in recent years has not been particularly high. In the previously mentioned analysis of twenty-nine important bills on aging introduced in the 1972 session of Congress, the rate of presidential acceptance was decidedly low. Of the twenty-nine, the essential features of sixteen bills managed to get through both houses, whence they went to the president's desk for signature or veto. In three of the sixteen cases (two in the health-care area and one relating to nutrition) the acts of Congress were generally regarded as involving measures contrary to those called for by the White House Conference. All three of these the president signed. Of the remaining bills, Mr. Nixon signed some into law and vetoed others; the veto rate considerably exceeded the rate of acceptance. And even among those Conference-supported bills to which he gave his assent—all in the income-maintenance area, as it happened—the president made clear his reluctance. Mr. Nixon was not happy, for example, with the 20 percent increase voted in Social Security benefits and would have much preferred the administration-backed five percent proposal.

Was Nixon's unwillingness to act more positively on demands endorsed by most senior-citizen spokesmen attributable to constraints inherent in the presidency or was it more a function of his Republican orthodoxy and anti–welfare state assumptions? While this is a significant question, it is not one which lends itself to an easy answer, considering the lack of any direct knowledge of Nixon's inner motivations and the complexity of all presidential decision-making. Yet by studying Nixon's overt behavior in comparison to that of other presidents, it should be possible to come up with suggestive evidence which points toward a tentative answer.

Various indices could be employed in comparing the responses of various presidents to a given policy issue; of these, one in particular recommends itself as both valid and accessible. On the premise that what presidents say in lengthy speeches before solemn state assemblages reflects reasonably well their personal policy preferences and priorities, the author surveyed for possible references to the aged and age-related concerns all of the State of the Union addresses for the past forty years. The first of these was Franklin Roosevelt's first such address, delivered in 1934, and the last one was Richard Nixon's last address, in 1974—a total of forty-two annual addresses. (The total is forty-two rather than forty-one because both Presidents Truman and Eisenhower presented State of the Union addresses in 1953). Aside from the obvious matter of simplicity and convenience, there are good reasons for dealing with the State of the Union address rather than with all presidential messages to Congress, since only the former is regularly delivered by the chief executive personally before the two houses, jointly assembled, and only it surveys national needs and objectives broadly rather than focusing on a single topic. The purpose of the survey, then, was to detect possible trends in the frequency of presidential comment on old-age concerns as a basis for judging the relative emphasis on these matters from one incumbent to another.[12]

In view of the fact that old-age issues have presented themselves in various forms over the years, the author scored any mention of the following items as a reference to the topic at hand: Social Security, old-age pensions, Medicare, the elderly, the aged—or any combination of these words. The length of the

comment generally was not considered important, though in one or two
cases where a president made a particularly lengthy comment on the topic
the fact was noted.

The findings reveal an interesting trend. Franklin Roosevelt mentioned an
age-related concern in seven of his twelve presidential addresses (1935, 1936,
1937, 1940, 1941, 1944, 1945), and his successor, Harry Truman, did so in
seven of his eight addresses (failing to mention the topic only in 1947).
Dwight Eisenhower was less consistent: after mentioning Social Security in
all four of the addresses during his first term, he failed to mention this, or
any other old-age concern, in the five speeches delivered during his second
term, 1957-61. As the issue of providing health care for the aged under
Social Security emerged in the 1960s, this became a regular item of
comment until it was enacted; John Kennedy referred to it in 1961, 1962,
and 1963, and Lyndon Johnson in 1964 and 1965. Moreover, Kennedy in his
1962 State of the Union address spoke of the elderly at some length, going
well beyond the Medicare issue in his treatment.

After 1965, interestingly, the picture changes. In his last four addresses,
1966, 1967, 1968, and 1969, Lyndon Johnson made reference to an
age-related issue on only one occasion, in 1967. And Richard Nixon, in his
five State of the Union addresses mentioned such an issue only once—in
1972 in the immediate aftermath of the White House Conference. While
there have been several significant increases in Social Security over the past
decade, all of them signed into law by the president, if not in all cases
enthusiastically advocated by him, it is noteworthy that Social Security was
mentioned only once (1967) in a State of the Union address during the
1965-74 period.

There is no obvious explanation for the paradoxical fact that the marked
decline in State of the Union references to old-age concerns has occurred in
just the period when the organized aged were coming into their own as a
political force. The resolution in part may lie in a flaw in the measurement
tool. State of the Union addresses are generally shorter nowadays; presidents
have less time in them to devote to matters of only marginal presidential
interest, the aged included. Moreover, the greater relative saliency of foreign
affairs and national defense in the past two decades may be a factor, though
the grave wartime emergencies faced by FDR and Truman did not prevent
either of them from discussing issues relevant to the aging. Presumably
Johnson and Nixon could have easily worked more such references into their
messages had they been so inclined.

Returning to the question posed earlier, the evidence at hand points to
the conclusion that the two Republican presidents, Eisenhower and Nixon,
have been less interested in the elderly than the four Democrats. Whereas all
four Democrats referred to matters particularly relevant to the aged in at
least half of their State of the Union addresses, Dwight Eisenhower did so on

only four of nine occasions and Richard Nixon on but one of five. With only four presidents identified with one party and two with the other, the number of cases is obviously too small to draw any firm conclusions, but on the basis of the evidence one cannot exclude differing partisan predispositions as a possible factor in the differences in presidential interest.

Yet the data also tend to support the hypothesis that the low level of commitment is a function of the nature of the presidency. Presidents of whatever political coloration have not chosen to address the needs of the elderly with the regularity and at the depth that they frequently bestow on the problems of other groupings more favored in American political folklore—farmers, school children, and the unemployed, for example. References to issues of direct concern to the aged are becoming a rare thing in State of the Union messages; leaving aside Medicare (an issue which in many respects transcended the aged per se), there have been only three direct references to the elderly since 1956! The presidency has changed over the past quarter of a century, as several observers have noted, and more and heavier burdens are being thrust on the office. Certain groupings in the population once of interest to incumbents have consequently tended to drop below the threshold of direct presidential concern, even though in other ways (often through White House subordinates) presidents still do manifest a concern in this area. As the office has changed, so too, it would seem, have presidential priorities.

While the two factors identified appear to be important independently in influencing presidential concern and involvement, they probably are not of equal weight. In all likelihood the partisan factor is the less significant one. Republican politicians, no less than Democratic, can ill afford to appear indifferent to senior-citizen needs, and by and large they have taken a positive interest in this area. The 1961 and 1971 White House conferences on aging were both organized by Republican administrations, and Arthur Flemming, a Republican of impeccable party credentials, has had as much to do with the growing national interest in aging as any recent federal official, Democratic or Republican. On the average the non-Southern wing of the Democratic party has been more actively interested in aging than has been true of Southern Democrats or Republicans, but the difference is not great and there is considerable overlap, some Republicans being substantially more interested in aging than is the case with a majority of northern Democratic lawmakers.

Assuming that I am correct in concluding that the nature of the office, not partisanship, is the primary factor in accounting for presidential hesitancy in the aging field, this finding can help to account for some things that would otherwise be puzzling, in particular the frequent gap between presidential rhetoric and behavior. In his appearance before the 1971 White House Conference, Richard Nixon said some things that were widely interpreted as

an endorsement of the central thrust of what the conferees had recommended. Yet within a year of the appearance, Nixon had vetoed the Older
Americans Comprehensive Service Amendments of 1972, had frozen all
federally-assisted public housing construction, not excluding the planned
specialized housing for the aged, and had made several other moves
generally regarded by old-age spokesmen as objectionable. While one could
easily charge that the president had been inconsistent (and even self-
contradictory), in all likelihood his behavior reflected a problem of relative
priorities. For a fiscal conservative and one concerned about maintaining
honest and efficient administration, the spending commitments implicit in
the Older Americans Act Amendments and the widespread scandals in
the housing program were considerations which overrode the old-age
dimension of the programs involved. There was also a possible inconsistency
involved when Lyndon Johnson discoursed at length on the needs of the
elderly in his 1967 State of the Union address and, at about the same time, approved (or his immediate White House subordinates approved) the bureaucratic downgrading of the Administration on Aging, a move abhorrent to
most senior-citizen spokesmen. Presumably the Johnson White House was
not indifferent to the issue of whether the aged enjoyed their deserved ''status'' in the executive branch but came to the conclusion that this must be
subordinated to the need for clear lines of managerial authority and for
grouping together related functional units in HEW to promote efficiency
and accountability.

   In identifying the presidency as an important constraint bearing on aging
activism, therefore, one is not suggesting that presidents are uninformed or
indifferent but that the way the office is structured requires policy demands
to be weighed against one another and that the way this is done frequently
causes the aged interest to come out on the light end. In part this is a
function of politicians' belief that the elderly vote is not likely to prove
decisive in presidential elections, unlike discontent among unionized
blue-collar workers or among farmers, for example, which can serve to tip
critical states from one party column into the other. Lacking campaign
funds, a deliverable bloc of votes, or any other sanctions impressive to
presidents or presidential aspirants, senior-citizen leaders are at a disadvantage. In their dealings with the chief executive, they have typically
learned to accept as a given the constraints imposed on them at that level
and to endeavor to present their demands in terms which do not involve a
clash with other, higher-order presidential priorities.

The Federal Bureaucracy

Of all the constraints affecting senior-citizen activism, none has been the
focus of more anger and frustration than the unwieldy character of the

federal bureaucracy. Since it is nominally answerable to the chief executive, the bureaucracy's structure is in part a manifestation of the presidential attitudes analyzed above. But White House initiatives are only one determinant of executive-branch structure and behavior. A federal bureaucrat who is inclined to resist the White House can usually find powerful allies, and for this reason among others the bureaucracy is a force unto itself.

As I have noted at various points in this work, senior-citizen groups have waged an arduous, uphill struggle to get the Administration on Aging situated securely under the immediate aegis of the HEW secretary in a position paralleling that of the Social Security Administration and other major subunits in the department. As a result of legislation adopted in early 1973 the AOA was removed from its former home in the Social and Rehabilitation Services (SRS) and was placed in the office of the secretary. As a result of a last-minute compromise, however, the statute was not written in such a way as to prevent the interposing of a new administrative layer between the AOA and the secretary, and in March of that year Secretary Weinberger established a new post, assistant secretary for human development, under whose aegis were grouped the Office of Child Development, AOA, and several other units. Though hailed by its sponsors as "a model of decentralized administration."[13] senior groups generally regarded the development as yet another setback in their continuing struggle to get "their" agency closer to the center of policymaking.

While it may be true that a success in this effort might achieve the increase in responsiveness and status hoped for by old-age organizations, it is just as possible (perhaps more so) that things will remain essentially unchanged. Professor Robert Binstock of Brandeis University forcefully articulated this latter position in responding to a question put to him in the course of 1972 Senate subcommittee hearings:

> The potential deficiency of these proposals [to elevate the status of AOA] is that titular changes and administrative location mean absolutely nothing if the executive branch is not willing or not forced to be committed to the success of such advocates. There are dozens of agencies in the Executive Office of the President that have little importance or strength. Conversely, an agency such as the Peace Corps, though structurally buried within the bureaucratic hierarchy of the State Department, had a great deal of power within the Federal government during the Kennedy Administration. If these grandly titled [agency] advocates that are proposed have no Presidential, Secretarial and Congressional commitment behind their advocacy activities, then it would be better if they were not created. Their nominal existence would delude older Americans into believing that they had an effective ally in high places, that they had won an important concession. Perhaps their demands for social and individual justice would be cooled down. This would be another in a series of cruel hoaxes for our Nation's elderly.[14]

In the same vein, a spokesman for the National Association of Social Workers reacted to Senator Frank Church's proposal to establish an assistant secretary for aging in HEW by remarking that "organizational charts are security blankets, which assume that by just setting up an organizational chart, presumably you solve a problem. What the aged need is a highly visible program, well funded, with a strong advocacy function and a clear mandate."[15]

Even if one were to assume that old-age associations succeeded in their bid to have AOA given status equal to that of the other major "administrations" in HEW and assuming as well that they got positive action on the related appeal for creating an aging unit in the Office of Management and Budget in the Executive Office of the President (or at some comparably high bureaucratic level), the labyrinth of the executive branch would continue to present them with intricate and bewildering problems. The structure of the federal bureaucracy provides no readily identifiable target upon which to focus senior-citizen pressure. Instead it presents numerous targets, each with its own unique administrative traditions and established lines of support into Congress and the universe of interest groups. In a recent report detailing significant federal programs in aging, the Senate Special Committee on Aging listed programs in no fewer than twenty-three federal agencies. Five of these (including the AOA) are subunits of the Department of Health, Education, and Welfare, while the remaining eighteen are scattered widely, from the Atomic Energy Commission to the Federal Trade Commission to the Department of Commerce, and so forth. Of the patients in Veterans Administration hospitals in October 1971, just over 20,000 or 24.9 percent were veterans over age sixty-five, and the budget for caring for these men exceeded by a wide margin the total for the Administration on Aging.[16] Moreover, the leading aging organizations can scarcely avoid devoting some of their energies to the activities of the Department of Labor; this agency carries on programs affecting the lives of many older persons, and a number of aging groups (NCOA, NCSC, NRTA) have entered into contractual arrangements involving hundreds of thousands of dollars annually for their role in administrating the agency's Operation Mainstream programs. And major efforts of the Department of Agriculture, especially Project FIND and the Food Stamp Program, involve the expenditures of millions of dollars annually in behalf of the elderly.

The aging groups have not even been in a position to insure that "their" agency, the AOA, has made significant gains in the scope of its administrative responsibilities. According to the Executive Reorganization Plan No. 1, promulgated by President Nixon in July 1971, the Foster Grandparents Program and the Retired Senior Volunteer Program (RSVP) were both transferred out of the Administration on Aging, which had initiated them, into the ACTION agency, where they are currently clustered along with other federal volunteer programs. While it is true that the AOA budget has continued to rise and that the agency continues to carry out important functions, its growth has been anything but spectacular. The notion held by many of its initial sponsors that AOA, in addition to administering a significant range of programs, would serve to "coordinate" federal programs in the aging field, has not been reflected in the agency's actual experience to date. The advisory council appointed by Senator Frank Church in 1971 summed up the problem in these terms:

> AOA falls far short of being the Federal "focal point in aging" sought by Congress. Instead, its concerns are splintered and scattered; there are limited, if any, policies and few clear-cut goals. Recent reorganizations have not strengthened Federal programs and commitment in aging in any way. Rather, they have fragmented an already flawed and feeble agency still further. This situation has created chaos as well as lack of direction in Federal and State programs.[17]

Depending on one's values and priorities, it may or may not be a good thing that AOA has had a difficult time carving out a secure niche in the federal establishment, and it is not the point of the present discussion to decide the question. The point is that the one agency in the federal establishment in which the aging associations by definition enjoy highly legitimate access and where they do not have to fend off the conflicting claims of numerous "strangers," has little if any of what politicians refer to as "clout." Lacking a central focus for their energies, the associations must do the best they can to make coherent sense of, and to influence, the behavior of a score or more of highly competitive and mutually jealous federal agencies.

I have offered evidence that the anxiety sometimes expressed that senior-citizen organizations are gaining unwarranted and dangerous levels of political power has no real basis in fact. In addition to the existence of marked structural cleavages among national senior organizations, there exist quite potent constraining factors in the political environment, in particular the predispositions that typify many members of the House, most presidents and numerous federal bureaucrats. While these constraints quite obviously have not entirely precluded old-age-group political effectiveness, they do tend to inhibit. Indeed, the aging associations and their congressional and AOA allies would be doing quite well if they could somehow muster the strength needed just to achieve the official recognition long since conferred on the organized veterans through a single executive-branch unit of dominant importance in the field (the Veterans Administration) and standing committees on veterans' affairs with general legislative powers in both House and Senate. When and if such an objective is achieved—a prospect that does not seem very likely at the moment—there will be time enough to worry about the possible risks of growing old-age influence.

4   Interpretation and
     Conclusion

13 The Senior Movement
in Perspective

In the preceding chapters it has become clear that the emergence of aging as a public-agenda priority has been related fundamentally to the existence of the modern senior movement. Because of the importance of this movement, these final chapters will treat it in fresh perspective, the better to judge its larger theoretical and practical significance. The commentary will focus on the writings of various theorists who have considered one or more facet of the topic at hand—the mass character of movements, their core organizations, and "policy systems" that may contain movement organizations as one of their essential components.

At the beginning of this work, I made use of the Cobb-Elder thesis, with its emphasis on public agenda-building, as a point of departure. It now seems fruitful to follow these authors in their analysis of rational group strategies aimed at expanding the scope of issues, intensifying group impact, and containing and combatting the political opposition. As the authors suggest is true of most successful group efforts, it has been an important asset for senior-group leaders to have acquired the necessary stature and influence to define (along with congressional allies) what the issues are for them, even though they lack the power to get their way always in final policy decisions. I have suggested as well that a marked contrast exists in the degree of pressure group success in the twenties and thirties as compared to the sixties and seventies and that this is to be accounted for at least partly by the greater skill shown by the more recent old-age activists in manipulating symbols, enlarging the size and attentiveness of relevant publics, and evolving an ideology capable of sustaining group commitment and élan. In structural terms, too, a marked contrast has been shown to exist, with the earlier groups having risen or fallen with the changing fortunes of a single leader who was essentially the embodiment of his organization, whereas the more recent ones have found a resource base and bureaucratic structure necessary for smooth succession of leadership and increasing political access.

I have indicated a need for caution in interpreting the data, lest one give the misleading impression that in all cases public policy successes are traceable, directly or indirectly, to prior senior-group effort. As has been mentioned, wide variations exist in the level of senior-group access, and instances exist where the organized elderly have been only marginal participants in significant policy breakthroughs. Yet, in a larger sense it is evident that the old-age lobby has been fundamental in the trend toward increased governmental responsiveness to old-age needs. Group activity has had a continuing impact on the general climate of opinion over the past two decades, and this in turn has had its effect on the calculations of lawmakers and politicians. While prior to the 1971 White House Conference old-age groups seem to have had only episodic direct political access, their effect on public opinion appears to have begun much earlier.

The perceptive reader will have noticed that, while the Cobb-Elder thesis was introduced at the outset and applied consistently in the earlier chapters, it tended to be laid aside in the later ones. Topics like group political access, administrative politics, and clientele group oversight of policy—all of them quite important in presenting a full picture of organized senior-citizen activity—are scarcely mentioned in *Participation in American Politics*. Moreover, the authors of that work have little to say about the origins and political behavior of social movements. Thus, without minimizing the suggestiveness of Cobb and Elder's thesis, I have found it necessary to introduce additional perspectives from time to time. Indeed, it is not too much to claim that what has been employed in the latter half of this work is a new and more encompassing general view.

I have pieced together the required theoretical perspective from the sociological literature dealing with social movements and collective behavior and from the political science literature on interest groups. For this reason names like Dawson and Gettys, David B. Truman, Robert Salisbury, Arnold Rose—each of whom has contributed to one or the other of these scholarly traditions—have been brought to bear. Yet, I am quite reluctant, for reasons that will become apparent, to adopt either an "interest group" or a "collective behavior" interpretation, or an uncritical amalgam of the two. Though both bodies of scholarship offer valuable and even indis-pensable insights that the analyst dare not ignore, each is also beset with significant bias, by which I mean a selective perception which tends to emphasize certain phenomena while minimizing or overlooking other important dimensions. Until this is recognized and in some way taken account of, any conclusions arrived at are likely to be flawed. The origin of such bias and its manifestation in previous studies will be treated in what is to follow. But more positively—and this is perhaps the most important methodological discovery of this work—I will argue that by bringing these two schools of thought into juxtaposition, the strengths of each can be used to offset the weaknesses present in the other, and the resulting synthesis can become a powerful tool in the understanding of senior-citizen activism or any similarly widespread collective phenomenon.

Interest Group Literature

The empirical studies which constitute the body of data in this field are quite varied both as to subject matter and theoretical perspective. To try to generalize about them would be extremely hazardous. As it turns out, this is unnecessary, since a relatively few books—mostly major synthetic works which undertake to distill the contributions of others and give fresh theoretical perspective—have been influential far out of proportion to their number. And when one examines these works, a striking parallelism does become apparent. The first pattern to be mentioned is what might be termed the "materialist" bias.

As a number of writers have pointed out, Arthur Bentley's 1908 work, *The Process of Government*, marked the beginning of scholarly attention to political groups as a major factor in public policy. Writers as diverse in outlook as Earl Latham, David Truman, and Robert Golembiewski all have acknowledged an intellectual debt to Bentley, and Mancur Olson is correct in suggesting that the work has been "probably one of the most influential in American social science."[1] While Bentley's contribution was many-faceted, one of his most influential opinions has been the notion that economic stakes are almost always fundamental in explaining why groups become potentially active and in accounting for their survival as organizational units. He was inclined to the view that economic stakes are fundamental, not only among organized businessmen, professional people, farmers, and the like, where such stakes are obvious, but also among most purportedly altruistic and community-minded groups, where such stakes remain hidden.

The origin of this notion in Bentley's mind came in part from his reading of Marx, whom he praised along with Ludwig Gumplowicz and George Simmel as the nineteenth-century theorists whose works most clearly brought to light the group process.[2] Though Bentley was not in any orthodox sense a Marxist, and indeed at one point in *The Process of Government* acknowledged that the "interests" which groups embody are diverse in nature and not in all cases economic in essence,[3] a close reading of his book nevertheless bears out the accuracy of Myron O. Hales's remark that he remained rooted in an economic interpretation of group behavior.[4] Since the economic motive was primary for Bentley and since he viewed the quest for material advantage as tending to displace other possible bases for group cohesiveness, it is not surprising that he should find the motive of self-interest at the base of many groups whose goals are not manifestly materialistic in nature—reform organizations, "public-spirited" citizens, groups, political parties. Remarking on a group of the "public-spirited" type in Chicago, Bentley observed that "every director or contributor to such an association may think of himself as participating out of disinterested regard for the public welfare ... [yet] usually we can find that the men most prominent in the leadership belong to some group that has a specially marked [economic] interest."[5] Similarly, in discussing political parties, Bentley's commentary is essentially concerned with the spoils system.[6]

Although *The Process of Government* was not especially influential in its own time, it gained an increasingly broad audience in the 1930s and 1940s, and its impact is readily apparent in the works of authors appearing in the past quarter-century. In *The Group Basis of Politics*, for example, Earl Latham largely concerns himself with the dialectic between public officials as a collective body and economically motivated groups. In a passing reference to nonmaterially based groups—to spiritual and philanthropic groups, mainly—Latham maintains that self-interest (presumably economic self-interest) is an important, if not dominant, motivating factor.[7] There is a parallel to this line of thought in a recent and highly regarded work by Grant McConnell, *Private Power and American Democracy*.[8] The book nowhere sets forth a formal definition of "private power," but from the context it is apparent that this term is meant to connote national organizations—of businessmen, cattlemen, labor union members—whose overriding concern is protection of economic stakes. Whether McConnell intends the term to apply as well to private, nonmaterially motivated associations, or whether he sees such bodies as too lacking in influence to affect the fundamental character of the power equation, is left ambiguous. Even assuming, however, that the author is not especially interested in public-regarding, purposive organizations, in which the quest for some larger definition of social good displaces the more typical emphasis on protecting material stakes and has left them deliberately out of the discussion, it is still arresting to find no mention of such organizations in chapters carrying titles like "The Progressive Legacy" and "The Search for the Public Interest." McConnell is obliged to come to terms with organizations professing purposive goals in the course of his lengthy chapter on the labor movement. He deals with this problem by regarding labor progressivism as an epiphenomenon, not a fundamental fact, of movement life: "Despite the frequently intense desire of some union leaders to enlarge the political and social horizons of their organizations," he writes, "the labor movement is ill-constituted to realize their hopes."[9]

A final example worth mentioning is the late E. E. Schattschneider's extremely influential work, *The Semi-Sovereign People: A Realist's View of Democracy*. Schattschneider was self-conscious about what he called the "drastic statements of the group theory" put forward by Bentley and certain followers wherein the group is made to appear the center of the political universe.[10] Yet, with regard to the relative importance of "public" and "private" interest groups, Schattschneider's thinking came to resemble Bentley's closely. While acknowledging that there are groups whose essential aim is to advance some goal which transcends the members' narrow self-interest, Schattschneider minimized their political significance and insisted instead that only "organized special interest groups," among which business groups are overwhelming in number and influence, are properly included within the boundaries of what he terms "the pressure system." In his passing comments on purposive organizations he confined attention to what might be called the "pure public" type (my term) as illustrated by the American League to Abolish Capital Punishment, whose members are involved out of a sense of public virtue, not for any fear of themselves being executed.[11] Schattschneider gave no consideration to groups of what might be termed the "mixed type" in which public-regarding and private-regarding goals are meshed and in which lobbying activities for larger social purposes are made possible through surpluses generated from providing private goods to members. While he was possibly correct in asserting that pure public groups are typically quite small and only of marginal political importance, it is by no means so obvious that groups of the "mixed" variety are of similarly little consequence.[12] In view of this, Schattschneider's contention that "public" goals are only to be realized through the instrumentality of the political party system and not through direct activity on the part of voluntary groups seems premature.[13]

A second bias which one can detect in systematic works dealing with political interest groups is the tendency for analysts to focus almost entirely on structured organizations—that is, on "pressure groups" and on their leaders and rank-and-file membership—while neglecting possible ongoing interactions between formal members and group-identified nonmembers. Though groups of all types suffer from what has been termed the "law of imperfect political mobilization," social-movement core organizations seem especially beset by the problem it refers to, namely, an inability among pressure groups to recruit as members more than a fraction of those who are eligible for membership and are supportive of the stated goals. In the case of social movements there is typically a large number of group-identified, but nonmember "fellow travelers," whose importance stems from their number and capacity to affect (often decisively) the level of goal achievement. This point has tended to be obscured in the interest-group literature, as will be evident from a brief consideration of one of its more distinguished works, V. O. Key's *Politics, Parties and Pressure Groups*. Key did allude to the fact that major political organizations often spring from prior social movements, and that in the cases of organized farmers and organized labor, among others, movement organizations were intimately associated with feelings of mass discontent. But social movements are treated by Key only in a historical context, and the bulk of his discussion is concerned with what happens after the well-nigh inevitable transition "from spontaneous movement to crystalized interest."[14] In his final paragraph on pressure groups, Key remarked that private associations, once in existence, come essentially to serve a "stabilizing and braking function"—this role being necessitated by the "oligarchies" and "hierarchies" which persist in power and insist on imposing "conformity and orthodoxy" within the group.[15] Alternative possibilities to how movement organizations behave after they mature are not explored in depth, and the possible significance of fellow travelers in such a context is disregarded.[16]

Criticism of the interest group literature on grounds of apparent materialist and organizational bias must be balanced by recognition of its several compelling virtues, two of which are important for present purposes. These are the appreciation: (1) that group leaders for the most part do accurately perceive the members' interests and generally pursue strategies rationally designed to advance those interests; and (2) that group political effort is properly viewed from the standpoint of the group itself (its internal processes, stakes, and aspirations) and not from the standpoint of officials and lawmakers, who often regard pressure group effort as distressing and inconvenient.[17] The significance of these analytic virtues will become apparent in the course of the following discussion.

Collective Behavior Literature

Systematic works on social movements have begun to appear only recently. For a long time scholars in the field would from time to time voice concern about the state of the discipline—its lack of balance, analytic depth, and so forth—but it was not until 1963, with the publication of Neil Smelser's book, *Theory of Collective Behavior*, that there was a serious effort to surmount some of the perennial problems associated with the field.[18] Even though it has now been in print for more than a decade, Smelser's book still is frequently cited by scholars. And since its contents are generally considered to reflect reasonably well the field as a whole, I shall use it as the focus for the present section.

A most compelling virtue of *Theory of Collective Behavior* is the recognition that people can be mobilized in large numbers for purposes that in part transcend their narrow self-interests and are related to some enlarged sense of societal need. Moreover, Smelser does not presuppose, as Dawson and Gettys and other earlier theorists tended to, that social movements as they mature tend inevitably toward ossification, rigidity, and bureaucracy. Movements not infrequently manage to resist this pathology, especially when the external environment is sufficiently acquiescent and when the leadership is flexible and innovative. Moreover, the notion that material stakes inevitably underlie group effort in politics is alien to Smelser.

In the second place, he makes clear that core organizations, while vital in providing a needed coherence and focus, are by no means all that matter in

terms of a social movement's political influence and potential. He maintains
that the mass of movement adherents—including both fellow travelers and
dues-paying, rank-and-file members—typically remain a significant force as
an influence on the top leaders. Smelser intimates, without using this
language, that it is precisely the ongoing interaction between the mass of
followers and the leaders that essentially distinguishes a movement organization from a typical pressure group with its characteristic "caucus" structure.[19] And as long as the fellow travelers and the rank and file retain this
influence the core structure is not likely to congeal into a vehicle for the
leaders' pursuit of narrowly personal aims and ambitions.

Despite the book's virtues, however, *Theory of Collective Behavior* has
come in for sharp criticism by some sociologists; it is a controversial work,
and arguments over its relative merit were still capable of dominating the
discussion in a social-movements panel discussion at a convention of social
scientists in 1974. Of the several lines of criticism that have been advanced, I
regard two as both cogent and pertinent in the present context.[20] In the first
place, Smelser makes use of a basic definition of "collective behavior" that
seems strained and far-fetched. For him the belief system which guides
collective behavior involves the "existence of extraordinary forces—threats,
conspiracies, etc.—which are at work in the Universe."[21] These beliefs,
involving both exceptional causes and exceptional consequences, lead to
behavior that "short-circuits" normal channels and constitutes what are for
him the characteristic forms of collective behavior—"panics," "crazes,"
"hostile outbursts," and other erratic and impulsive forms of social action.[22]
It is axiomatic, given this definition, that rational and prudent individuals,
ones mindful of their immediate and long-term interests, would avoid
becoming involved in such behavior. But this definition poses problems
even within Smelser's own scheme of things, since toward the end of the
book, especially in the ninth chapter on "norm-oriented" social movements, he cites numerous cases of groups and individuals acting in a
nonerratic and apparently rational manner in pursuit of their goals.

Second, following from the notion that collective behavior is essentially
disruptive, discordant, and crazed, Smelser adopts the perspective that
presence in society of this behavior makes necessary its "control" or
"containing" or "handling" by public authorities and social control
agents.[23] His sympathies are ultimately with the managers in society and the
law and order forces, and he is not warmly responsive to whatever frustration
and sense of rage may give rise to a movement initially and carry it onward.
His analysis has the unfortunate effect of leading the reader's thinking away
from how social movements might more successfully gain their ends, and
instead toward how society should control them and check their political
consequences.

To conclude this discussion of how sociology and political science have treated political groups, it appears that the overemphasis in the interest group literature on material stakes and narrowly conceived organizational behavior can be offset if one takes account of purposive incentives and ongoing interactions between mass-movement adherents and movement leaders as discussed in the collective behavior literature. Conversely, the latter literature's tendency to overstate the elements of panic and impulsiveness among movement activists and to adopt an essentially managerial perspective can be countered through attention to the interest group literature's stress on group rationality, prudence, and change-oriented collective effort animated by a well-justified sense of grievance. All this has significant application to the matter of senior-citizen activism.

The national groups which have been at the focus of attention in this study—in particular AARP/NRTA, NCSC, and NCOA—have responded in part to their own internal dynamics and maintenance needs (to be treated in more detail in the following chapter) and in part to the larger senior movement of which they are important functioning elements. The senior movement did not altogether lose its spontaneous and impulsive aspects once it had passed beyond its "popular" phase in the 1950s. Instead, like the lava of some brooding volcano, movement adherents—many of them not formally affiliated with any national old-age organization—have constituted a seething force, ready at any moment to erupt. Thus Commissioner on Aging Martin in 1969 and 1970 was startled by the number of elderly persons who poured forth to participate in state-level pre-White House Conference planning meetings—the number of such meetings eventually was many times larger than originally planned for. His experience was reminiscent of the time ten years previous when the McNamara Committee on Problems of the Aged and Aging found old people flooding in to voice their frustrations and anxieties in the course of the committee's hearings throughout the country. The emergence of the Gray Panthers and another new group, Senior Advocates International, in the early 1970s is testimony to the fact that even now the senior movement retains significant spontaneous elements.

The growth of the national old-age groups has been conditioned in part by their ability to respond to this continuing mass restlessness, a factor that has an obvious bearing on why senior leaders repeatedly voice dissatisfaction with what federal officials and lawmakers do in behalf of the elderly. The competition and rivalry among national senior groups is of sufficient consequence that none of them can afford to rest on their political oars. Moreover, significant numbers of constituents are prepared in crisis moments to lend their numerical strength to group lobbying efforts; since this potential exists, it increases the likelihood that senior leaders will make use of it.

Senior movement leaders appear to have gained widespread acceptance among constituents for both their diagnosis and their programmatic suggestions for achieving amelioration of old-age suffering. Implicit in most statements of purpose has been the notion that the evil to be attacked and overcome is a set of societal attitudes whose effect is to place old people at a severe disadvantage.[24] It is a structured predisposition that is objected to, and one which prevails not only among younger persons afflicted with "gerontophobia" but also a fair proportion of those over age sixty-five, in whom it takes the form of self-abnegation and occasionally even self-hate. This is not a case of simple prejudice, since the attitudes have found their way into societal structures and mores such as compulsory retirement ages and arbitrary cut-off ages in deciding insurance eligibility. "Institutionalized agism" seems a proper term for it. Whatever their differences on other matters, the leading senior organizations have been at one in objecting to such discriminatory patterns and in demanding corrective governmental action.

If the social movement literature demonstrates anything, it is that such collective efforts often do not succeed in realizing their stated goals. Many factors are involved in the case of failure, but one important factor is a lack of tactical flexibility resulting from doctrinaire adherence to a predefined program or ideology. Following the collapse of the ill-fated Townsend movement of the thirties, the emergence of what was to become the modern senior movement easily could have fallen victim to political palliatives and quixotic nostrums. Instead, it seems to have profited from the Townsend experience and managed to keep long-term goals in mind while casting about for effective political instruments for the immediate combat. Some in the fifties focused their energies at the state level; others found in John F. Kennedy a presidential aspirant whose policies and goals they could identify with; still others sought initially to avoid identification with governmental solutions and seek improvement in the elderly's status through private voluntarism. The specific results of all this diverse activity are not easy to assess, but it is clear enough that the general outcome was a gradual coalescence around a set of goals which national opinion leaders—leading politicians included—found attractive and could support.

This final point is quite important, since the senior movment probably could not have sustained its moderate and reformist character had public opinion at any point crystallized against it. The literature on social movements is fairly consistent in showing that, unless the agents of social control are to some extent receptive and responsive, a social movement is likely either to collapse out of sheer frustration or to veer off in the direction of political extremism. Francis E. Townsend did this when he joined a far-right third party effort in the 1936 election, and it is interesting that this occurred after leading politicians (including President Roosevelt) earlier had refused to meet with him or seriously consider his "plan."

As was brought out in the chapter on old-age politicization and later on when discussing the 1972 Social Security amendments, senior-citizen leaders have managed to achieve increasing levels of generalized acceptance in Washington. This has come about because their constituents have a well-documented basis for making claims on society and because the leaders have learned to present their case in a manner appealing to politicians. Congressmen and senators need specialized, technical information as a basis for legislation—senior groups stand ready to provide it; lawmakers want reassurance that by responding positively to the elderly other articulate groups will not charge that their needs have been ignored—senior-group leaders can help them weigh the political costs and rationalize a positive posture; politicians want to be reelected—old-age associations, though not able to deliver votes or participate directly in campaigns, do have access to a large home-district reading audience, and a favorable personal reference in one of their house organs presumably can make a decided impression on an election-conscious lawmaker.

The emphasis in this chapter has been on the senior movement in its entirety. In the chapter to follow, I shall present some final thoughts on a crucial aspect of movement life, namely its core organizations.

14 Senior Movement Core Organizations: Concluding Commentary

By dealing at length in the preceding chapter with the collective behavior literature, I have given prominence to the fact that purposive incentives, which are centrally important in all social movements, have been a primary source of senior-citizen cohesiveness. It is my contention that the senior movement has gained adherents largely because millions of aging persons have come to identify with its objectives and are prepared to make sacrifices, material and otherwise, in furtherance of its ends. In the vocabulary of economic theory its leaders have succeeded in attracting followers in part by offering a range of "public goods"—mainly consisting in a concerted effort to achieve expanded governmental benefits and protections which are of sufficient magnitude in the "utility function" of many retirees to justify their attending rallies, paying dues, and otherwise foregoing alternative consumption and expressive possibilities.

Yet, while admitting the importance of public goods as an inducement, one should not assume that essentially "private goods," meaning ones that can be enjoyed and consumed by senior citizens individually without regard to wider social benefit or purpose, have been irrelevant or unimportant to the movement. And there is reason to suspect that private goods are of considerable importance in accounting for the origins and growth of the senior movement's major core organizations—in particular for such mass-membership groups as AARP and NCSC and, more indirectly, for groups like NCOA, which are nominally composed of specialists in the field but also are responsive to wider constituencies. While core organizations are not by any means all there is to a social movement, they are typically its central focus. In the words of political scientist Jo Freeman:

> . . . . [the] core groups of a movement not only determine much of its conscious polity but serve as foci for its values and activities. Just as it has been argued that society as a whole has a cultural and structural "center" about which most members of the society are more or less "peripheral," so too a social movement can be conceived of as having a center and a periphery.[1]

Considering the importance of core organizations, it is worthwhile to devote attention in this chapter to their role in the senior movement, building on the empirical data presented in Chapter 7 and making use of a more rigorous theoretical model. The distinction between public and private goods, derived from the field of economics, will serve as the point of departure.

The most distinguished application of the public goods/private goods literature to the understanding of political interest groups is Mancur Olson, Jr.'s work, *The Logic of Collective Action*. David B. Truman, a leading student of group behavior and one who is not given to exaggeration, avers that the work is "perhaps the most suggestive contribution at the abstract level [in recent years]" and one containing insights both "numerous and valuable."[2] In the course of his analysis Olson presented a convincing argument that much otherwise puzzling political involvement among business, labor, and professional associations and other groups grounded primarily on material incentives can be accounted for on the basis of his general theory of groups.

Olson also maintained, though on this point his supporting case material was decidedly meager, that his theory could be applied with similarly successful results to reform groups, social movements, and other such associations where purposive incentives are a major factor.[3] Olson was working on the premise that most individuals, at least those who are prudent and self-regarding, would not be so "irrational" as to support an organization from which they derived no direct, tangible benefit, even assuming that they identified with its social goals. Movement organizations, catering in many cases to the needs of the marginally influential in society, are normally unable to offer the material incentives that may be available in abundance to groups composed of the affluent. Olson implies that in the former case some private-regarding and self-interested motive other than money may be at work, but he provides only a vague notion of what this might consist of concretely.[4]

The apparent reason for Olson's failure to develop at more depth his theory's implications for noneconomic groups is that, as an economist schooled in the classical tradition, he is most comfortable in analyzing behavior which is reducible to rational monetary calculations. "The theories developed in this study," he remarked, "thus appear to account for the main *economic* pressure groups" (emphasis added).[5] This cast of mind led him into two closely related misconceptions. The first, involving an overemphasis on economic motives, is answered by James Q. Wilson: "not all or perhaps most members of an economic association join for economic (i.e. money seeking) reasons and for many who do join the cost of membership in dues will exceed any material gain they receive."[6] Purposive and solidary incentives, in other words, are often significant even among groups whose manifest goals are material in character, and these incentives are probably primary in the case of movement organizations like the National Farmers Union, whose existence Olson seeks to account for on a rational, income-maximizing basis.[7]

Secondly, Olson is not entirely persuasive in his insistence on a sharp distinction between small groups, where nonmonetary motives are seen as the primary basis for member involvement, and large groups, where in his view only a private benefit ("selective incentive") will cause a rational person to voluntarily contribute. It has been demonstrated recently that even in large voluntary groups social pressures are not necessarily diluted to the point of impotence and may even be pervasive. Given the importance of "reference individuals" and "opinion leaders"—a factor ignored by Olson—social pressures often can be maintained even as group size increases.[8] In a utility model, then, revised so as to account for the importance of altruistic behavior stimulated by one's identification with a reference group, the question of whether the rational individual will pay dues to and otherwise support a voluntary organization becomes one of probabilities, not certainty. Given certain conditions, it may well be rational for him to do so. A somewhat similar objection to Olson's analysis is presented by James Q. Wilson, but I am less persuaded than Wilson that the difficulty involved here requires that one throw out economic models altogether.[9] For these reasons, I propose to adopt such a modified utility model in the present chapter.[10]

As noted previously, the leading old-age membership groups have offered—in addition to public goods—a range of private benefits attractive to members. Some of these have an obvious monetary value, while others are private benefits in which a monetary value can be arrived at only indirectly. Benefits of the former type are everywhere apparent among the groups in question. The leading case would appear to be AARP, which has made available to members a seemingly endless array of insurance plans, cut-rate prescription drugs, travel programs, retirement planning institutes, and so forth—all offered at prices which are competitive, or can be made to appear competitive, with their "free market" (that is, nonmembership related) counterparts. Other national aging groups also make private benefits available, some in a wide assortment, others on a more limited basis. Even among those groups whose only significant private good is the association's monthly house organ—distributed "free" to members while denied to nonmembers—there is an obvious value involved; such publications typically contain at least as much worthwhile information as do general-circulation magazines sold at a newstand for fifty cents or a dollar.

The range of inducements offered by associational leaders also includes a variety of other, less obvious, private items. There are decals, posters, and pins which are prepared by the national headquarters and passed out "free" to members. (The 1971 tenth-anniversary NCSC convention, for example, was awash with "Senior Power" medallions and lapel pins.) In addition, the leaders and staff endeavor within limits to assist elderly constituents with their personal finances, their role in this regard often becoming especially significant when the problem relates to some federal retiree-benefit, on which the national association is likely to be well informed and in a position to wield some influence. As noted in Chapter 7, NARFE executives concern themselves with casework arising under the Federal Employees Retirement Act; similarly, staff personnel in several other aging organizations from time to time assist constituents with problems relating to Social Security, SSI and other kinds of old-age benefits. Also in the category of associational benefits with a calculable market value are chartered buses in which elderly persons at bargain rates are enabled to attend rallies and political caucuses in which the national association has taken an interest. And the list of such benefits could be extended.

Important as such monetarily calculable items as these are in the lives of senior-movement organizations, they by no means exhaust the range of private benefits offered. There are other inducements of an essentially nonmonetary variety. One of these is the ability of the national association to relieve constituents of what otherwise might be distressing and uncomfortable social pressure. The general principle is that, if a potential contributor to a voluntary association feels he will suffer the disapproval of others when he doesn't contribute and this disapproval causes him a utility loss, then there will be a cost (tax) to him of noncontributing; conversely, if he does contribute, he may expect approval if he is known to give, and, assuming that the approval of others gives him satisfaction, this may amount to a positive incentive.[11]

While they have not formulated the matter in these abstract terms, the leaders of the senior-citizen core organizations have adopted this as an operative principle. Throughout the thirteen-year existence of NCSC its executives have stressed the importance of maintaining and fostering the three thousand affiliated retiree clubs throughout the country. Club news is given prominence in *Senior Citizen News*, and both the current and past executive directors, William Hutton and Blue Carstenson, respectively, have regarded healthy clubs as essential to the survival and well-being of the national association. Other national senior organizations have similarly worked to foster a grass-roots structure—regional and local affiliates in the case of AARP and NARFE, senior centers in the case of NCOA, regional research and training centers in the case of the Gerontological Society, and so forth. Evidently, an important function of all such local structures has been that of fostering face-to-face relationships among dues-paying national members and between members and potential members now in the "fellow traveler" category. It is a plausible hypothesis that these personal relationships have been a significant factor in the substantial enlargement in national associational memberships that has been a distinctive feature of recent years; current members have been reinforced in their loyalty to the national association, and the proportion of "free riders," who benefit from associational activity while avoiding commitment, has been held to a minimum.

The state and local affiliates also give additional strength to the national association by helping to reward those persons who stand out by their depth of commitment and their contribution to leadership. The possibility that one might be elected to some high office in a local or regional chapter, an office carrying honor and prestige and few additional burdens, may serve as an inducement to faithful, imaginative, and dedicated service. An association organized only at the national level can offer but a small number of such private nonmonetary incentives, whereas associations with extensive grass-roots structures may offer them to substantial numbers of persons.[12]

Considering the apparent importance of private incentives—both material and nonmaterial—to the senior movement, it is an interesting question why private, for-profit firms do not enter the "market" in significant numbers and attempt to offer the "goods" at a more competitive price. (A recently founded, for-profit organization, Senior Advocates International, Inc., led by William C. Fitch, is in essence testing the validity of this proposition, but its survival over a long period has yet to be proved.) It might be imagined that profit-oriented firms would be at an advantage in such competition since they (unlike nonprofit movement organizations) presumably would not be obliged to divert scarce resources into expensive lobbying campaigns aimed at realizing public benefits. How, then, is one to account for the virtual absence of such firms from the field? It would appear that an answer is to be found in the substantial competitive advantage enjoyed by the existing, nonprofit senior organizations on both their supply and demand sides.

On the supply side several factors serve to increase prohibitively the costs incurred by for-profit firms relative to those of the nonprofit type: (1) the fact that nonprofit associations enjoy tax exemption on income generated by the sale of any private goods which are directly related to their educational and philanthropic purposes (in the case of the aging associations this exemption includes virtually all their operations); (2) as nonprofit institutions, the major aging organizations receive an indirect government subsidy in the form of lower postal rates for bulk solicitations; (3) an additional subsidy exists in the form of reduced rates charged nonprofit institutions for radio and TV advertising—local TV stations, for example, frequently run AARP advertisements as public service announcements.

Other advantages accrue to the nonprofit association on the demand side. Among these are (1) donations made to them are exempt from the donor's personal income tax, and this effectively lowers the after-tax price the donor faces in considering nonprofit vs. for-profit output of identical goods; (2) there is a higher demand for the output of nonprofit organizations, resulting from the popular tendency to be suspicious of the profit motive, identifying it with "rip-offs," "profiteering," "pocket-padding," and the like. The advantage enjoyed by nonprofit firms in this respect is probably especially impressive for large national associations, such as AARP and NCSC, which rely heavily on the mails to advertise and supply goods to members, and where alternative sources of objective information about the organization are not generally accessible. While it is true that the reputations of some nonprofit organizations (not in the aging area, but elsewhere) have come under suspicion, the general effect of their nonprofit legal status is still, on balance, to enhance their general respectability.

What the above adds up to is a general explanation for the remarkable growth of national senior-citizen organizations in the past several years, most obviously in the case of AARP/NRTA, but also with NCSC, NCOA, and others. By identifying positively with growing reformist sentiment among the elderly, these groups have tapped a reservoir of purposive sentiment and willingness to take collective action. The fact that the groups are all legally nonprofit organizations and have grass-roots affiliates where a sense of solidarity can be engendered has enhanced their appeal to prospective members. As the groups have gained legitimacy in the eyes of members and of fellow travelers, their packages of optional benefits have come to seem even more attractive, and the sale of these to members has helped produce surpluses in organizational treasuries from which they can finance, among other things, expanded recruiting drives.

Indeed, the goods offered for sale to members have figured so prominently in the growth of these organizations, especially in the AARP case, that some analysts would single out this aspect for central emphasis. One must take this view seriously even if, finally, it seems best not to accept it. The position of these observers is that senior-citizen organizations are properly regarded not as core units of a social movement, not as committed to larger social goals, and not as purposive in any genuine sense; but as business firms seeking to make a "profit" or, to be more precise (since one is dealing here with legally nonprofit organizations), a "surplus." Those who espouse this view point to the fact that from time to time AARP uses its identification with senior-citizen uplift so as to gain access to potential new members and otherwise unavailable income sources. Heads of corporations, for example, are commonly asked if they would like AARP to come in and give their soon-to-retire employees a guidance course on retirement problems and options; many executives have agreed willingly, the courses being free of charge to the firm and generally popular among interested employees. There is an obvious payoff for AARP in this, since the courses permit its representatives to outline the benefits of AARP membership and to distribute educational and propaganda materials. They make the case for the wide-ranging AARP benefit package, though presumably they do not mention the opinion of several independent analysts that more adequate benefits, at lower prices, frequently are available on the open market.[13] Another point used in support of the contention that profit lies at the root of all that AARP undertakes is the fact that Leonard Davis, the organization's co-founder, has become personally wealthy in the course of his long association with the group.

Insofar as this view calls attention to a certain ambiguity in AARP involvement in the senior movement, it seems a useful corrective. Yet, I do not accept it as a valid general perspective, for the reason that it fails to account convincingly for much of the behavior of AARP leaders. Much of what these leaders do, while seemingly irrational and pointless from the standpoint of organizational profit, is entirely comprehensible when viewed as a manifestation of purposive goals. An essentially profit-motivated organization, for example, would scarcely commit significant resources to lobbying for broadly encompassing ends like national health insurance, public transit subsidies for the elderly, the extension of the Older Americans Act, and other programs whose beneficiaries would include large numbers of persons who are not dues-paying AARP members. Nor is it consistent with the view mentioned that a number of AARP activists whom the author has conversed with stress the importance for them of the organization's larger social purposes and their feelings of solidarity with other activists. If these people are really in it for reasons of economic gain—"a piece of the pie," so to speak—they manage to convey no indication whatever of that.

If my argument is correct that a sense of purposiveness is fundamental to most recent senior-citizen groups, it follows that any decline that might occur in the members' zeal for reform would have major organizational consequences. Quite possibly, such a change already is under way. Perhaps the aging organization's very success in achieving protective legislation and in increasing general public awareness of old-age needs may have disruptive organizational consequences. As Meyer Zald and Robert Ash have suggested is the case with social movements generally, complete success constitutes a threat to a movement no less serious than the opposite danger of having its demands totally rejected by society; either event may be the occasion for rank-and-file disillusionment and apathy. A perfectly stable organization, they remark, would be one which, among other things, always seems to be getting closer to its goals without quite attaining them.[14]

There have been several instances among the groups considered in this work in which complete success served to generate organizational problems. In the case of two groups active in the 1930s, the AALL and AASS, it has been noted that the passage of the Social Security Act—which both groups were identified with, even if their leaders did not approve all of its provisions—made it possible for many present and potential supporters to conclude that further contributions were unnecessary. Though Abraham Epstein had managed on an earlier occasion (1933) to reorient both the goals and the name of his organization so as to take account of legislative successes, he seemed unable to do so a second time in 1935. Epstein expressed vehement dissatisfaction with the Social Security Act in its initial form, but his anxiety and sense of concern seemed an insufficient antidote to growing rank-and-file apathy, and at the time of his death in the early 1940s AASS was already in a state of serious decline. The fate of AALL followed a similar downward course, though its demise (more so than with AASS) probably reflected the success of the whole New Deal package of which Social Security was but a part.

In 1965 the National Council of Senior Citizens was faced with a comparable problem, but in this case its leaders were able to come up with a solution. Although the organization had been initially created to mobilize support for a hospital-care-for-the-aged program to be financed through Social Security, the authoritative acceptance of this principle as embodied in the 1965 Medicare legislation had the effect of rendering this objective obsolete. Rather than allow the organization to pass out of existence, NCSC leaders proposed to enlarge the scope of their goals so as to include a broad range of old-age legislative concerns, and the question then became whether the proposal would gain constituency acceptance. In commenting on movement organizations facing the "success" problem, Zald and Ash suggest that "if the movement organization has its own member and fund-raising support base and if there are solidary or short-run material incentives that bind members to each other and to the organization," then leaders may be able to deal with the problem effectively.[15] NCSC seems to have fulfilled both these conditions. On the first point, by the time Medicare passed Congress NCSC had an inclusive, mass-membership structure built upon numerous senior-citizen clubs and local chapters one of whose purposes was to raise money. Also, the leaders of the nation's larger industrial unions had become a major source of financial support, and the purposes for which these union donations were made in no way were inconsistent with the proposed goal-redefinition. On the second point, while it is true that purposive incentives implicit in the Medicare crusade had served as the professed or manifest reason for NCSC's existence at the outset, there had also arisen other types of incentives whose effect was to glue the organization into a cohesive whole. As suggested above, nonmonetary, private incentives offered by the leaders and actively desired by members appear to have been important. As a consequence NCSC was in a position not only to survive the redefinition but to prosper as never before in its history.

A full decade has now elapsed since Medicare, and in a strictly legislative sense the period has been one of many victories and only a handful of genuine setbacks, and this has implications for all national aging associations, NCSC included. While the aging remain a disadvantaged group in American society, a broad range of protective legislation has come into existence which, if adequately funded and fully implemented, would substantially alleviate their distress. The possibility cannot be excluded that

the ultimate effect may be a sense of apathy among rank-and-file constituents and a feeling among the more politically acute among them that
whatever legislative breakthroughs are yet to come will occur, not on the
basis of a continued "old age" focus, but by piecing together a new
coalition of reform forces aimed at some more inclusive concern, for
example, universal health-care protection. If this were to occur, it might not
endanger the survival of the aging organizations as such (at least not in the
short run), but it nevertheless might mark the end of their status as the
vanguard of a social movement and have adverse consequences for the sense
of élan and commitment among constituents.

In summary, senior-movement organizations have managed to survive
and prosper for much the same reason that allows for the survival of many
charities which rely on philanthropic outlays from business firms. In neither
case are considerations of monetary gain entirely absent from the thinking of
the supporting donor. But in their efforts to maximize utility, both dues-
paying senior-group members in the former case and donating firms in the
latter also respond to altruistic motives, as made salient in their behavior by
social pressure, by the need for social acceptance, and by desire for approval
from reference-group individuals. The willingness of people to heed appeals
to their altruism is strongly conditioned by the general opinion climate, and
thus changes in that climate are likely to have wide organizational ramifi-
cations.

15 The Old-Age Policy System

On the basis of evidence presented in the main body of this work and in the light of other analysts' findings, there appears to be compelling evidence that an old-age policy system has come into existence in national government. The participants in this triangular alliance—appointive officials in the executive branch, committee and subcommittee leaders in Congress, and leaders of the major clientele groups in the aging field—deal with one another not only through formal, structured channels but also on a regular and informal basis. These ongoing relationships are significant at all stages of the policy process—formulation, initiation, decision-making, and legitimation. The system, of course, is not wholly self-contained and autonomous, since from time to time key decisions affecting it are made by "outside" actors, such as the president or presidential aides. But on all matters of routine importance—and this inlcudes a broad range of issues— the system functions relatively autonomously as a "subgovernment," having broad powers within its domain.

The existence of this subgovernment was first noted by political scientist Dale Vinyard in a paper which addressed itself primarily to one facet of the system, the Senate Special Committee on the Aging. While Vinyard did not undertake to define the precise limits and extent of this system of power, he left no doubt of its existence and of the identity of its core elements, comprising (in addition to the Special Committee) key appropriation and substantive subcommittees in the House, the Administration on Aging in HEW and other executive units administering special programs for the aged, and various professionals in the field identified with social welfare agencies, universities, and institutes. With regard to the role of major clientele associations, Vinyard expressed some uncertainty as to their extent of participation. While remarking on the one hand that groups like NCSC "are also involved," he went on to comment that "groups of and for the aged have been slow to develop . . . [and] they generally do not have the degree of cohesion or power often found in other interest groups . . . . in this [aging] area interest groups are generally weaker than in other policy systems."[1] Since Vinyard's remarks on the extent of interest-group involvement have a direct bearing on the overall thesis of the present work, I shall consider them in more detail later on. For the moment, it is sufficient to note the existence of a policy system and the fact that it is one from which clientele groups are by no means excluded.

What then, is the scope or domain of this system? What are the payoffs accruing to its various participants? What is its probable future, assuming the continuance of important societal trends bearing on the aging? How is one to evaluate the system normatively in terms of some larger conception of the public interest? It seems appropriate that this final chapter should address itself to these issues.

Scope and Substance of the Subsystem

While the analyst can identify with some confidence the central actors in the aging policy system, it is by no means an easy task to establish criteria by which to delimit its outer boundaries. Though one could make a plausible argument that the system includes all of the score or more federal agencies with special programs for the aging alluded to in Chapter 12, as well as the entire memberships of such major congressional standing committees as the House Appropriations Committee and the Senate Finance Committee, to do so would be to introduce an element of unreality. Granted that any decision as to what to include and to exclude will necessarily contain an arbitrary element, it would seem wise to exclude those actors whose role in decision-making is only episodic, and to include only those who are self-conscious about the aging as a societal grouping and who are involved on a fairly regular formal and informal basis in decision-making. I have decided to exclude the House Select Committee on Aging in the following enumeration since its exact role is yet to be defined clearly.

The evidence leads one to suspect that what appears at first glance to be a single aging policy system, can more usefully be regarded as two, and perhaps three, semiautonomous subsystems, each with a particular substantive focus and membership. In the first place there is what may be termed the "income and health maintenance" system, whose focus is on Social Security (OASI), Medicare, the Supplemental Security Income system (SSI), and other related programs concerned with guaranteeing minimal levels of security and income in old age. The actors in this system include: on the congressional side, the Ways and Means and the Commerce and Health committees in the House, key individuals in the Senate Finance Committee and the Senate Special Committee on Aging; in the executive branch, the Social Security Administration and the Commissioner on Aging; and among clientele groups, the National Council of Senior Citizens (especially Nelson Cruikshank, its president) and, to a lesser degree, AARP.

A second system might be labeled the "universal services" system. Here the focus is more on governmental services in kind and includes such

programs as Foster Grandparents, RSVP, Meals-on-Wheels, and programs
under Title III of the Older Americans Act. The participants include, on the
congressional side, the Senate Special Committee on Aging, the Subcommittee on Aging of the Senate Committee on Labor and Public Welfare (these
two bodies having a high degree of overlapping membership), the Special
Education Subcommittee of the House Education and Labor Committee; in
the executive branch, the Administration on Aging and ACTION, which
have operating responsibility in these areas; and among clientele groups,
AARP and NCOA. (NCSC generally has manifested a lesser level of concern
with these programs than has characterized its interest in income maintenance). When matters of particular relevance to them arise, the participants
also presumably include spokesmen for the National Association of State
Units on Aging (NASUA), the Gerontological Society, the four leading trade
associations, and the National Caucus on the Black Aging, though with
regard to such involvement data are lacking.

A third system, which I shall designate the "older workers manpower
system," has as its focus the need to train able-bodied workers over age fifty
for available jobs and to protect others already employed. In the executive
branch the operating agency in this area is the Operation Mainstream
Program of the Department of Labor; the congressional participants include
the General Subcommittee on Labor of the House Education and Labor
Committee, the Subcommittee on Labor-HEW Appropriations of the
Senate Appropriations Committee. The interest-group participants include
all those with Labor Department contracts—the National Farmers Union,
which runs the so-called "Green Thumb" and "Green Light" programs for
older farmers, the National Council on the Aging, the National Retired
Teachers Association, NCSC, NASUA, and the Gerontological Society. The
combined dollar amount for these contracts in the fiscal year 1972 was in
excess of $21 million.[2]

Though other federal agencies and committees of Congress do from time to
time address the specialized needs of senior citizens as one category within
their larger clienteles (for example, the housing affairs "subgovernment"
occasionally does so), it seems inappropriate to include such cases within the
scope of the definition. Yet, the very fact that HUD and numerous other
agencies and congressional committees do have a pronounced senior-citizen
impact serves to call attention to a fundamental fact conditioning senior-
citizen groups and other old-age spokesmen in Washington, namely, that
with few exceptions the major cabinet departments as well as bureaus within
departments are organized along functional rather than clientele lines. This
functional pattern is an important factor in the existence of the three
subsystems mentioned above. The organization of both legislative and
executive branches of government along functional lines virtually assures a
lack of clear focus on aging and tends to frustrate even rather modest efforts
at interagency coordination.[3]

There are, admittedly, exceptions to the general pattern of functionally organized federal Agencies, most notably embodied in the Department of Labor, Agriculture, and Commerce, all of which are organized along clientele lines. Though the spokesmen for senior citizens from time to time have contemplated the creation of an agency, either autonomous or within HEW, which would similarly bring together all or most age-related programs in the executive branch, it seems highly unlikely that any such sweeping reorganization will occur. The existing clientele-based departments and agencies at their outset invariably represented accommodations to forces in society which were sufficiently cohesive and militant as to demand "recognition" from policymakers. And while the aging have increased in political visibility in recent years, they seem far from having achieved the kind of leverage which inheres in organized business, labor, and agriculture in the United States, a leverage which at one time served to justify an exception to the general practice of functionalism.

Payoffs

In arguing that senior-citizen spokesmen often are frustrated and confused by efforts to wield political influence, I do not mean to imply any real possibility of their choosing to withdraw from public policy involvement. One must bear in mind the payoffs which are present. Such involvement among other things serves to confer status and legitimacy on nongovernmental actors. In modern industrial societies government fulfills an integrating and regulating function, both for the society as a whole and for various population groupings within it, and senior-citizen leaders, by identifying with public authority, are enabled better to regularize the internal affairs of their associations and reduce what is from their standpoint potentially disruptive factionalism. On the other hand, of course, the leaders of insurgent factions within the various associations may correspondingly come to resent what they construe as unwarranted efforts to cloak the established leaders with the mantle of majesty and respectability.

Involvement with government also helps voluntary associations to increase the supply of private goods with which to reward supporters and, by withholding them, to punish nonsupporters. A wealthy organization like AARP may have such a large fund of internally generated incentives that a government contract—even one of substantial amount—may have little consequence as a source of monetary incentives. Yet, this is probably not true of most national aging groups. A particularly impressive case was noted in Chapter 8, where it was seen that NCOA, as a result of a government contract signed in the middle-1960s, was able to realize a substantial increase in its annual budget. I have no in-depth information as to how these various contracts have affected the internal life of the organizations in question, but it is a plausible hypothesis that the effect has been substantial.

While the primary effect of such federal funding presumably has been an enlargement of material incentives, it may also have the incidental effect of increasing the fund of nonmaterial ones as well—a sense of camaraderie, for example.

In any arrangement involving obvious payoffs to one party in a transaction, one can anticipate corresponding benefits for the others—assuming, that is, that all parties choose to continue their relationship. Federal officials and lawmakers would appear to have major incentives to draw upon the resources that are uniquely available from nongovernmental groups and individuals. In Chapter Six, under the heading "Elements of Old-Age Political Access," it was noted that nongovernmental groups are in a position to provide specialized knowledge and information to lawmakers and public officials, among whom expertise is rare in the social gerontology field. Even though the Department of Health, Education, and Welfare has trained personnel on its staff and the resources to contract with outside consultants, there often have been times when specialized studies prepared under the auspices of AARP, the Gerontological Society, or NCSC has been read with obvious interest by policymakers, and reflected in major decisions. It is difficult to place a dollar value on such research, but presumably it is substantial.

By allowing the recognized spokesmen for senior citizens into the policy process, lawmakers and officials also help to legitimate actions which otherwise might be vulnerable to attack as cases of alleged political posturing or demagoguery. It was not by accident, for example, that in justifying their vote in favor of the allegedly "inflationary" Social Security increases of 1972 a number of congressmen and senators alluded specifically to the demands of national senior-citizen groups. Similarly, it may well have been a factor in President Nixon's thinking that the compromise Older Americans Amendments proposal which was thrust into his hand by Congressman Waggoner had the explicit endorsement of the 6 million-strong AARP.

Partnership Status for the Clientele Groups

Earlier in this chapter I referred several times to the major senior-citizen clientele groups in a context implying their full acceptance as partners in a policy process. While this view does not exactly contradict Dale Vinyard's view that was mentioned earlier, there is at least some tension between what I have been saying and his picture of these groups as relatively weak and of low cohesion. Before proceeding further, it therefore seems important to inquire further into this.

Although his initial paper was presented at a conference early in 1972, the interviews on which Vinyard drew in reaching his conclusion, as reported in a recent personal conversation, were conducted roughly two years previous, in 1970. Bearing in mind the dates, it would appear that his argument may not contradict my own, since I too have argued that prior to the 1971 White House Conference the major old-age mass-membership groups were only episodically involved in the policy process. Though the circumstances varied from one group to another, the basic reason for such lack of involvement at that time seems to be that they had yet to complete the task of basic organizational construction and were thus without the needed "profits" and "surpluses" that Robert Salisbury has suggested are often a necessary prerequisite to sustained group lobbying activity.[4] Lacking the necessary surpluses, even a relatively politicized group like NCSC had experienced difficulty in achieving genuine political effectiveness.

Yet, in a prescient passage, Vinyard remarked that at the time of his interviews the situation regarding interest groups was "uncertain," and he ventured the suggestion that with greater group consciousness more powerful organizations of and for the aged well might develop. In the roughly four years that have intervened between Vinyard's interviews and the present writing, it would seem that just such a development has occurred. The data presented in Chapters 9, 10, and 11 of this work lend considerable support to Binstock's recent assessment that, "in the classic pattern of American interest group politics, public officials and other politicians [now] feel it incumbent upon them to invite these groups to participate in most policy activities relating to aging."[5]

It would seem that the 1971 White House Conference marked a watershed in terms of old-age associational involvement. Although in the long run the aging groups might have achieved increased political stature even in its absence, the conference was significant in at least three ways. First, it provided a forum so conducive to interest-group involvement that even the most narrowly focused and apolitical among them (for example, NARFE) were obliged to give attention to broadly defined needs. Groups like AARP and NCOA whose earlier political objectives may have been somewhat indistinct now were obliged to clarify their policy objectives and give greater attention to implementation. Second, the conference heightened the level of general old-age awareness in high official circles, both in Congress and in the executive branch, and as a consequence interest-group leaders gained increased confidence that in approaching officials and lawmakers they would not likely be rebuffed. And third, the conference served to heighten retirees' awareness that national old-age associations were in existence and that support of such groups might have beneficial consequences both for the individual and for old people collectively. It was not an accident that in the period after the close of the conference the national mass-membership associations—already of substantial size—continued a growth in numbers.

Future of the System

Attempts at looking into the future are inevitably hazardous, especially when one's object of study is set in a fluid and dynamic environment. Yet, without venturing into the realm of sheer conjecture, one can seek to identify dominant environmental trends impinging on the aging and, by projecting the trends forward, to offer some predictions as to how things may unfold in the future. It seems reasonable to expect that four trends, already apparent in the past few years, will continue to exert a powerful influence on the attitudes, expectations, and behavior of decision-makers in the aging field:

—continued growth in the old-age population, both absolutely and relatively, with the effects of this change being potentially quite pro- nounced after the year 2000 and more modest in the decades prior to that;
—persistence of the trend toward increased self-consciousness of the aging as a collective grouping, although without elimination of the divisions along racial, social class, partisan, sectional, and other lines.
—continued viability of the senior movement as a social entity, with large mass participation and reasonably cohesive ''core'' organizations, and further expansion in the number of professionals in social gerontology and related fields who likewise will cluster into national voluntary associations with social policy goals;
—continued generalized support among the younger, nonretiree population for the ''legitimate'' demands put forward in the name of old-age people, even though there may be taxpayer ''backlash'' over specific proposals, for example, continued increases in payroll taxes to finance enlarged Social Security benefits.

The first and most obvious consequence, assuming the continuation of these trends, is the likelihood of an enlargement in the scope of the aging policy system. Up to the present the participants in the policy system have focused their energies almost exclusively on issues which are manifestly of concern to senior citizens—enactment of the Older Americans Act, passage of Medicare, the Foster Grandparents Program, increased monetary benefits for the elderly. But with a continued growth in relative numbers, coinciding with increased cohesiveness, the spokesmen for the aging may well find that the doors of other decision-making centers in the federal government are opened to them—in agricultural policy, for example, or veterans' affairs.

In the second place, one can anticipate efforts on the part of presidents, governors, and mayors to at least loosen the grip of policy system participants on substantive policy affecting the aging within their respective governmental domains. Even in the years of its greatest cohesiveness, the national aging policy system has been resaonably responsive to White House initiatives; but, if the actions of the White House in the latter part of the Nixon era can be taken as indicative, the extent of presidential control on aging matters has not always been as great as that desired. As Charles J. Parrish has maintained in a recent paper, a basic appeal of revenue-sharing legislation was a desire of Republican policymakers to place sharp limits on the power of various policy systems in the federal government which were dominated (so it was believed) by holdover Democrats in the federal bureaucracy and by Democratic majorities in Congress. Parrish writes:

> these systems had come, by the beginning of the Nixon Administration, to be a major basis of support for the liberal policies of the national Democratic Party in the domestic policy arena. . . . The prospect of a broad revenue sharing approach which would hand over a large portion of the funds that had gone into the categorical grant system, could conjure up the image of the formerly powerful groups which have supported the expansion of social legislation for the past 40 years having to divide their efforts between 38,000 general purpose governments. . . . The import of this aspect of the New Federalism for the area of the aging is the same as for other policy areas. The national interest groups which have been important in the development and sustaining of the policy efforts which have helped expand the interest in the aging over the past years may well have more difficulty in the future finding the proper fulcrum for moving policy in one direction or another.[6]

At the present writing it is premature to say whether the enactment of the Older Americans Comprehensive Services Amendments of 1973, a statute which in essence applies the New Federalism approach to the field of aging, will have the consequences which presidential advisors apparently intended. The point is, however, that, assuming the correctness of the earlier prediction regarding an expansion of the aging policy system's scope, it cannot fail to have consequences for presidential mastery of the bureaucracy. Quite possibly, then, presidential efforts to "coordinate and control" the executive branch will be pitted against the policy system's determination to "maintain a proper aging focus" within the larger pattern of U.S. domestic policy.

Third, spokesmen for senior citizens in Washington can expect that high officials and members of Congress will become more openly skeptical than in prior years of claims that any one leader, or group of leaders, can validly speak for the nation's 20 million elderly persons, or any substantial fraction thereof. It has not always been made apparent in published accounts that major breakthroughs on the aging front have occurred typically as a result of coalitions between old-age representatives and the spokesmen for other constituencies (labor, the financially hard-pressed children and grandchildren of old people in need of medical care, and so on). Whatever may be the value of "senior power" as a rhetorical device, there can be no reasonable expectation that the elderly will become the autonomous, independent force in elective politics that any strict definition of the term would seem to imply. As I have intimated at a number of points, spokesmen for the aging have achieved their most impressive legislative results in circumstances where the balance of forces already leaned in their favor and they were able to capitalize on initial advantages. It is arguable, however, that such advantageous circumstances may not be so commonplace in the future; assuming this to be the case, appeals to "senior power" and unsupportable claims of mass rank-and-file support for a given policy proposal may have the result, not of increasing interest-group leverage, but of decreasing it.

Finally, within the old-age subgovernment itself, one can expect that the stature and influence of clientele group representatives will increase somewhat relative to the lawmakers and federal officials who are also members of the old-age policy system; clientele groups, it will be recalled, are by a number of years the most recent entrants into the system and as such their representatives have been junior in status to the others. (Nelson Cruikshank may be an exception to this generalization). Given turnover in personnel and a continuation of the already apparent pattern for key persons to shuttle about among various jobs within the system—from official posts to nongovernmental groups, and vice versa—this status differential will likely decline markedly. One consequence presumably will be that interest-group leaders, for the sake of institutionalizing their political access, will be obliged to yield up some of their former independence of action—a situation that is by no means without parallel in other policy arenas in Washington.

To summarize, it is quite likely that the next several years will see organized senior citizens becoming a more established part of an ongoing aging policy system, even though the dramatic policy changes which characterized the aging field in the sixties and early seventies will not likely recur. From time to time spokesmen for the elderly may try to wring concessions from budget-conscious lawmakers and officials by alleging support from a cohesive and militant constituency, but the response is likely to be skeptical. More and more the attitude among federal policymakers is likely to be that the problems of the elderly, instead of requiring a unique policy response, should be looked at as one set of problems among others—and not always of highest priority. Incremental change, not sweeping innovation, is the most probable course.

To repeat, I feel hesitant about offering any such predictions, since there are so many imponderables that could drastically alter the situation. Among the unknowns, one in particular—the matter of who will succeed Arthur S. Flemming as commissioner on aging—merits special attention. Since Flemming has passed seventy, his retirement can not be a long way off, though it is still conjectural when it will occur. Because the post of commissioner is central to the whole policy system, a choice of successor will have important repercussions for other system participants. Will the person chosen be of Flemming's commanding prestige, one who—like him—is temperamentally inclined to give ear to group requests and in a position administratively to act on many of them? Or will the successor be in the mold of Flemming's two predecessors—knowledgable professionals but political nonentities—who may elect to keep senior groups at a distance while building up their support elsewhere? The second of these possibilities seems the more likely. If it occurs, the aging organizations could be in for a difficult time. Flemming's extraordinary stature cannot be emphasized too strongly. One would have difficulty naming another subcabinet level official whose influence extended into the Oval Office of the White House and who has been in a position, as is reliably reported, to more than once head off a threatened veto by contacting the president directly. To the degree, therefore, that senior groups' policy-level stature has depended on Flemming's presence, a successor who was cast in a different mold—for example, William Bechill—would adversely affect it. Even under these circumstances, it seems improbable that the national groups would find themselves altogether frozen out. But, at minimum, their path toward increased legitimacy and access would be made more tortuous and uncertain.

A Normative Postscript

The purpose of this work will have been fulfilled if it succeeds in adequately depicting what has occurred and in offering reasoned explanations of major trends. It is in order, however, to venture at least tentatively into the treacherous realm of normative values and at least pose the fundamental question of whether the system described has any justification for existence. Can its existence be squared with some larger conception of the public interest?

In the political science literature one can find two conflicting responses to this issue. On the one hand are the views of Grant McConnell and Theodore Lowi, who in separate works warned of the dangers of essentially self-defined subgovernments having little real answerability to the formal elective representatives. "The underestimation of this pattern of power," McConnell writes, "is also partly a product of the cautious language used to describe it by scholars. 'Clientele relationships' (or even less happily 'clientelism'), the term usually applied to this phenomenon, not only confers an aura of professional respectability on the participants in these relationships; it also obscures the fact that they are power relationships.... When, under the guise of serving an ideal of democracy as the self-government of small units, the coercive power of public authority is given to these groups, their internal government becomes a matter of serious concern."[7] In a similar vein Lowi warns against the potentially corrupting influence of what he terms "interest group liberalism," in which clientele groups are welcomed into the policy process at the sacrifice of any larger or more encompassing conception of the public interest.[8]

Without directly contradicting the points expressed above, two other observers, David B. Truman and Harold Seidman, have addressed themselves to the dangers inherent when population groupings, broadly affected by public policy, fail to organize and gain access to the centers of decision-making. After alluding to the existence of "multiple power centers" in the federal government (his term for subgovernment), Seidman remarks that, "Effective functioning of the governmental machine requires a high degree of stability, uniformity, and awareness of the impact of new policies, regulations, and procedures on the affected public . . . [for example] if the Department of Health, Education and Welfare discarded all previous standards applicable to grants-in-aid, the public outcry against innovation would shake the Congress and the White House."[9] The regular gathering together of officials, lawmakers, and clientele group-leaders, in other words, may have positive consequences in terms of predictability, orderliness, and rationality. Truman worries over the widespread tendency for major publics in American society to remain alienated and unorganized and, by their silence, to convey a false sense of harmony and stability to decision-makers. In a society which not only affirms the rights of groups to organize in their own behalf but also is structured so as to respond readily, a group's failure to organize and to become politically involved becomes a fundamental public problem—in Truman's words the problem of "morbific publics."[10]

Any final sizing up of the aging policy system must remain tentative and subject to revision based on a longer view of things. The system as it currently functions seemingly avoids some of the most serious risks of "interest group liberalism" and "clientelism" by virtue of the fact that on the interest-group side what one confronts is not a handful of essentially narrowly focused and self-seeking "private" bodies but core organizations whose persistent tendency has been to enlarge the size of their constituencies and at the same time to welcome newly formed groups (for example, the recent National Caucus on the Black Aging) into their midst. One is dealing here with a set of groups similar to those which Theodore Lowi in a recent work referred to in a rather abstract, but highly suggestive, commentary; the very size and inclusiveness of such associations, he asserted, becomes a check against the pathologies of "clientelism."[11] Moreover, by opting for inclusive memberships drawn to them by purposive and solidary incentives, and while not seeking to wield coercive sanctions over members, the core organizations constituting the senior movement would seem for the most part to avoid the danger McConnell alluded to, namely, that "the conditions and qualifications of membership may exclude significant num-bers of people who are affected by the group's actions and the public regulations it influences."[12] If I am correct in these assumptions, then it would seem that on balance the senior-citizen policy system contributes decidedly more to the public interest than it threatens that interest.

Appendix

Statement by the Executives of Six National Organizations (Read to the Opening Session of the White House Conference on Aging, November 28, 1971)

Our members have invested substantial amounts of time and resources in the preparations for the White House Conference on Aging.

Their futures are linked in a very real way to what happens at the Conference and, above all, to what happens after the Conference.

It is our hope, therefore, that the discussions that take place and the conclusions that are reached will contribute to just one objective. That objective is: The enlistment of widespread support from all social, economic, religious and political groups in behalf of action programs that will make available to older persons increased resources, services and opportunities and that will remove existing inequities which ethnic and other minority groups have had to bear.

Our most serious problem is a lack of commitment to action in the field of aging within all of our social, economic, religious and political groups. The White House Conference must devote itself to this problem. We must not drive persons within these groups apart as they confront issues in the field of aging. Instead, we must seek a clear agreement on goals and a unity of purpose which is reflected by commitments from them to increase resources, services and opportunities for older persons and to remove existing inequities which ethnic and other minority groups have had to bear.

We join all who have planned this Conference in the desire to open it up to full, uninhibited discussion of issues even where there may be sharp differences of opinion. Any attempt to utilize the Conference for partisan political advantage will be a violation of the spirit which has permeated the planning of the Conference.

Statement of the Executives of Six National Organizations (Read to the Closing Session of the White House Conference on Aging, December 2, 1971)

In a message to the delegates at the opening of this Conference, we stated that it was our hope that the discussions and the conclusions reached would contribute to just one objective. That objective is: The enlistment of widespread support from all social, economic, religious, and political groups in behalf of action programs that will make available to older persons increased resources, services and opportunities and that will remove existing inequities which ethnic and other minority groups have had to bear.

We believe that the discussions and the conclusions reached by the delegates could set in motion forces that can lead to the achievement of this objective.

What is now required are commitments to action.

The Chairman has reviewed with us the plans for sending a communication to the national organizations that have participated in this Conference. We believe that an approach of this kind would help to provide an opportunity to make meaningful commitments for action. We also believe, however, that it should be made clear that participation by voluntary organizations in the Post-Conference Year can be meaningful only if there is commitment of substantial resources and leadership by government at all levels.

Our organizations will take advantage of this opportunity. We hope that hundreds of other organizations will do likewise.

In responding to this communication, we intend to underline the following points in connection with those specific Conference recommendations with which each of our organizations finds itself in agreement:

1. We will monitor on a continuous basis what is happening to those recommendations addressed to that public sector at all levels, but especially those which are addressed to the Federal Government, and will speak out in no uncertain terms when actions do not keep pace with rhetoric.
2. We wil do everything possible to develop strong political backing at all levels of government for such recommendations.
3. We will take seriously the recommendations addressed to the private sector and will make significant investments of time, energy and resources in order to implement them.

The Chairman advised us that he recognized the importance of commitments for action from the public sector to parallel those he is seeking from the private sector. He is going to urge public agencies at all levels to make their own commitments.

We are convinced that an immediate and vigorous effort is going to be made to determine just where we are in terms of a willingness on the part of public and private organizations to follow up on the White House Conference recommendations. We are convinced further that once this information is available, it will provide the basis for developing strategies for action—strategies that could produce unprecedented actions in behalf of older persons on the part of all segments of our society during the Post-Conference Year.

The millions of older persons we represent will be satisfied with nothing less. We are confident that the delegates to this Conference will be satisfied with nothing less.

Notes

Chapter 1

1. Edwin Dale, "The Security of Social Security, The Young Pay for the Old," *New York Times Magazine*, January 14, 1973, p. 8.

2. See "Federal Outlays in Aging, Fiscal Years 1967-72," *Facts and Figures on Older Americans,* no. 4, Administration on Aging of HEW (June 1971).

3. Dale Vinyard, "A Policy System for the Aged: Some Preliminary Observations," Paper delivered for the annual meeting of the Midwest Political Science Association, Chicago, April 27, 1974.

4. The phrase is Robert Binstock's, in "Interest Group Liberalism and the Politics of Aging," *The Gerontologist* 12, no. 3, pt. 1 (Autumn 1972): 265.

5. " 'Senior Power'—A Growing Force in Politics," *U.S. News and World Report*, May 24, 1971, p. 63; Barbara Isenberg, "Aging Increasingly Flex Their Political Muscle," *Wall Street Journal*, November 17, 1972, p. 1.

6. Bernard Berelson, "Democratic Theory and Public Opinion," *Public Opinion Quarterly* 16 (1952); Bernard Berelson et al., *Voting* (Chicago: University of Chicago Press, 1954); Robert Dahl, *A Preface to Democratic Theory* (Chicago: University of Chicago Press, 1956); Robert Dahl, *Who Governs?* (New Haven: Yale University Press, 1961); Nelson Polsby, *Community Power and Political Theory* (New Haven: Yale University Press, 1963); V. O. Key, "Public Opinion and the Decay of Democracy, *Public Opinion Quarterly* 37 (1961): 481-94.

7. Jack L. Walker, "A Critique of the Elitist Theory of Democracy," *American Political Science Review* 60, no. 2 (1966): 293.

8. Roger Cobb and Charles Elder, *Participation in American Politics: The Dynamics of Agenda-Building* (Boston: Allyn and Bacon, 1972).

9. Ibid., p. 160.

10. Ibid., pp. 112-16; 130-50.

11. Theron F. Schlabach, *Edwin E. Witte: Cautious Reformer* (Madison: Wisconsin State Historical Society, 1969), p. 157; Arthur Altmeyer, "Twenty Years of Social Security," address of August 15, 1955, Box 259, Witte Papers, Wisconsin State Historical Society (cited in Schlabach).

12. Ernest Griffith, *Congress, Its Contemporary Role*, 2d ed., rev. (New York: New York University Press, 1956), pp. 37-39.

13. Dale Vinyard, "The Senate Special Committee on the Aging," *The Gerontologist* 12, pt. 1 (Autumn 1972): 298-303.

Chapter 2

1. The following discussion draws heavily on Schlabach, *Edwin E. Witte,* chap. 5.

2. Clark Chambers, *Seedtime of Reform: American Social Service and Social Action, 1918-1933* (Minneapolis: University of Minnesota Press, 1963), p. 174.

3. Barbara Armstrong, *Insuring the Essentials* (New York: Macmillan, 1932), pp. 432–38.

4. Lloyd F. Pierce, "The Activities of the American Association for Labor Legislation in Behalf of Social Security and Protective Legislation," (Ph.D. diss., University of Wisconsin, 1953), p. 391.

5. Schlabach, *Edwin E. Witte*, pp. 91–92.

6. Arthur Altmeyer, *The Formative Years of Social Security* (Madison: University of Wisconsin Press, 1966), p. 8.

7. Irving Bernstein, *The Lean Years: A History of the American Worker, 1920–1933* (Boston: Houghton Mifflin, 1960), pp. 490–91.

8. Frank B. Freidel, *Franklin E. Roosevelt: The Triumph* (Boston: Little Brown, 1956), p. 41.

9. Edwin E. Witte, *The Development of the Social Security Act* (Madison: University of Wisconsin Press, 1962), p. 74 and passim.

10. Bernstein, *The Lean Years,* p. 487.

11. Carl H. Voss, ed., *Stephen S. Wise, Servant of the People: Selected Letters* (Philadelphia: The Jewish Publication Society of America, 1969), p. 147.

12. Freidel, *The Triumph*, p. 42.

13. Bernstein, *The Lean Years*, p. 492.

14. Abraham Epstein, *Insecurity, A Challenge to America*, 2d ed., rev. (New York: Random House, 1938), pp. 533, 536.

15. Chambers, *Seedtime*, pp. 211–12.

16. Ibid., p. 169.

17. Schlabach, *Edwin E. Witte*, p. 97.

18. Witte, *Development of Social Security*, pp. 82n, 83n.

19. Schlabach, *Edwin E. Witte,* p. 138.

20. Ibid., p. 139.

21. Ibid., pp. 121–22.

22. Ibid., p. 140.

23. Epstein, *Insecurity*, chap. 36.

24. *New York Times*, August 15, 1935, p. 3; July 15, 1965, p. 13; July 31, 1965, p. 8.

25. Epstein, *Insecurity*, p. 677.

26. Roy Lubove, *The Struggle for Social Security* (Cambridge: Harvard University Press, 1968), p. 140.

27. Ibid., pp. 141–43.

28. Letter from Andrews to Paul Douglas, February 15, 1927, Andrews Collection, Cornell University. Quoted in Pierce, "The Activities of the American Association for Labor Legislation," p. 391.

29. Ibid., p. 392.

30. Cobb and Elder, *Participation,* pp. 115–16.

31. *Old Age Security Herald*, September–October, 1931, p. 1.

32. *Old Age Security Herald*, July 30, 1930, pp. 3–5.

33. Quoted in ibid., November 1930, p. 2.

34. Peter Odegard, *Pressure Politics: The Story of the Anti-Saloon League* (New York: Columbia University Press, 1928); Joseph R. Gusfield, *Symbolic Crusade: Status Politics and the American Temperance Movement* (Urbana: University of Illinois Press, 1963).

35. Bernstein, *The Lean Years*, pp. 97, 238.

36. For example, *Old Age Security Herald*, February 1930, p. 8.

37. James Q. Wilson, *Political Organizations* (New York: Basic Books, 1973), p. 217.

38. Abraham Epstein, *The Challenge of the Aged* (New York: Macy-Masius, 1928), p. 291.

39. Chambers, *Seedtime of Reform*, p. 164.

40. Abraham Holtzman, *The Townsend Movement* (New York: Bookman Associates, 1963), p. 87. Holtzman maintains that "the Townsend plan and the Social Security Act are inextricably linked together, the inclusion of an old-age insurance provision within the Act represented a direct response to Townsend pressure. The Townsend Movement must be credited with having crystallized tremendous populist sentiment in favor of old age security." His view on this point is directly contradicted by at least two authorities: Altmeyer, *The Formative Years*, pp. 10-11; and Arthur Schlesinger, Jr., *The Politics of Upheaval*, (Boston: Houghton-Mifflin, 1958), pp. 40-41. Other writers, while not dealing directly with the "Townsend Movement thesis," have discussed the passage of the act in terms which either minimize or disregard entirely the Townsend efforts in the legislative process: Max J. Skidmore, *Medicare and the American Rhetoric of Reconciliation* (University, Alabama: University of Alabama Press, 1970) and Wilbur Cohen, *Social Security: The First Thirty Years* (Ann Arbor: Institute of Gerontology, University of Michigan, 1970). The man remembered as the "father" of Social Security, Edwin E. Witte, goes so far as to suggest that if any relationship exists between the Townsend forces and the 1935 act, it is a negative one, since the movement's efforts served to delay the act's passage (Witte, *Development of Social Security*, pp. 95-96).

41. Schlesinger, *Politics of Upheaval*, p. 38.

42. Ibid., p. 40.

43. Cobb and Elder, *Participation,* p. 35.

44. David B. Truman, *The Governmental Process* (New York: Knopf, 1951), 265 and passim.

45. Ibid.

46. Jack Nagel, "Some Questions About the Concept of Power," *Behavioral Science* 13 (1968): 130 (cited in Cobb-Elder, *Participation in American Politics*, p. 23).

Chapter 3

1. Pierce, "The Activities of the American Association for Labor Legislation," p. 416.

2. *Social Security*, June–July, 1940, p. 8.

3. "Life of Abraham Epstein: An American Epic," *Social Security*, September–October, 1942, p. 5.

4. *Social Security*, March, 1942, p. 6; *New York Times* (obituary), May 3, 1942, p. 53.

5. Altmeyer, *The Formative Years,* pp. 4, 31-33; *Social Security*, September–October, 1939, p. 3.

6. Holtzman, *The Townsend Movement*, pp. 106, 108, 203.

7. Edna C. Wentworth, "Income of Old-Age and Survivor's Insurance Beneficiaries, 1941 and 1949," *Social Security Bulletin*, May 1950, p. 4.

8. Ibid., p. 3.

9. Arthur J. Altmeyer, "The First Decade of Social Security," *Social Security Bulletin*, August 1945, p. 5.

10. James O. Morris, *Conflict Within the AFL: A Study of Craft Versus Industrial Unionism* (Ithaca, New York: Cornell University Press, 1958), pp. 271-72.

11. Philip H. Taft, *The A.F. of L. from the Death of Gompers to Merger* (New York: Harper and Bros., 1959), p. 284.

12. Stephen K. Bailey, *Congress Makes a Law: The Story Behind the Employment Act of 1946* (New York: Columbia University Press, 1950).

13. On newspapers and magazine vendors, see U.S., Congress, House, Committee on Ways and Means, *Newspaper Vendors*, 80th Congress, 1st session (June 12, 1947), pp. 23-25 (hereafter referred to as Hearings, *Newspaper Vendors*); U.S., Congress, Senate, Committee on Finance, *Social Security Status Quo Resolution*, 80th Congress, 2d session (April 1-2, 1948), pp. 125-29 (hereafter referred to as Hearings, *Status Quo Resolution*).

14. Hearings, *Newspaper Vendors*, p. 12; Hearings, *Status Quo Resolution*, p. 75; *New York Times*, June 5, 1948, p. 1.

15. *New York Times*, April 21, 1948, p. 24.

16. *Congressional Record*, vol. 94, pt. 6 (June 14, 1948), 80th Congress, 1st session, pp. 8139-44.

17. Susan Hartmann, *Truman and the 80th Congress* (Columbia, Missouri: University of Missouri Press, 1971), p. 128.

18. *Harry S. Truman: Containing the Public Messages, Speeches, and Statements of the President: January 1 to December 31, 1948.* The Public Papers of the Presidents of the United States (Washington, D.C.: United States Government Printing Office, 1962), p. 3.

19. U.S., Congress, House, Committee on Ways and Means, *Social Security Amendments* of 1949, 81st Congress, 1st session (March/April, 1949), p. 1987.

20. U.S., Congress, Senate, Committee on Finance, *Social Security Revision*, pt. 3, 81st Congress, 2d session (February/March 1950), p. 2093.

21. *Statistical Abstract of the United States*, 1972 edition.

22. Jackson K. Putnam, *Old-Age Politics in California: From Richardson to Reagan* (Stanford, California: Stanford University Press, 1970), pp. 126-30; Frank A. Pinner, Paul Jacobs, and Philip Selznick, *Old Age and Political Behavior: A Case Study* (Berkeley and Los Angeles: University of California Press, 1959), pp. 253-60.

Chapter 4

1. Michael Kaye Carlie, "The Politics of Age: Interest Group or Social Movement," *The Gerontologist* 9, no. 4 (Winter 1969): 262.

2. Abraham Holtzman, "Analysis of Old Age Politics in the United States," *Journal of Gerontology* 9, no. 1 (January 1954): 63.

3. Angus Campbell, "Social and Psychological Determinants of Voting Behavior," in *Politics of Age*, ed. Wilma Donahue and Clark Tibbetts (Ann Arbor: University of Michigan Press, 1962), p. 98.

4. Arnold M. Rose, "Organizations for the Elderly: Political Implications," in Donahue and Tibbetts, *Politics of Age*, pp. 138-41.

5. M. W. Riley and Anne Foner, *Aging and Society* (New York: Russell Sage, 1960), p. 509.

6. Rose, "Organizations for the Elderly," p. 509. Rose remarks: "Irregularity of participation due to ill health, physical inability to participate in many kinds of activities, faltering attention on the part of those whose mental powers are occasionally shaky, and the lack of sustained interest on the part of those who look toward the future are some of the serious difficulties.... A large proportion of older persons (even when their mental and physical abilities have not markedly deteriorated) seem to want things to be done for them, even expect things to be done to them, rather than having things done by them."

7. Theodore Marmor, *The Politics of Medicare* (Chicago: Aldine, 1973), p. 16.

8. Council of State Governments, *The States and Their Older Citizens* (Chicago, 1955), pp. 161-64.

9. U.S., Congress, Senate, Subcommittee on Problems of the Aging, Committee on Labor and Public Welfare, *The Aged and the Aging in the United States: A Report*, 86th Congress, second session, 1960, p. 25; James L. Sundquist, *Politics and Policy: The Eisenhower, Kennedy and Johnson Years* (Washington, D.C.: Brookings Institution, 1968), pp. 287-321.

10. Milton Barron, "Minority Group Characteristics of the Aged in American Society, *Journal of Gerontology* 8 (1953): 477-81.

11. Jean Maxwell, *Centers for Older People: Guide for Programs and Facilities* (New York: National Council on the Aging, 1962), p. 8.

12. Robert J. Havighurst, "Life Beyond Family and Work," in *Aging in Western Societies*, ed. Ernest W. Burgess (Chicago: University of Chicago Press, 1960), p. 342.

13. Maxwell, *Centers for Older People*, pp. 23-24.

14. Ibid., p. 74.

15. Wilma Donahue and Clark Tibbetts, "Summary and Forecast," in Donahue and Tibbetts, *The Politics of Age*, p. 216.

16. James E. Trela, "Some Political Consequences of Senior Center and Other Old-Age Memberships," *The Gerontologist,* Summer 1971, pp. 118-23 (quotation, p. 119).

17. Ibid., p. 120.

18. Arnold M. Rose, "Group Consciousness Among the Aging," in *Older People and Their Social World: The Sub-Culture of the Aging*, ed. Arnold M. Rose and Warren M. Peterson (Philadelphia: Davis, 1965), p. 24.

19. Ibid., pp. 33-35.

20. Barron, "Minority Group Characteristics of the Aged," pp. 477-81.

21. Richard H. Kern, " 'Too Old to Work and Too Young to Die,' An Examination of the UAW Program for its Retired Workers" (Master's thesis, Institute of Industrial Relations, University of Wisconsin, 1974), pp. 52, 83, 106.

22. Ibid., pp. 61-66.

23. In ibid., p. 54.

24. Arnold M. Rose, "The Impact of Aging on Voluntary Associations," in *Handbook of Social Gerontology*, ed. Clark Tibbetts (Chicago: University of Chicago Press, 1960), pp. 676, 677.

25. Robert and Leona Rienow, "The Desperate World of the Senior Citizen," *Saturday Review*, January 28, 1961, pp. 11-12.

26. Margaret Abrams, "The Story of AARP," *Modern Maturity*, October-November, 1971, pp. 72-73.

27. Bernard E. Nash, "The Changing Look of Aging," *NRTA Journal*, January-February, 1972, p. 4.

28. Charles F. Odell, "Attitudes Toward Political Activities Among the Aging," in Donahue and Tibbetts, *Politics of Age*, p. 34.

29. *Parade Magazine*, January 28, 1973 (n.p.). See also *New York Times*, May 21, 1972, p. 48.

30. Arnold M. Rose, "The Subculture of Aging: A Framework for Research in Social Gerontology," in Rose and Peterson, *Old People and Their Social World*, p. 13.

31. Richard Harris, *A Sacred Trust* (New York: Penguin, 1969), p. 73.

32. Ibid., pp. 99-100.

33. Ibid., p. 100.

34. Sundquist, *Politics and Policy*, p. 299.

35. U.S., Congress, Senate, Subcommittee on Problems of the Aged and Aging, Committee on Labor and Public Welfare, *Report*, 86th Congress, second session, 1960, p. 25.

36. Carl A. Dawson and Warner Gettys, *An Introduction to Sociology* (New York: Ronald Press, 1929), chap. 20. The Dawson-Gettys work is mentioned favorably in Herbert Blumer, "Social Movements," in *Principles of Sociology*, rev. ed., ed. A. M. Lee (New York: Barnes and Noble, 1955), p. 203; compare also, Theodore Lowi, *The Politics of Disorder* (New York: Basic Books, 1971), pp. 35-53.

37. Dawson and Gettys, *Introduction to Sociology*, p. 798.

38. Ibid.

Chapter 5

1. Lloyd H. Fisher, "Research in the Politics of Age," in Donahue and Tibbetts, *Politics of Age*, pp. 41-45; Frank A. Pinner, "Theories of Political Participation," ibid., pp. 63-73. These authors make it clear that a number of factors contributed to the lack of such organizations.

2. Truman, *The Governmental Process*, p. 511. "Any mutual interest," Truman asserts, "any shared attitude, is a potential interest group."

3. Survey Research Center, The University of Michigan, *Who Votes for Whom* (mimeographed, July 6, 1965).

4. Angus Campbell, "Voting Behavior," p. 91; interview with James C. O'Brien, August 21, 1965.

5. Fred I. Greenstein, *The American Party System and the American People* (Englewood Cliffs, N.J.: Prentice-Hall, 1963), p. 28.

6. Warren Miller, "The Political Behavior of the Electorate," in Raymond Wolfinger, ed., *Readings in American Political Behavior* (Englewood Cliffs, N.J.: Prentice-Hall, 1966), p. 252.

7. V. O. Key, *The Responsible Electorate* (Cambridge: Harvard University Press, 1966), p. xi.

8. Campbell, "Voting Behavior," pp. 93-97.

9. Social Security Administration, *The Health Care of the Aged* (Washington, D.C.: U.S. Government Printing Office, 1962), p. 121; Richard A. Cloward and Frances F. Piven, "A Strategy to End Poverty," *The Nation*, May 2, 1966.

10. Campbell, "Voting Behavior," p. 94.

11. Interview with James C. O'Brien, August 21, 1965; also with Alexander Barkan, November 18, 1966.

12. Angus Campbell et al., *The American Voter* (New York: John Wiley, 1964), p. 98.

13. Interviews with James O'Brien, July 21, 1965; with Charles E. Odell, August 10, 1965; and with Lizabeth Bamberger, August 15, 1967.

14. Congress, U.S., Senate, Committee on Labor and Public Welfare, Hearings, *Health Needs of the Aged and Aging*, April 4-13, 1960.

15. *New York Times*, May 3, 18, 1960.

16. *Business Week*, June 17, 1960.

17. *New York Times*, June 23, 1960.

18. The following account, except where noted, is based on interviews with Blue Carstenson, James V. O'Brien, and Harold Sheppard.

19. Blue Carstenson, memorandum (typed), July 14, 1960.

20. Interview with Alexander Barkan, November 18, 1966.

21. The growing interest in the political potential of the elderly was reflected in the 1960 Democratic platform. In addition to a section on "Medical Care for Older Persons," the platform for the first time had a separate section entitled, "A Program for the Aging."

22. The following account is based on interviews with Blue Carstenson, Richard Donahue, and James O'Brien.

23. Theodore H. White, *The Making of the President, 1960* (New York: Atheneum, 1961), p. 247.

24. The information that follows in the text is taken from interviews with Carstenson and O'Brien and from the roster drawn up at Senior Citizens headquarters at the beginning of October 1960: Carstenson and O'Brien, "Memorandum to all Senior Citizens for Kennedy Chairmen, Coordinators and Liaison Persons" (mimeographed), Washington, October 4, 1960.

25. Charles E. Odell, letter to Peter A. Corning, September 26, 1967.

26. Blue Carstenson and Lawrence O'Brien, "Report to the National Chairman," Democratic National Committee, 1960.

27. These figures were not corroborated in the roster published in October. Chairmen, coordinators, local staffers, and other liaison people were listed for only thirty-one states and numbered only 134 altogether. However, the correspondence files of Senior Citizens for Kennedy headquarters indicate that a number of workers were added in subsequent weeks, almost up to election day, in fact. But even if we base our estimate of the scope of Senior Citizens for Kennedy on the October 4 roster, it is clear that, on paper at least, the operation was nationwide and extensive.

28. *The Senior Citizens Sentinel*, November, 1960.

29. On the aggregate shift between 1956 and 1960, U.S. Bureau of the Census, *Statistical Abstract of the United States: 1965*, 86th ed., (Washington, D.C., 1965), p. 373; on Gallup Poll, *Congressional Quarterly Almanac*, 1964 ed., p. 1013; Survey Research Center, *Who Votes for Whom*.

30. Survey Research Center, *Who Votes for Whom*.

31. Lenore A. Epstein and Janet H. Murray, *The Aged Population of the United States* (Washington, D.C.: Government Printing Office, 1967), p. 23; Survey Research Center, *Who Votes for Whom*.

32. *New York Times*, Septermber 7, 8, 14, 20, 22, 23, and October 7, 1960.

33. V. O. Key, *Politics, Parties and Pressure Groups*, 5th ed., (New York: Crowell, 1964), pp. 482–85.

34. Paul F. Lazarsfeld and W. N. McPhee, *Voting* (Chicago: University of Chicago Press, 1954).

35. Carstenson and O'Brien, *Report to the National Chairman*.

36. Cited in Greenstein, *The American Party System and the American People*.

37. Interviews with Myer Feldman, Richard Donahue, Alexander Barkan, and Harold Sheppard.

38. Democratic National Committee, *The Democratic Campaign Manual, 1964* (Washington, D.C.: Democratic National Committee, 1964).

39. Interview with Richard K. Donahue, June 22, 1966.

40. Interview with Gertrude Landau, Director of Hudson Day Center, New York City, February 7, 1966.

41. Key, *Politics, Parties and Pressure Groups*, pp. 466–76, 479. Though all of the concluding points listed are at least implied by material in the body of this chapter, fuller documentation may be found in Corning, "Senior Citizens for Kennedy: An Effector of a Political Subsystem."

Chapter 6

1. Robert H. Salisbury, "An Exchange Theory of Interest Groups," *Midwest Journal of Political Science* 13, no. 1 (February 1969): 4–5. (Reprinted in *Interest*

Group Politics in America, ed. Robert Salisbury [New York: Harper and Row, 1970], pp. 35–36.)

2. Truman, *The Governmental Process*, p. 502.

3. For a more extended discussion of the role of the aged in pre-industrial society, see Simone de Beauvoir, *The Coming of Age* (New York: Putnam, 1972).

4. See Helen B. Shafer, "Plight of the Aged," *Editorial Research Reports*, November 10, 1971, p. 879; and Clare Townsend, *Old Age: The Last Segregation* (New York: Grossman, 1971).

5. In 1900, for instance, more than 66 percent of the aged population was still involved in the work force. By 1970, the proportion had dropped to less than 25 percent, and by 1972 it had dropped still further to 17 percent. The first two statistics appear in Herman B. Brotman, "Facts and Figures on Older Americans," *Retirement Life* (Official Publication of the National Association of Retired Federal Employees), March, 1972, p. 14. The last statistic appears in Senator Frank Church, "State of the Aging, Legislative Relief" (delivered in U.S. Senate, February 7, 1972), *Vital Speeches* 38 (March 1, 1972): 301.

6. Church, "State of the Aging," p. 301.

7. George Maddox and Marvin J. Taves, "Research Development on Behavior and Social Scientific Aspects of Aging," 1971 White House Conference on Aging, *Proceedings*, p. 1.

8. Michael C. Jensen, "Harsh Arithmetic of Old Age in America," *Saturday Review*, April 8, 1972, pp. 42, 44. A study conducted by the Subcommittee on Labor of the Senate Committee on Labor and Public Welfare found that since 1950 nine-tenths of workers covered by plans requiring eleven years of service and three-fourths of workers covered by plans requiring ten years of service did not qualify for benefits when they left their jobs.

9. On Social Security as income source, see Shafer, "Plight of the Aged," pp. 865–82. According to the *Saturday Review* article cited above, less than one-fourth of all retirees are expected to receive benefits from private pension plans. On old-age poverty, see Senator Frank Church, "A Time for Security and Dignity," *Perspective on Aging*, Spring 1972, p. 5; idem, "State of the Aging," p. 301; Vernon Pizer, "Duck! Geriatric Lib is on the March," *Magazine of the Washington Star*, January 24, 1971, p. 7. The "poverty line," according to the Bureau of the Census, is $1,852 for a single person and $2,328 for an aged couple. HEW officials set a slightly higher standard: $2,315 per individual and $2,910 per couple. By these criteria 25 percent of aged couples and 60 percent of aged individuals could be considered "poor."

10. On per capital health care spending, see "Accent on Youth," *U.S. News and World Report*, February 8, 1971, p. 35. On old people's medical spending, see Brotman, "Facts and Figures on Older Americans," p. 14; Jensen, "Harsh Arithmetic of Old Age," p. 41; Shafer, "Plight of the Aged," p. 875. On Medicare inadequacies, see Shafer, "Plight of the Aged," p. 876; Brotman, "Facts and Figures on Older Americans," p. 14.

11. Shafer, "Plight of the Aged," p. 875.

12. Barbara Isenberg, "Out to Pasture," *Wall Street Journal*, November 15, 1972, p. 1.

13. On property tax rise, see AARP/NRTA, "Platform Proposals for 1972 National Political Conventions," Washington: AARP/NRTA, 1971, p. 18. On impact on aged, see Shafer, "Plight of the Aged," p. 877.

14. Matilda White Riley, ed., *Aging and Society* (New York: Russell Sage Foundation, 1968), 1:130; U.S. Congress, National Commission on Urban Problems, Joint Economic Committee, *Impact of the Property Tax: Its Economic*

Implications for Urban Problems (Washington, D.C.: Government Printing Office, May, 1968), p. 16.

15. On aged in substandard housing, see Paul M. Milbanck, *The Elderly in Older Urban Areas* (Philadelphia: University of Pennsylvania Press, 1968), p. 52; *Congressional Record*, October 4, 1972, p. S16751. On old people's housing expenditures, see Riley, *Aging and Society*, 1:102.

16. Townsend, *Old Age: The Last Segregation*, p. x.

17. M. Seligson, "Social Crime of Growing Old," *Life*, May 19, 1972, p. 22.

18. The "case study" presented is actually a composite of several factual case histories.

19. Shafer, "Plight of the Aged," p. 876.

20. If our hypothetical case had occurred before the enactment of the 1971 Social Security amendments, the widow would have received only 82.5 percent of the benefits her husband would have received if he were alive.

21. Congress, U.S., Senate, Subcommittee on Health of the Elderly, Special Committee on Aging, *Hearings*, 92d Congress, first session, pt. 3, September 20, 1971, p. 265.

22. Isenberg, "Out to Pasture," p. 4.

23. Yonina Talmon, "Aging: Social Aspects," in David Sills, ed., *International Encyclopedia of the Social Sciences* (New York: Macmillan, 1968), 1:192.

24. Ibid.

25. Isenberg, "Out to Pasture," p. 4.

26. R. O. Beckman, "A Cold Shoulder for the Elderly," *Perspectives on Aging*, Autumn 1972, p. 8.

27. George R. Peters, "Self-Conceptions of the Aged, Identification and Aging," *The Gerontologist*, Winter, 1971, pt. 2, p. 70.

28. Quoted in Pizer, "Duck! Geriatric Lib is on the March," p. 30.

29. Harris, *A Sacred Trust*, p. 74. As a way of not appearing hostile to the aging as such, the AMA established a so-called "Joint Council to Improve the Health Care of the Aged." Harris remarks that "the title turned out to be a misnomer, for the council's chief conclusion was that health care of the aged didn't need improving" (ibid).

30. Truman, *The Governmental Process*, p. 512.

31. White House Conference on Aging, 1971, *Proceedings*.

Chapter 7

1. Theodore Lowi, *The End of Liberalism* (New York: W. W. Norton, 1969), pp. 64–65.

2. Walter Polner, "The Aged in Politics, A Successful Example: The NPA and the Passage of the Railroad Retirement Act of 1934," *The Gerontologist* 2 (1962) 2:207–15; Pinner, Jacobs, and Selznick, *Old Age and Political Behavior;* Putnam, *Old Age Politics in California*.

3. The list is from Binstock, "Interest Group Liberalism and the Politics of Aging," p. 269.

4. Richard Harris, "Annals of Legislation," *The New Yorker*, July 16, 1966, p. 51.

5. Ibid.

6. Ibid.

7. Sundquist, *Politics and Policy*, pp. 310–11, 314; J. David Greenston, *Labor and American Politics* (New York: Knopf, 1969), p. 338; Harris, *A Sacred Trust*, pp.

148, 153, 177, 183, 189–90. At least one informed observer passes over the NCSC role in silence: Marmor, *The Politics of Medicare*.

8. Interview with William R. Hutton, NCSC executive director, January 1972.

9. The following section is based on Margaret Adams, "The Story of AARP," *Modern Maturity*, October–November, 1971, pp. 72–74.

10. *Washington Post*, February 13, 1972, p. 1.

11. U.S., Congress, House, Committee on Ways and Means, *Hearings on Hospital, Nursing Home and Surgical Benefits for OASI Beneficiaries*, H.R. 4700, 86th Cong., 1st sess., July 13–17, 1959, pp. 510–11.

12. *Retirement Life*, selected issues, 1956, 1960, 1971.

13. "Fact Sheet," December 1969 (mimeo., available in NCOA Library, Washington, D.C.).

14. The description that follows in the text of NCOA's early history is based on an interview with NCOA President, Albert J. Abrams, September 1974.

15. Interview with Robert E. Sarvis, chairman, Social Action Committee, National Institute of Senior Centers, September 1974.

16. Sheldon H. Messinger, "Organizational Transformation: A Case Study of A Declining Social Movement," *American Sociological Review* 20, no. 1 (February 1955): 3–10; Pinner, Jacobs, and Selznick, *Old Age and Political Behavior*, passim.

17. Interview with William R. Hutton, January 1971.

18. *Washington Post*, February 13, 1972, p. A21.

19. "The National Council on the Aging: An Historical Perspective," prepared for NCOA staff meeting, September 24, 1969 (mimeo., on file in NCOA Library, Washington, D.C.), p. 11.

20. Ibid., p. 19.

21. "Summary of NCOA Financial Activities for Calendar 1969" (mimeo., available in NCOA Library, Washington, D.C.).

22. Putnam, *Old Age Politics in California*, p. 57; Holtzman, *The Townsend Movement*, p. 92.

23. Binstock, "Interest Group Liberalism and the Politics of Aging," p. 278.

24. Lowi, *End of Liberalism*.

25. Binstock, "Interest Group Liberalism," pp. 273–77.

26. Skidmore, *Medicare and the American Rhetoric of Reconciliation*, chap. 5.

27. "The National Council on the Aging: An Historical Perspective," p. 15.

28. Binstock, "Interest Group Liberalism," pp. 273–77.

29. *Senior Citizen News*, November 1971, p.1.

30. Ibid., p. 3.

31. *AARP News Bulletin*, January 1972, pp. 1, 6.

32. National Council of Senior Citizens, *A Platform for the Seventies for All Americans* (policy statement prepared for 1971 White House Conference on Aging), p. 2.

33. *AARP News Bulletin*, January 1972, p. 6.

34. U.S., Congress, Senate, Special Committee on Aging, Subcommittee on Health of the Elderly, *Barriers to Health Care for Older Americans*, Hearings, 93d Cong. 2nd sess. (March 12, 1974), p. 730.

35. Ibid., pp. 703–13.

36. "Health Report," *National Journal*, January 18, 1975, pp. 93–99.

37. Cobb and Elder, *Participation in American Politics*, pp. 104–8.

Chapter 8

1. Robert Binstock, *Planning: Background* (Washington, D.C.: White House Conference on Aging, March 1971); Robert Binstock, Carolyn M. Cherington, and

Peter Woll, "Federalism and Leadership Planning: Predictors of Variance in State Behavior," *The Gerontologist* 14, no. 2 (April 1974): 114-21; Robert B. Hudson, "State Politics, Federalism and Public Policies for Older Americans," paper delivered before the 1973 meeting of the American Political Science Association, New Orleans, La.; Robert B. Hudson, "Rational Planning and Organizational Imperatives: Prospects for Area Planning in Aging," *The Annals* (September 1974) 415:41-54; Robert B. Hudson and Martha B. Veley, "Federal Funding and State Planning: The Case of State Units on Aging," *The Gerontologist* 14, no. 2 (April 1974): 122-28.

2. See, for example, Dale Vinyard, "The Senate Special Committee on the Aging," p. 300.

3. U.S., Congress, House, Committee on Education and Labor, Subcommittee on Safety and Compensation, *Hearings on Bureau of Older Persons*, 85th Congress, second session, March-April, 1958, p. 151.

4. Ibid., p. 2.

5. Ibid., p. 10 (emphasis added).

6. Ibid., p. 157.

7. Ibid.

8. Ibid., p. 92.

9. Ibid., p. 157.

10. The 1961 White House Conference on Aging, *Basic Policy Statements and Recommendations,* prepared for Special Committee on Aging, U.S. Senate, May 15, 1961, pp. 156 and 165.

11. See, for example, Sundquist, *Politics and Policy*, pp. 308-9.

12. *New York Times*, February 22, 1963, p. 2; interviews with William Bechill, November, 1973.

13. Harris, *A Sacred Trust*, p. 121.

14. Interview with William C. Fitch, November 1973.

15. U.S., Congress, House, Committee on Education and Labor, Subcommittee on Education, *Administration of Aging: Hearings on H.R. 7957 and Similar Bills*, 88th Congress, first session, 1963.

16. Ibid., pp. 138-39.

17. Ibid., p. 185.

18. Ibid., p. 239.

19. Ibid., pp. 25, 27.

20. Ibid., pp. 16-18.

21. Ibid., p. 144.

22. Vinyard, "The Senate Special Committee on the Aging," p. 300.

23. Interview with William Bechill, November 1973.

24. A knowledgeable informant in the National Council of Senior Citizens has given the following version of how the bargain was struck which paved the way for the Bechill nomination. The author has been unable to verify the account with any of the principals directly involved, but it is worthwhile recording the incident as described. After the nomination of William D. Bechill had been held up in the Senate for some time, President Johnson called a meeting in his office to hammer out a compromise. At one point in the conversation the president turned to Andrew Biemiller, the chief Washington lobbyist for the AFL-CIO and enquired whether labor had any objection to Bechill's confirmation. Whether through ignorance of the stand being taken by labor-oriented groups like NCSC (which seems unlikely) or as a result of other considerations, Biemiller responded that labor trusted Wilbur Cohen (then undersecretary of HEW and the man under whose jurisdiction the Administration on Aging was to be placed) and since Cohen wanted Bechill, labor would not oppose the nomination. Since labor had constituted the most powerful interest

working for Odell, Biemiller's statement settled the issue. As a face-saving gesture, it was agreed that Charles Odell should be appointed to the newly created Advisory Council on Older Americans, a nonsalaried group of notables being established to advise the commissioner on aging.

25. U.S. Congress, House, Committee on Education and Labor, General Subcommittee on Education, *Problems of the Aged and Aging,* 87th Congress, second session, pt. 1 (February, April, May 1962), pp. 506–8; *Hearings on HR 7959 and Similar Bills* (September 17, 1963).

26. Hudson, "State Politics, Federalism, and Public Policies for Older Persons," p. 18.

27. Ibid., p. 6.

28. Interview with William Bechill, November 1973.

29. Interview with William Fitch, November 1973.

30. Interview with William Bechill, November 1973.

31. Robert H. Binstock, "Interest-Group Liberalism," p. 275.

32. Quoted by Robert H. Binstock, interview, January 1975.

33. Binstock, "Interest-Group Liberalism," p. 236.

34. Interview with William Bechill, November 1973.

35. Interview with John Martin, November 1973.

36. "The Second White House Conference on Aging—A Summary Prepared by the Staff of the White House Conference on Aging, September, 1971," reprinted in Subcommittee on Education, House Education and Labor Committee, *Hearings on H.R. 12071 and Related Bills,* pt. 1, 92d Congress, first session (September, October, November 1971), p. 43.

37. Interview with John B. Martin, November 1973.

Chapter 9

1. For a discussion of the role of private groups serving on "intercessor" function in behalf of clients, see Gilbert Y. Steiner, *The State of Welfare* (Washington, D.C.: Brookings Institution, 1971), p. 321.

2. U.S., Congress, Senate, Committee on Labor and Public Welfare, *White House Conference on Aging: Report to Accompany S. J. Resolution 117,* 90th Congress, second session (May 1, 1968), p. 2n and passim.

3. U.S., Congress, House, Committee on Education and Labor, *White House Conference on Aging: Report to Accompany H. J. Resolution 1371,* 90th Congress, second session (July 25, 1968).

4. Henry J. Pratt, *The Liberalization of American Protestantism: A Case Study in Complex Organizations* (Detroit: Wayne State University Press, 1972), pp. 223–25, 248, 264.

5. *National Journal,* September 25, 1971, p. 1969.

6. Ibid.

7. The joint committee subsequently, in April and May 1971, went into the field to conduct additional hearings at various regional centers, and there the dominance of the proceedings by national groups no longer occurred. But it was the Washington hearings, not the regional ones, that had a dramatic impact, and that is the reason for stressing them at this point.

8. U.S., Congress, Senate, Special Committee on Aging and Subcommittee on Aging of the Committee on Labor and Public Welfare, *Evaluation of Administration on Aging and Conduct of White House Conference on Aging,* Joint Hearings, 92d Congress, first session, March 31, p. 227 (Fitch); March 30, p. 191 (Nash); March 25,

p. 25 (Cohen); March 29, p. 151 (Walters); other witnesses: March 29, pp. 136–37; March 25, pp. 46–48, 50–52; March 31, pp. 234–35.

9. U.S., Congress, Senate, Special Committee on Aging, *The Administrating on Aging or a Successor*, 92d Congress, first session (October 1971), passim.

10. Interview with John Martin, November 1973.

11. "The Second White House Conference on Aging—A Summary Prepared by the Staff of the White House Conference on Aging, September 1971," reprinted in Subcommittee on Education, House Education and Labor Committee, *Hearings on H.R. 12017 and Related Bills*, pt. 1, 92d Congress, first session (September, October, and November 1971), pp. 53, 241.

12. U.S., Congress, House, Subcommittee on Education, *Hearings on H.R. 12017 and Related Bills*, p. 241; *National Journal*, September 25, 1971, p. 1969.

13. Hudson, "State Politics, Federalism and Public Policies for Older Americans," pp. 10–12, 16, 23.

14. Interview with John Martin, November 1972.

15. E. Pendleton Herring, *Group Representation Before Congress* (Baltimore: Johns Hopkins University Press, 1929), p. 75; Bertram M. Gross, *The Legislative Struggle* (New York: McGraw-Hill, 1953), p. 31; Abraham Holtzman, *Interest Groups and Lobbying* (New York: Macmillan, 1966), pp. 38–39; Donald C. Blaisdell, *American Democracy Under Pressure* (New York: Ronald Press, 1957), p. 106.

16. Donald R. Hall, *Cooperative Lobbying: The Power of Pressure* (Tucson: University of Arizona Press, 1969), pp. 185–86, 209, and chap. 5–8 inclusive.

17. Truman, *The Governmental Process*, pp. 85–91.

18. Lester Milbrath, *The Washington Lobbyists* (Chicago: Rand McNally, 1963), pp. 171–72, 174.

Chapter 10

1. Quoted in photocopy of the talk furnished by NCSC, p. 1.

2. The source for this summary is the 1971 White House Conference on Aging, *Basic Policy Statements and Recommendations*.

3. U.S., Congress, Senate Special Committee on Aging, *Developments in Aging: 1972 and January–March 1973*, 93d Congress, first session (May 10, 1973), p. 60.

4. Ibid., p. 3.

5. Ibid., p. ix.

6. U.S., Congress, House of Representatives, Committee on Education and Labor, Select Subcommittee on Education, *Hearings on H.R. 12017 and Related Bills*, pt. 2 (March–April, 1972), p. 1209.

7. Interview with anonymous informant, AOA, September 1973.

8. Interview with Jack Duncan, September 1973; interview with Jay Constantine, Senate Finance Committee staff, September 1973.

9. U.S., Congress, Senate, Special Committee on Aging, *Future Directions in Social Security*, 93d Congress, first session (July 26, 1973), pt. 5.

10. Interview with John Martin, November 1973.

11. Interview with Bernard Nash, November 1973.

12. Ibid.

13. Interview with Peter Hughes, AARP, November 1973.

14. Interview with John Martin, November 1973.

15. Interview with William Hutton, NCSC, February 1974.

16. Robert Salisbury, "An Exchange Theory of Interest Groups," pp. 27-28.

Chapter 11

1. U.S. Department of Health Education and Welfare, 1971 Advisory Council on Social Security, Report, 92d Congress, 1st session, 1971, p. 64–65.

2. The Advisory Council on Social Security comprised the following:

Arthur S. Flemming, president, Macalaster College, Chairman
Bertha S. Adkins, former undersecretary of the Department of Health, Education, and Welfare
J. Douglas Brown, provost and dean of the faculty, emeritus, Princeton University
Walter J. Burke, secretary-treasurer, United Steel Workers of America
Kermit Gordon, president, Brookings Institution
Gabriel Hauge, chairman of the board, Manufacturers Hanover Trust Company
Arthur Larson, director, Rule of Law Research Center, Duke University
Bert Seidman, director, Department of Social Security, AFL-CIO
Charles A. Seigfreid, vice chairman of the board and chairman of the executive committee, Metropolitan Life Insurance Company
Joseph P. Tonelli, president-secretary, International Brotherhood of Pulp Sulphite and Paper Mill Workers of the United States and Canada
Robert C. Tyson, director and former chairman of the Finance Committee, United States Steel Corporation
Dwight L. Wilbur, M.D., past president, American Medical Association
Whitney M. Young, Jr., executive director, National Urban League.

3. Whitney Young was not literally a representative of a labor union but he allied with the labor representatives throughout the deliberations. For proof of this alliance see "Statement of Walter J. Burke, Bert Seidman, Joseph Tonelli and Whitney M. Young, Jr." in "Report of the Advisory Council," p. 74.

4. Ibid. Also note implications of independence in Recommendation 5, which stated: "The Council recommends that two nongovernment members be appointed by the President subject to confirmation by the Senate and be added to the boards of trustees of the Social Security trust funds as a means of assuring public understanding and confidence in the funds management" (p. 63).

5. Truman, *The Governmental Process*, p. 459.

6. *New York Times*, March 31, 1972.

7. *Congressional Record,* July 31, 1972, 92d Congress, 1st session, p. S12244.

8. Aaron Wildavsky, *The Politics of the Budgetary Process*, (Boston; Little Brown, 1964), p. 132.

9. U.S. Government, "Toward a National Policy on Aging," 1971 White House Conference on Aging—Final Report, vol. I (Washington, D.C.), p. x.

10. Much of the information presented within this chapter is derived from lengthy interviews with senior and junior staff members for senators, congressmen, and committees. In order to guarantee that their remarks would be candid and accurate the persons interviewed were assured that their requests for anonymity would be respected.

11. Compare, "Report of the Advisory Council on Social Security," April 5, 1971, with *Congressional Record*, 92d Congress, second session, Friday, June 30, 1972.

12. *Congressional Record*, 92d Congress, second session, Friday, June 30, 1972, p. H6513, statement by Representative Goldwater.

13. Church's own amendment would have provided the graduated scale of benefit increases mentioned previously. See *Congressional Record*, Monday, February 14, 1972, 92d Congress, second session, p. S1604.

14. Natalie Davis Spingarn, "Economic Report/Congress Debates Application of Billions in Social Security Funds," *National Journal,* 29 April 1972, p. 733.

15. "Forces Reshaping Social Security," *Business Week*, July 15, 1972, p. 69.

16. See *Congressional Record,* June 30, 1972, p. S10789.

17. Ibid.

18. Ibid., 28 February 1972, p. H1492.

19. Ibid., 30 June 1972, p. H1329.

20. The information concerning the lobbying techniques of the Chamber of Commerce is taken from Patricia A. Goldman, "Washington Pressures/U.S. Chamber Works to Erase Negative Image and Improve Grass-Roots Clout," *National Journal*, 1 April 1972, pp. 558-70.

Chapter 12

1. F. G. Dickinson, "Economic Aspects of our Population," in *Problems of America's Aging Population: A Report of the First Annual Southern California Conference on Gerontology* (Gainsville: University of Florida Press, 1951).

2. ESSO, *Preparation for Retirement*, Standard Oil Company of New York, 1950.

3. "The Center Eclectics" (Interview with Harvey Wheeler), *Center Reports,* Center for the Study of Democratic Institutions, Santa Barbara, June 1974, p. 22.

4. Leaving out those with purely housekeeping and internal organizational functions (for example, the Select Committee on the House Beauty Shop, the House Select Committee on Committees), and focusing on ones with a manifest legislative role, the number of select or special Senate committees in a recent year exceeded the House total by 7 to 2 (Source: *1973 Congressional Directory*).

5. *Congressional Record*, 93d Congress, 2d session (October 2, 1974), p. H9812.

6. House of Representatives, Select Committee on Committees, *Committee Structure Hearing*, September 16, 1973, mimeo, pp. 13, 16.

7. Ibid., p. H9810.

8. Dale Vinyard, "The Senate Special Committee on the Aging," p. 301.

9. Interview with Jack Duncan, Select Subcommittee on Education staff, House Education and Labor Committee, September 1973.

10. Lewis A. Froman, Jr., *Congressmen and their Constituencies* (Chicago: Rand McNally, 1963), chap. 6.

11. Several explanations suggest themselves in accounting for the greater tendency for senators to specialize in one or more policy areas. One possible factor is the more heterogeneous character of their constituencies and the impossibility of having detailed, in-depth knowledge of the needs of all the various groupings in the home district (state); by becoming knowledgeable in one area, therefore, the senator may earn a reputation for effectiveness—one that may serve to impress not only the grouping immediately affected, but others as well. There is, secondly, the sheer fact of greater senatorial visibility and the resulting knowledge that the senator's expertise will gain him a respectful audience. There are fewer senators than congressmen and they serve for longer periods, and what senators have to say on national and world issues traditionally has commanded serious attention in the mass media, attention usually denied to all but a handful of outstandingly effective House members—a Wilbur Mills, for example.

12. For the addresses through 1966 a source book was employed: Fred L. Israel, ed., *The State of the Union Messages of the Presidents, 1790-1966* (New York: Chelsea House/Robert Hector, 1966), vol. 3; for 1967-74, the texts were consulted in the *New York Times*.

13. *The National Journal*, 21 April 1973, p. 580.

14. U.S., Congress, Senate, Committee on Labor and Public Welfare, Subcommittee on Aging, *Hearings on S. 50, S. 491 and S. 375,* 93d Congress, second session, 2 February 1973, pp. 440, 444.

15. Ibid., p. 282.

16. U.S., Congress, Senate, Special Committee on Aging, *Developments in Aging: 1972 and January–March 1973* (Washington, D.C.: Government Printing Office, 10 May 1973), p. 247.

17. U.S., Congress, Senate, Special Committee on Aging, *The Administration on Aging—Or a Successor?* (Washington, D.C.: Government Printing Office, October, 1971), p. 2.

Chapter 13

1. Olson, *The Logic of Collective Action* (Cambridge, Mass.: Harvard University Press, 1965), p. 119; Truman, *The Governmental Process,* p. ix; Robert Golembiewski, "The Group Basis of Politics," *American Political Science Review* 14, no. 4 (December 1960): 962–71; Earl Latham, *The Group Basis of Politics: A Study in Basing Point Legislation* (Ithaca: Cornell University Press, 1952), p. 10.

2. Arthur Bentley, *The Process of Government* (Chicago: University of Chicago Press, 1908), pp. 465–72.

3. "The word 'interest'," Bentley remarked, "in social studies is often limited to the economic interest. There is no justification for such a limitation. I am restoring it to its broader meaning coextensive with all groups whatsoever that participate in the social process" (ibid., p. 212).

4. Myron Q. Hale, "The Cosmology of Arthur F. Bentley," *American Political Science Review* 14, no. 4 (December 1960): p. 959. While the economic tone which Hale alludes to pervades Bentley's book, it is most fully apparent in the Appendix, pp. 487–94. Here Bentley offers a series of brief case studies of group involvement in politics, and it is significant that on close reading every one turns out to involve groups concerned with protecting and advancing material stakes of some kind.

5. Bentley, *The Process of Government,* p. 492.

6. Ibid., pp. 15–18, 421.

7. Latham, *The Group Basis of Politics,* pp. 17, 28, and passim.

8. New York: Knopf, 1966.

9. Ibid., pp. 333–34.

10. E. E. Schattschneider, *The Semi-Sovereign People* (New York: Holt, Rinehart and Winston, 1960), p. 21.

11. Ibid., pp. 25–32.

12. Schattschneider devotes an entire chapter to the American labor movement. But instead of treating the AFL-CIO as a case of the "mixed type" with some socially expansive goals and others narrowly self-serving, he treats it as part of the "pressure system" and thus one with only self-interested ends. See ibid., chap. 3.

13. Ibid., pp. 56–60. There is at least one very noteworthy exception to the pattern traced above, namely, James Q. Wilson's recent book, *Political Organizations* (New York: Basic Books, 1973). Wilson is careful to distinguish groups whose dominant incentives are material benefits from ones essentially purposive in character, and he avoids any suggestion that either type is a priori of greater political importance; in this respect, as in others as well, Wilson's book marks an important theoretical breakthrough. But its existence does not vitiate the general bias alluded to, one whose influence remains pervasive.

14. Key, *Politics, Parties and Pressure Groups,* p. 29 (see also pp. 47–48).

15. Ibid., pp. 70–71.

16. A more positive treatment of how fellow travelers can affect the life of political organizations is to be found in Truman, *The Governmental Process*. Truman avoids the "crystallization" imagery of Key and makes the point that "retaining the loyalty of such members" [fellow travelers] may be important to the successful achievement of the group's claims" (p. 158). It is not clear, however, that Truman fully grasps how profoundly such members can affect social movement core organizations. He mentions such actors in only four rather incidental passages and his specific application of the concept is to such nonmovement groups as the American Association of University Professors and the American Medical Association.

17. Expressive of these virtues is Truman, *The Governmental Process*, passim.

18. Neil Smelser, *Theory of Collective Behavior* (Glencoe: The Free Press, 1963). Earlier commentaries include Rudolph Heberle, "Observations on the Sociology of Social Movements," *American Sociological Review*, 14, no. 3 (1949): 347; Herbert Blumer, "Collective Behavior," in Joseph R. Gittler, ed., *Review of Sociology, An Analysis of a Decade* (New York: Wiley, 1957), p. 146. A commentary contemporary with Smelser's is Lewis M. Killian, "Social Movements," in R. E. L. Faris, ed., *Handbook for Modern Sociology* (Chicago: Rand McNally, 1964), p. 426.

19. Smelser, *Theory of Collective Behavior*, pp. 296-306.

20. The following discussion draws on Elliot Currie and Jerome H. Skolnick, "A Critical Note on Conceptions of Collective Behavior," *The Annals of the American Academy of Political and Social Science*, 391, no. 3 (September 1970): 34-35.

21. Smelser, *Theory of Collective Behavior*, p. 8.

22. Ibid., p. 72, 79-130.

23. Ibid., pp. 222-68.

24. For example, Bernard Nash, executive director of the relatively conservative AARP, commented with reference to the conclusion of the 1971 White House Conference: "While I was optimistic about the overall results of the conference, I was disappointed that certain recommendations did not impart a sense of urgency—a need for immediate action ... the discussion of health care, and particularly national health insurance, was, in my opinion, not specific enough. And the mandatory retirement recommendation did not address itself to the basic issues—age discrimination in firing should be as illegal as age discrimination in hiring" (*AARP News Bulletin*, January 1972, p. 6). Elsewhere in the same issue of the publication (p. 3), considerable space was devoted to a resolution condemning "age motivated mandatory retirement policies in business, government and industry."

Chapter 14

1. Jo Freeman, "The Origins of the Womens' Liberation Movement," *American Journal of Sociology* 78, no. 4 (January 1973): 793.

2. Olson, *The Logic of Collective Action;* Truman, *The Governmental Process*, pp. xxvii, xxx.

3. Olson, *The Logic of Collective Action*, pp. 159-65.

4. His most specific comment on the point is expressed in a footnote: "The veterans' organizations are not primarily economic organizations, or even political. Their main functions are social, and they attract most of their members because of the social benefits they provide.... All of their social and other benefits go only to those who join; they provide selective incentives.... The political power of the veterans' lobbies is accordingly a by-product of the social and economic services provided by the veterans' organizations" (ibid., pp. 159-60n).

5. Ibid., p. 159.

6. Wilson, *Political Organizations*, p. 25.

7. Olson, *The Logic of Collective Action*, pp. 158–59.

8. Bruce Bolnick, "Toward a Behavioral Theory of Philanthropic Activities," in Edmund S. Phelps, ed., *Altruism, Morality and Economic Theory* (New York: Russell Sage, 1975), p. 215.

9. Wilson, *Political Organizations*, chap. 2.

10. The author is indebted to Stephen Long, Ph.D. candidate in economics, University of Wisconsin-Madison, for his extremely helpful suggestions concerning this section.

11. The concept involved here is roughly equivalent to what James Q. Wilson in a different context has denoted a "collective solidary incentive." See Wilson, *Political Organizations*, pp. 39–45.

12. The concept involved here is roughly equivalent to Wilson's "individual solidary incentive" (ibid.).

13. For a good summary of the view that AARP benefits are overpriced, see Jeremy Main, "A Word to the Wise About Old Age Groups," *Money*, March 1975, pp. 44–48.

14. Mayer N. Zald and Roberta Ash, "Social Movement Organizations: Growth, Decay and Change," *Social Forces* 44, no. 3 (March 1966): 333.

15. Ibid.

Chapter 15

1. Dale Vinyard, "The Senate Committee on the Aging and the Development of a Policy System," paper delivered at the Political Science Section of the Michigan Academy, East Lansing, March 1972, pp. 3, 20. A slightly amended version of this paper was published under the title, "The Senate Special Committee on the Aging," *The Gerontologist* 12, (Autumn 1972), pt. 1, pp. 298–303 (see especially p. 302).

2. Senate Special Committee on the Aging, *Developments in Aging, 1972* (Washington, D.C.: U.S. Government Printing Office, May 10, 1973), p. 191.

3. Vinyard, "A Policy System for the Aged: Some Preliminary Observations," pp. 28–30.

4. Salisbury, "An Exchange Theory of Interest Groups," pp. 25–30.

5. Robert H. Binstock, "Aging and the Future of American Politics," *The Annals* 415 (September 1974): 206.

6. Charles J. Parrish, "Policy-Making and the Aged: Problems for the Future," paper presented at the Annual Meeting of the American Society for Public Administration, Syracuse University, May 1974, pp. 4, 14.

7. Grant McConnell, *Private Power and American Democracy* (New York: Knopf, 1966), pp. 339, 341–42.

8. Lowi, *The End of Liberalism*, chap. 3.

9. Harold Seidman, *Politics, Position and Power: The Dynamics of Federal Organization* (New York: Oxford University Press, 1970), p. 76.

10. Truman, *The Governmental Process,* pp. 516–24.

11. Theodore Lowi, *The Politics of Disorder* (New York: Basic Books, 1972), pp. 55–58.

12. McConnell, *Private Power*, p. 342.

Bibliography

Books and Scholarly Essays

Altmeyer, Arthur. *The Formative Years of Social Security*. Madison: University of Wisconsin Press, 1966.

Barron, Milton. "Minority Groups Characteristics of the Aged in American Society." *Journal of Gerontology* 8 (1953): 477–81.

Beauvoir, Simone de. *The Coming of Age*. New York: Putnam, 1972.

Beckman, R. O. "A Cold Shoulder for the Elderly." *Perspectives on Aging*, Autumn 1972, p. 8.

Bentley, Arthur F., *The Process of Government*. Chicago: University of Chicago Press, 1908.

Berelson, Bernard. "Democratic Theory and Public Opinion." *Public Opinion Quarterly* 16 (1952): 324–26.

Bermeo, Nancy Gina. "Aged Activism: Causes, Effects, and Future Trends." Honors thesis, Mount Holyoke College, 1973.

Bernstein, Irving. *The Lean Years: A History of the American Worker, 1920–33*. Boston: Houghton Mifflin, 1960.

Binstock, Robert. "Aging and the Future of American Politics." *Annals of the American Academy of Political and Social Science* 415 (September 1971): 199–212.

———. "Interest Group Liberalism and the Politics of Aging." *Gerontologist* 12, no. 3, pt. 1 (Autumn 1972): 265–80.

———, Carolyn M. Cherington and Peter Woll. "Federalism and Leadership Planning: Predictors of Variance in State Behavior." *Gerontologist* 14, no. 2 (April 1974): 114–21.

———, and Robert B. Hudson. "Political Systems and Aging." In Robert Binstock and Ethel Shanas, eds., *The Handbook of Aging and the Social Sciences*. New York: Van Nostrand Reinhold Company, 1976.

Bolnick, Bruce. "Toward a Behavioral Theory of Philanthropic Activities." In Edmund S. Phelps, ed., *Altruism, Morality and Economic Theory*. New York: Russell Sage, 1975.

Campbell, Angus. "Social and Psychological Determinants of Voting Behavior." In Wilma Donahue and Clark Tibbetts, eds., *Politics of Age*. Ann Arbor: University of Michigan Press, 1962, pp. 87–100.

Carlie, Michael Kaye. "The Politics of Age: Interest Group or Social Movement." *Gerontologist* 9, no. 4 (Winter 1969): 259–63.

Chambers, Clark. *Seedtime of Reform: American Social Service and Social Action, 1918-33*. Minneapolis: University of Minnesota Press, 1963.

Church, Frank. "A Time for Security and Dignity." *Perspectives on Aging*, Spring 1972, p. 5.

Cobb, Roger, and Charles Elder. *Participation in American Politics: The Dynamics of Agenda-Building*. Boston: Allyn and Bacon, 1972.

Corning, Peter, "Senior Citizens for Kennedy: An Effector in a Political Subsystem." Master's thesis, New York University, 1969.

Council of State Governments. *The States and Their Older Citizens*. Chicago: Council of State Governments, 1955.

Dawson, Carl A., and Warren Gettys. *An Introduction to Sociology*. New York: Ronald Press, 1929.

Donahue, Wilma, and Clark Tibbetts, eds. *Politics of Age*. Ann Arbor: University of Michigan Press, 1962.

Epstein, Abraham. *Insecurity: A Challenge to America*. New York: Random House, 2d rev. ed., 1938.

Fisher, Lloyd H. "Research in the Politics of Age." In Wilma Donahue, ed., *Politics of Age*. Ann Arbor: University of Michigan Press, 1962, pp. 41-45.

Freidel, Frank B. *Franklin E. Roosevelt: The Triumph*. Boston: Little Brown, 1956.

Greenstein, Fred I. *The American Party System and the American People*. Englewood Cliffs, N.J.: Prentice-Hall, 1963.

Griffith, Ernest. *Congress: Its Contemporary Role*. 2d ed., rev. New York: New York University Press, 1956.

Hale, Myron Q. "The Cosmology of Arthur F. Bentley." *American Political Science Review* 14, no. 4 (December 1960): 955-61.

Harris, Richard. *A Sacred Trust*. New York: Penguin, 1969.

Hartmann, Susan. *Truman and the 80th Congress*. Columbia, Missouri: University of Missouri Press, 1971.

Havighurst, Robert J. "Life Beyond Family and Work." In Ernest W. Burgess, ed., *Aging in Western Societies*. Chicago: University of Chicago Press, 1960.

Holtzman, Abraham. "Analysis of Old Age Politics in the United States." *Journal of Gerontology* 9, no. 1 (January 1954): 56-66.

———. *The Townsend Movement*. New York: Bookman Associates, 1963.

Hudson, Robert B. "Rational Planning and Organizational Imperatives: Perspectives for Area Planning in Aging." *Annals of the American Academy of Political and Social Science* 415 (September 1974): 41-54.

———. "State Politics, Federalism and Public Policies for Older Americans." Paper delivered before the annual meeting of the American Political Science Association, New Orleans, 1973.

Hudson, Robert, and Martha Veley. "Federal Funding and State Planning: The Case of State Units on Aging." *Gerontologist* 14, no. 2 (April 1974): 122-28.

Key, V. O. *Politics, Parties and Pressure Groups*. 5th ed. New York: Crowell, 1964.

————. "Public Opinion and the Decay of Democracy." *Public Opinion Quarterly* 37 (1961): 481–94.

————. *The Responsible Electorate*. Cambridge: Harvard University Press, 1966.

Korn, Richard. " 'Too Old to Work and Too Young to Die': An Examination of the UAW Program for its Retired Workers." Master's thesis, Institute of Industrial Relations, University of Wisconsin, 1974.

Latham, Earl. *The Group Basis of Politics*. Ithaca: Cornell University Press, 1952.

Leotta, Louis, Jr. "Abraham Epstein and the Movement for Old Age Security." *Labor History* 10 (Summer 1975): 359–77.

Lowi, Theodore. *The Politics of Disorder*. New York: Basic Books, 1971.

Lubove, Roy. *The Struggle for Social Security*. Cambridge: Harvard University Press, 1968.

Marmor, Theodore. *The Politics of Medicare*. Chicago: Aldine, 1973.

Maxwell, Jean. *Centers for Older People: Guide for Programs and Facilities*. New York: National Council on the Aging, 1962.

McConnell, Grant. *Private Power and American Democracy*. New York: Knopf, 1966.

Messinger, Sheldon. "Organizational Transformation: A Case Study of a Declining Social Movement." *American Sociological Review* 20, no. 1 (February 1955): 3–10.

Milbanck, Paul M. *The Elderly in Older Urban Areas*. Philadelphia: University of Pennsylvania Press, 1968.

Odell, Charles. "Attitudes Toward Political Activities Among the Aging." In Wilma Donahue, ed., *The Politics of Age*. Ann Arbor: University of Michigan Press, 1962.

Olson, Mancur, Jr. *The Logic of Collective Action: Public Goods and the Theory of Groups*. Cambridge: Harvard University Press, 1965.

Peters, George R. "Self-Conceptions of the Aged." *Gerontologist* 11 (Winter 1971), pt. 2, pp. 69–73.

Pierce, Lloyd E. "The Activities of the American Association for Labor Legislation in Behalf of Social Security and Protective Legislation." Ph.D. dissertation, University of Wisconsin, 1953.

Pinner, Frank A., Paul Jacobs and Philip Selznick. *Old Age and Political Behavior: A Case Study*. Berkeley and Los Angeles: University of California Press, 1959.

————. "Theories of Political Participation." In Wilma Donahue, ed., *The Politics of Age*. Ann Arbor: University of Michigan Press, 1962, pp. 63–73.

Polner, Walter. "The Aged in Politics, A Successful Example." *Gerontologist* 2 (1962): 207–15.

Pratt, Henry. "Old Age Associations in National Politics." 415 *Annals of the American Academy of Political and Social Science* 415 (September 1974): 106–19.

Putnam, Jackson K. *Old Age Politics in California: From Richardson to Reagan*. Stanford: Stanford University Press, 1970.

Riley, M.W. and Anne Foner. *Aging and Society.* 3 vols. New York: Russell Sage, 1960, 1968, 1973.

Rose, Arnold. "Group Consciousness Among the Aging." In Arnold Rose and Warren M. Peterson, eds., *Older People and Their Social World: The Sub-Culture of the Aging.* Philadelphia: Davis, 1965.

———. "The Impact of Aging on Voluntary Organizations." In Clark Tibbitts, ed., *Handbook of Social Gerontology.* Chicago: University of Chicago Press, 1960.

———. "Organizations for the Elderly: Political Implications." In Wilma Donahue, ed., *The Politics of Age.* Ann Arbor: University of Michigan Press, 1962, pp. 138-41.

Salisbury, Robert H. "An Exchange Theory of Interest Groups." *Midwest Journal of Political Science* 13, no. 1 (February 1969): 1-32.

Schattschneider, E. E. *The Semisovereign People.* New York: Holt, Rinehart and Winston, 1960.

Schlabach, Theron F. *Edwin E. Witte: Cautious Reformer.* Madison: Wisconsin State Historical Society, 1969.

Seidman, Harold. *Politics, Position and Power: The Dynamics of Federal Organization.* New York: Oxford University Press, 1970.

Skidmore, Max J. *Medicare and the American Rhetoric of Reconciliation.* University, Alabama: University of Alabama Press, 1970.

Skolnick, Jerome, and Elliott Currie. "A Critical Note on Conceptions of Collective Behavior." *Annals of the American Academy of Political and Social Sciences* 391, no. 3 (September 1970): 34-45.

Smelser, Neil. *Theory of Collective Behavior.* Glencoe: The Free Press, 1963.

Steiner, Gilbert. *The State of Welfare.* Washington, D.C.: Brookings Institution, 1971.

Sundquist, James. *Politics and Policy: The Eisenhower, Kennedy and Johnson Years.* Washington, D.C.: Brookings Institution, 1968, chap. 7.

Tolman, Yonina. "Aging: Social Aspects." In David Sills, ed., *International Encyclopedia of the Social Sciences.* New York: Macmillan, 1968, 1:186-96.

Townsend, Claire. *Old Age: The Last Segregation.* New York: Grossman, 1971.

Trela, James E. "Some Political Consequences of Senior Center and Other Old-Age Memberships." *Gerontologist* 11 (Summer 1971): 118-23.

Truman, David B. *The Governmental Process.* New York: Knopf, 1951.

Vinyard, Dale. "A Policy System for the Aged: Some Preliminary Observations." Paper delivered for the annual meeting of the Midwest Political Science Association, Chicago, April 1974.

———. "The Senate Special Committee on Aging." *Gerontologist* 12, pt. 1 (Autumn 1972): 298-303.

Voss, Carl H. *Stephen S. Wise: Servant of the People.* Philadelphia: The Jewish Publication Society of America, 1969.

Walker, Jack L. "A Critique of the Elitist Theory of Democracy." *American Political Science Review* 60, no. 2 (1966): 285-95.

Wilson, James Q. *Political Organizations.* New York: Basic Books, 1973.

Zald, Mayer N., and Roberta Ash. "Social Movement Organizations: Growth, Decay and Change." *Social Forces* 44, no. 3 (March 1966): 327-41.

Mass-Circulation Periodicals

Abrams, Margaret. "The Story of AARP." *Modern Maturity*, October-November 1971, pp. 72-73.

Church, Frank. "State of the Aging, Legislative Relief" (delivered in U.S. Senate, February 7, 1972), *Vital Speeches*, March 1, 1972, pp. 301-02.

Dale, Edwin. "The Security of Social Security, The Young Pay the Old." *New York Times,* January 14, 1973, p. 8.

Isenberg, Barbara. "Aging Increasingly Flex their Political Muscle." *Wall Street Journal,* November 17, 1972, p. 1.

Jenson, Michael. "Harsh Arithmetic of Old Age in America." *Saturday Review,* April 8, 1972, pp. 42, 44.

"Life of Abraham Epstein: An American Epic." *Social Security,* September-October, 1942, pp. 3-6.

Main, Jeremy. "A Word to the Wise About Old Age Groups." *Money*, March 1975, pp. 44-48.

Nash, Bernard. "The Changing Look of Aging." *NRTA Journal*, January-February 1972, pp. 4-5.

Pizer, Vernon. "Duck! Geriatric Lib is on the March." *Magazine of the Washington Star.* January 24, 1971, p. 7.

Rienow, Robert, and Leona Rienow. "The Desperate World of the Senior Citizen." *Saturday Review*, January 28, 1961, pp. 11-12.

Seligson, M. "Social Crime of Growing Old." *Life*, May 19, 1972, p. 22.

"'Senior Power'—A Growing Force in Politics." *U.S. News and World Report*, May 24, 1971, p. 63.

Shafer, Helen B. "Plight of the Aged." *Editorial Research Reports*, November 10, 1971, pp. 875-89.

"White House Conference on Aging: Preparations." *National Journal,* September 25, 1971, p. 1969.

Government Publications

Altmeyer, Arthur, "The First Decade of Social Security." *Social Security Bulletin*, August 1945, pp. 5-8.

Basic Policy Statements and Recommendations, 1961 White House Conference on Aging. Prepared for Senate Special Committee on Aging, May 15, 1961.

Binstock, Robert, *Planning: Background.* Washington, D.C.: White House Conference on Aging, March 1971.

Committee on Education and Labor, House. *White House Conference on Aging: Report to Accompany S.J. Res. 117.* 90th Congress, 2d session (May 1, 1968).

Epstein, Lenore A., and Janet H. Murray. *The Aged Population of the United States.* Washington, D.C.: U.S. Government Printing Office, 1967.

"Federal Outlays in Aging, Fiscal Years 1967-72." *Facts and Figures on Older Americans*, no. 4. Administration on Aging of HEW, June 1971, pp. 1-4.

Maddox, George, and Marvin J. Taves. "Research Development on Behavior and Social Scientific Aspects of Aging." 1971 White House Conference on Aging, *Proceedings.* Washington, D.C.: U. S. Government Printing Office, 1972.

Social Security Administration. *The Health Care of the Aged.* Washington, D.C.: U.S. Government Printing Office, 1962.

Special Committee on Aging, Senate. *The Administration on Aging—Or a Successor?* Washington, D.C.: U.S. Government Printing Office, October 1971.

Special Committee on Aging, Senate. *Developments in Aging: 1972 and January-March, 1973.* Washington, D.C.: U.S. Government Printing Office, May 1973.

Special Committee on Aging, Senate. *Evaluation of Administration on Aging and Conduct of a White House Conference on Aging.* Joint Hearings, 92d Congress, 1st session, March 1971.

Special Committee on Aging, Senate. *Future Directions in Social Security.* 93d Congress, 1st session, July 26, 1973, pt. 5.

Wentworth, Edna E. "Income of Old Age and Survivor's Beneficiaries, 1941 and 1949." *Social Security Bulletin*, May 1950, p. 4.

Index

247